THE MUSICIAN'S GUIDE TO AURAL SKILLS

THE MUSICIAN'S GUIDE TO AURAL SKILLS

Ear-Training

THIRD EDITION

Paul Murphy
Muhlenberg College

Joel Phillips
Westminster Choir College of Rider University

Elizabeth West Marvin
Eastman School of Music

Jane Piper Clendinning
Florida State University

W. W. NORTON & COMPANY
NEW YORK • LONDON

W. W. Norton & Company has been independent since its founding in 1923, when William Warder Norton and Mary D. Herter Norton first published lectures delivered at the People's Institute, the adult education division of New York City's Cooper Union. The Nortons soon expanded their program beyond the Institute, publishing books by celebrated academics from America and abroad. By mid-century, the two major pillars of Norton's publishing program—trade books and college texts—were firmly established. In the 1950s, the Norton family transferred control of the company to its employees, and today—with a staff of four hundred and a comparable number of trade, college, and professional titles published each year—W. W. Norton & Company stands as the largest and oldest publishing house owned wholly by its employees.

Copyright © 2016, 2011, 2005 by W. W. Norton & Company, Inc.

All rights reserved
Printed in the United States of America

Third Edition

Editor: Justin Hoffman
Editorial assistant: Grant Phelps
Managing editor, College: Marian Johnson
Associate project editor: Michael Fauver
Copyeditor: Elizabeth Bortka
Proofreader: Debra Nichols
Electronic media editor: Steve Hoge
Electronic media editorial assistant: Stephanie Eads
Production manager: Andy Ensor
Design director: Rubina Yeh
Music typesetting and page composition: David Botwinik; CodeMantra
Manufacturing: Quad Graphics-Taunton

ISBN 978-0-393-26406-7 (pbk.)

W. W. Norton & Company, Inc., 500 Fifth Avenue, New York, NY 10110
www.wwnorton.com
W. W. Norton & Company, Ltd., 15 Carlisle Street, London W1D 3BS

2 3 4 5 6 7 8 9 0

Contents

Preface

The Musician's Guide series is the most comprehensive set of materials available for learning music theory and aural skills. Consisting of a theory text, workbook, and anthology, along with a two-volume aural-skills text, the series features coordinated resources that can be mixed and matched for any theory curriculum.

The two volumes of *The Musician's Guide to Aural Skills* teach the practical skills students need as professional musicians—dictation, sight-singing, rhythm-reading, keyboard harmony, improvisation, ear-training, and composition—through real music. Though the two volumes of this book correspond to *The Musician's Guide to Theory and Analysis* in ordering and terminology, they are designed to be used together, individually, or in conjunction with other theory texts.

This Ear-Training volume develops listening and writing skills, including composition, in assignments that students may complete in class or as homework. The companion Sight-Singing volume emphasizes the skills required for real-time performance, and also includes strategic, progressive training in rhythm-reading, improvisation, and keyboard skills. Both volumes feature a wide range of real musical repertoire—including classical, popular, and folk selections—throughout.

The Musician's Guide to Aural Skills, 3rd Edition, Ear-Training is distinctive in several significant and intertwined ways. First, it emphasizes small- and large-scale listening through pattern-based dictations and literature-based analytic exercises. Second, the text draws on music from a wide range of styles and periods, from popular (Broadway musicals, movies and television, classic rock, jazz, and blues) to common-practice, as well as twentieth- and twenty-first century music literature. Moreover, these examples feature a variety of timbres and ensembles, such as: keyboard (piano, pianoforte, harpsichord, and organ); vocal (solo voice and chorus); solo strings (violin, viola, and cello sonatas); chamber ensembles (string trios and quartets, clarinet quintet, chamber orchestra); large ensembles (orchestra, band); woodwinds; and jazz combo. With few exceptions, literature-based dictations are high-quality acoustic recordings, not MIDI files. Third, the text provides abundant feedback and cues for students: self-check answers at the end of the text for each *Try It* dictation; notation tips and cues to get started; and probing questions that encourage students to reexamine previous answers and build on what they have already discovered. Fourth, the text offers the greatest flexibility in learning and teaching. All material may be completed in class as teacher-led inquiry or outside of class with students working by themselves or with classmates.

Using This Volume

This Ear-Training volume is divided into 40 chapters to align with both the Sight-Singing volume and *The Musician's Guide to Theory and Analysis*. Composition exercises are linked with specific chapters in the text. We hope that this organization will make it easier for instructors to plan for class and to coordinate aural skills with written theory.

As students move through the Ear-Training volume, learning objectives at the beginning of each chapter identify the specific concepts and skills to be addressed, and summarize what students will learn. All audio examples are available online. Students can access the recordings by going to digital.wwnorton.com/auralskills3et and registering with the code inside their texts.

Each chapter begins with *Try It* exercises. These self-led, self-evaluated dictations reinforce chapter concepts in short, targeted ways to help students succeed with longer excerpts from the literature. Answers for all *Try It* exercises appear in the Teacher's Edition, and in an appendix of the Student Edition. Students will want to return to these dictations throughout their study, using them for additional practice and review.

Following each set of *Try It* exercises are Contextual Listening activities, which present real musical excerpts and complete compositions to analyze aurally. Contextual Listening exercises were pioneered in the first edition of this text and have been refined ever since. These exercises are graduated from easiest to most difficult in each chapter and are strategically structured to guide students through each listening example with thoughtful analytical questions and a step-by-step process for taking dictation. Annotated scores and answers to all Contextual Listening examples appear in the Teacher's Edition.

New to this edition, Contextual Listening exercises feature Workspaces, where students work from the outsides inward in a strategic process that results in accurate notation of what they hear. Students might begin by notating meter and rhythm on a single staff, to which they then assign solfège syllables or scale-degree numbers. They then map this information onto notes on the staff to complete accurate transcriptions. Targeted analytic questions guide students through the process.

The main goal of the Contextual Listening assignments is to develop and improve students' strategies for thinking and listening. Striving for perfection is admirable, but students shouldn't be discouraged if they don't get everything right. For that reason, teachers might evaluate this work in a more holistic manner, focusing on whether students have understood the main concepts of an exercise, rather than on every small detail of their answers. For some of the more challenging exercises, students might be instructed to work with a partner. Long examples, such as those for invention, fugue, and sonata, may be assigned in parts so that teachers can check the work on each part before assigning the next one. Contextual Listening exercises are graduated from easiest to most difficult so that teachers can customize their assignments to the skill and experience of their students. Tasks are broken up to make the process easier and to highlight the areas in which difficulties occur. For example, students might be asked to notate the melody using solfège syllables or scale-degree numbers; to notate only the pitches of the bass part or melody; to notate only the first bass pitch of each measure; or to identify meter types, chord qualities, patterns, and so on.

The Ear-Training volume culminates with guided composition exercises designed to let students create their own music for a variety of vocal and instrumental ensembles through model composition of forms, genres, and styles they have experienced throughout their study. Students often progress in a spiral fashion, for example, developing their initial work with phrases to create period structures that are later used for both small- and large-scale forms. Students explore twentieth-century practices working with nontonal motives and sets, serialism, indeterminacy, and a great number of rhythmic techniques. Students are encouraged to listen to and perform not only their own work, but also that of their classmates, which can be an exciting and rewarding experience.

Planning Your Curriculum

The Musician's Guide covers concepts typically taught during the first two years of college instruction in music. For instructors who adopt both the *Theory and Analysis* and *Aural Skills* texts, we know you will appreciate the consistent pedagogical approach, terminology, and order of presentation that the two texts share. Nevertheless, you may find at times that students' aural and practical skills develop more slowly than their grasp of theoretical concepts. There is no harm done if aural/practical instruction trails slightly behind conceptual understanding. For this reason, we summarize the organization of the volumes and suggest strategies for using them. Typically deployed over four or five semesters, most college curricula might be addressed by one of the following two models.

Plan 1 (**four semesters, including one semester dealing with musical rudiments**)

	Sight-Singing	Ear-Training
Term 1	Chapters 1-10 including Keyboard Lessons	Chapters 1-10 and Compositions 1-4
Term 2	Chapters 11-21 including Keyboard Lessons	Chapters 11-21 and Compositions 5-11
Term 3	Chapters 22-33 including Keyboard Lessons	Chapters 22-33 and Compositions 12-13
Term 4	Chapters 34-40 including Keyboard Lessons	Chapters 34-40 and Compositions 14-17

Alternatively, the following organization is one suggestion for those curricula that offer a dedicated rudiments class in addition to a four-semester core sequence.

Plan 2 (**a rudiments class followed by four semesters**)

	Sight-Singing	Ear-Training
Rudiments	Chapters 1-8 omitting modal melodies in Chapter 5; Keyboard Lessons 1-8, omitting Lesson 5.2	Chapters 1-8 and Compositions 1-2
Term 1	Chapter 5 (modal melodies), and Chapters 9-14; Keyboard Lessons 5.2 14	Chapters 9-14 (with review of modes from Chapter 5) and Compositions 3-7
Term 2	Chapters 15-21 and Keyboard Lessons	Chapters 15-21 and Compositions 8-11
Term 3	Chapters 22-33 and Keyboard Lessons	Chapters 22-33 and Compositions 12-13
Term 4	Chapters 34-40 and Keyboard Lessons	Chapters 34-40 and Compositions 14-17

Applying Solfège Syllables and Scale-Degree Numbers

All singing systems have merit and choosing *some* system is far superior to using none. To reinforce musical patterns, we recommend singing with movable-*do* solfège syllables and/or scale-degree numbers, but we provide a summary explanation of both the movable- and fixed-*do* systems in Chapter 1 to help students get started. (A quick reference for diatonic and chromatic syllables also appears at the front of this volume.) For solfège in modal contexts, we present two systems in Chapter 5, one using syllables derived from major and minor, and one using relative (rotated) syllables. (A quick reference also appears at the back of this volume.)

Applying a Rhythm-Counting System

Many people use some counting system to learn and perform rhythms—in effect, "rhythmic solfège." For example, a rhythm in $\frac{2}{4}$ meter might be vocalized "du de, du ta de ta" (Edwin Gordon system), or "1 and, 2 e and a" (McHose/Tibbs system), or "Ta di Ta ka di mi" (Takadimi system). We leave it to the discretion of each instructor whether to use such a system and which to require.

Our Thanks to . . .

A work of this size and scope is helped along the way by many people. We are especially grateful for the support of our families and our students. Our work together as coauthors has been incredibly rewarding, a collaboration for which we are sincerely thankful.

For subvention of the recordings, we thank James Undercofler (director and dean of the Eastman School of Music), as well as Eastman's Professional Development Committee. For audio engineering, we are grateful to recording engineers John Ebert and John Baker. For audio production work, we thank Glenn West, Christina Lenti, and Lance Peeler, who assisted in the recording sessions. We also thank our colleagues at both Westminster Choir College of Rider University and the Eastman School of Music who gave of their talents to help make the recordings. The joy of their music making contributed mightily to this project.

We are grateful for the thorough and detailed work of our prepublication reviewers, whose suggestions inspired many improvements, large and small: Michael Berry (University of Washington), David Castro (St. Olaf College), Melissa Cox (Emory University), Gary Don (University of Wisconsin-Eau Claire), Terry Eder (Plano Senior High School), Jeffrey Gillespie (Butler University), Melissa Hoag (Oakland University), Rebecca Jemian (University of Louisville), Charles Leinberger (University of Texas-El Paso), David Lockart (North Hunterdon High School), Robert Mills (Liberty University), Daniel Musselman (Union University), Kristen Nelson (Stephen F. Austin State University), Shaugn O'Donnell (City College, CUNY), Tim Pack (University of Oregon), Scott Perkins (DePauw University), and Sarah Sarver (Oklahoma City University). For previous editions, reviewers have included: Jeff Donovick (St. Petersburg College), Bruce Hammel (Virginia Commonwealth University), Ruth Rendleman (Montclair State University), Alexander Tutunov (Southern Oregon University), and Annie Yih (University of California at Santa Barbara).

We are indebted to the staff of W. W. Norton for their commitment to this project and their painstaking care in producing these volumes. Most notable among these are music theory editor Justin Hoffman, whose knowledge of music, detailed, thoughtful questions, and genuine support for this project made him a joy to work with, and Maribeth

Anderson Payne, whose vision helped launch the series with great enthusiasm. Michael Fauver was project editor of the volume, with assistance from copyeditor Elizabeth Bortka and proofreader Debra Nichols. We appreciate the invaluable assistance of media experts Steve Hoge, Stephanie Eads, Meg Wilhoite, and Timothy Bausch. Grant Phelps was editorial assistant, David Botwinik was typesetter, and Andy Ensor was production manager.

Paul Murphy, Joel Phillips, Elizabeth West Marvin, and Jane Piper Clendinning

THE MUSICIAN'S GUIDE TO AURAL SKILLS

Elements of Music

Pitch and Pitch Class

In this chapter you'll learn to:

- Use this book and its related materials
- Identify melodic contour and organization
- Identify whole and half steps
- Map pitches to notes, solfège syllables, scale-degree numbers, and letter names
- Analyze melodic patterns to transpose a melody

Dictation and Pattern Recognition

Taking dictation is the process of listening to music and capturing one or more of its elements by memorizing, performing, analyzing, and notating what you hear. These elements—such as pitches, rhythms, harmonies, and form—fall into patterns, so pattern recognition is fundamental to understanding music and improving aural skills.

Choosing Audio Playback Equipment

When listening, use a high-quality playback system. Connect your device's audio output to an external amplifier and speakers or use ear buds or headphones. The built-in speaker on your device will not provide satisfactory audio output to complete these activities.

Contour

Contour is melodic shape. Successive pitches ascend, repeat, or descend, creating the simple contours ⁄, —, and ⟍.

Mapping Pitch

Pitches may be represented as notes on a staff; pitch classes may be represented as solfège syllables, scale-degree numbers, and letter names. Associating a pitch with a note, syllable, number, and letter is called "mapping."

Movable Systems:

- With **scale degrees**, you sing a number for each step of the scale; the numbers are the same for major and minor.

- With **movable *do***, each note of the scale is associated with a syllable, some of which change between major and minor.
- The following table shows how scale degrees correlate with movable-*do* solfège syllables in major keys with the changes for minor shown in parentheses.

SCALE DEGREE	SOLFÈGE SYLLABLE
1	*do*
7 = "sev"	*ti (te)*
6	*la (le)*
5	*sol*
4	*fa*
3	*mi (me)*
2	*re*
1	*do*

Fixed Systems:

- With **letter names**, you sing the name of each note, dropping any accidentals. For example, C, C♯, and C♭ are all sung as "C."
- With **fixed-*do* solfège**, each solfège syllable is associated with a note name regardless of key.
- The following table shows how note names correlate with fixed-*do* syllables.

LETTER NAME	SOLFÈGE SYLLABLE
C (C♯, C♭)	*do*
B (B♯, B♭)	*ti*
A (A♯, A♭)	*la*
G (G♯, G♭)	*sol*
F (F♯, F♭)	*fa*
E (E♯, E♭)	*mi*
D (D♯, D♭)	*re*
C (C♯, C♭)	*do*

Preparatory Listening

Complete the *Try It* dictations to familiarize yourself with the following concepts and skills:

- Recognizing simple contours
- Distinguishing between half steps, whole steps, and skips
- Notating melodic fragments with note heads only

Try It

Listen to short melodies that are played twice with a pause in between. The first note of each dictation is provided to help orient you.

- Notate the pitches of each dictation on the staff provided with solid note heads.
- If you are working by yourself, sing the melody aloud with solfège syllables, scale-degree numbers, and/or letter names.

Contextual Listening

To begin a Contextual Listening (CL) assignment, first review the concepts and skills that will be covered in each exercise. Follow the instructions in the exercise making sure always to sing the excerpts aloud. Again, don't worry about rhythmic notation for now. Several of the questions require you to transpose the melody. One of the most helpful aspects of using solfège syllables or scale-degree numbers is the ease with which you can do this.

NAME ______________________________

Contextual Listening 1.1

In this CL exercise you will:

- Identify the melodic contour and organization of a children's song
- Map a stepwise melodic line to notes, solfège syllables, scale-degree numbers, and letter names
- Analyze melodic patterns to transpose the melody

Listen to part of a children's song, and complete the following exercises. The excerpt consists of two segments, each one five pitches long.

Listening Strategies

- Memorize what you hear as quickly as possible. Perform it in your imagination as many times as you like, and at any tempo, in order to comprehend what you heard.
- Focus on only one musical element at a time, such as contour or pitch.

1. Pitches 1–2 create which contour?
   (a) 
   (b) 
   (c) 
2. Pitches 3–5 create which contour?
   (a) 
   (b) 
   (c) 
3. Segment 1 (pitches 1–5) creates which contour?
   (a) 
   (b) 
   (c) 
   (d) 
4. Segment 2 (pitches 6–10) creates which contour?
   (a) 
   (b) 
   (c) 
   (d) 
5. Segments 1 and 2 can be considered individual musical ideas. Which best describes the melody's organization?

	Segment 1	*Segment 2*
(a)	idea 1	idea 1 repeated exactly
(b)	idea 1	idea 1 repeated, but higher in pitch
(c)	idea 1	idea 1 repeated, but lower in pitch
(d)	idea 1	idea 2

6. Use the workspace provided to capture the melody and analyze its construction.
   (a) In the blanks provided, begin with the given solfège syllable, scale-degree number, and letter name, and write solfège syllables, scale-degree numbers, or letter names for the entire melody.
   (b) The starting pitch is C3. On the staff, write an appropriate clef and notate the melodic pitches using solid note *heads* only; don't worry about the rhythm. For help, refer to your solfège syllables, scale-degree numbers, and letter names.
   (c) Beneath and between each pair of pitches, write **S** for same pitch, **W** for whole step, and **H** for half step.
   (d) Play your answer at the keyboard and sing it with solfège syllables, scale-degree numbers, and letter names.

Workspace

Solfège syllables: d ___ ___ ___ ___ ___ ___ ___ ___ ___

Scale-degree numbers: $\hat{1}$ ___ ___ ___ ___ ___ ___ ___ ___ ___

Letter names: C ___ ___ ___ ___ ___ ___ ___ ___ ___

Notation starting on C3:

Analysis:

7. Compare what you wrote with what you heard. Use Sing-Check to check the pitches.

Sing-Check

Play *do* ($\hat{1}$) and sing the first melodic pitch with its solfège syllable or scale-degree number. Sing pitch 2, then check it by playing it. Continue until you finish the melody, always singing the pitch first, then checking it by playing.

8. (a) Use the analysis from question 6 to help transpose the melody to begin on the given pitch. Before each pitch you write, notate an accidental—♭, ♯, or ♮.

   (b) Play your answer at the keyboard, singing it with the same solfège syllables or scale-degree numbers as you did the original.

Listening Strategy

Sing a transposed melody with the same solfège syllables or scale-degree numbers as the original.

9. Follow the procedure from question 8 and transpose the melody to begin on the given pitch.

NAME ______________________

Contextual Listening 1.2

In this CL exercise you will:

- Identify melodic contour and organization of a children's song
- Recall noncontiguous pitches
- Map a melodic line to notes, solfège syllables, scale-degree numbers, and letter names
- Analyze melodic patterns to transpose the melody

Listen to part of a children's song, and complete the following exercises. The excerpt consists of four segments.

1. Segment 1 (pitches 1–4) creates which melodic contour (shape)?
   (a) ／
   (b) ＼
   (c) ／＼
   (d) ＼／

2. Focus on the end. The last segment creates which melodic contour (shape)?
   (a) ／
   (b) ＼
   (c) ／＼
   (d) ＼／

3. Segments 1, 2, 3, and 4 can be considered individual musical ideas. Which of the following best describes how the segments are organized?

	Segment 1	*Segment 2*	*Segment 3*	*Segment 4*
(a)	idea 1	idea 1 repeated	idea 2	idea 1 return
(b)	idea 1	idea 1 repeated	idea 2	idea 2 repeated
(c)	idea 1	idea 2	idea 3	idea 4
(d)	idea 1	idea 2	idea 1	idea 2

4. Use the workspace provided to capture the melody and analyze its construction.

Listening Strategies

- If a segment repeats, write a shortcut, such as ⁒ (meaning "repeat") or c 1 (meaning "copy segment 1").
- After each melodic skip you hear a pitch you've heard before. Recalling a previously heard pitch may be easier than figuring out a skip.

   (a) In the blanks provided, begin with the given solfège syllable, scale-degree number, and letter name, and write solfège syllables, scale-degree numbers, or letter names for the entire melody.

   (b) The starting pitch is C4 on the staff. Write an appropriate clef and notate the melodic pitches using solid note *heads* only; don't worry about the rhythm. For help, refer to your solfège syllables, scale-degree numbers, and letter names.

   (c) Beneath and between each pair of pitches, write **S** for same pitch, **W** for whole step, and **H** for half step. For skips, write **W** + **W** or **W** + **H**.

Workspace

Solfège syllables: d ___ ___ ___ | ___ ___ ___ ___ | ___ ___ ___ | ___ ___ ___

Scale-degree numbers: $\hat{1}$ ___ ___ ___ | ___ ___ ___ ___ | ___ ___ ___ | ___ ___ ___

Letter names: C ___ ___ ___ | ___ ___ ___ ___ | ___ ___ ___ | ___ ___ ___

Segment 1 *Segment 2* *Segment 3* *Segment 4*

Notation starting on C4:

Analysis:

5. Compare what you wrote with what you heard. Play your answer at the keyboard, singing it with solfège syllables, scale-degree numbers, and letter names.

6. (a) Use your analysis from question 4 to help you transpose the melody to begin on the given pitch. Before each pitch you write, notate an accidental—♭, ♯, or ♮.

(b) Play your answer at the keyboard, singing it with the same solfège syllables or scale-degree numbers as the original.

(c) Play and sing again, this time doubling the melody in your left hand one octave lower.

7. Following the procedure from question 6, transpose the melody to begin on the given pitch.

NAME ______________________________

Contextual Listening 1.3

In this CL exercise you will:

- Identify melodic contour and organization of a children's song
- Begin a melody with a pitch other than *do* ($\hat{1}$)
- Map a melodic line to notes, solfège syllables, scale-degree numbers, and letter names
- Analyze melodic patterns to transpose the melody

Listen to part of a children's song, and complete the following exercises.

1. Pitches 1-5 create which melodic contour (shape)?
   (a) 
   (b) 
   (c) 
   (d) 
2. The final 3 pitches create which contour (shape)?
   (a) 
   (b) 
   (c) 
   (d) 
3. Compared with the first half of the melody, the second half has
   (a) the same beginning and ending. (b) the same beginning, different ending.
   (c) a different beginning, same ending. (d) a different beginning and ending.
4. Use the workspace provided to capture the melody and analyze its construction.

Listening Strategies

- If a segment repeats, write a shortcut, such as ⁒ (meaning "repeat") or c 1 (meaning "copy segment 1").
- Identify any melodic skip by filling in the "missing" pitch.

  (a) In the blanks provided, begin with the given solfège syllable, scale-degree number, and letter name, and write solfège syllables, scale-degree numbers, or letter names for the entire melody.

  (b) The starting pitch is E5 On the staff, write an appropriate clef and notate the melodic pitches using solid note *heads* only; don't worry about the rhythm. For help, refer to your solfège syllables, scale-degree numbers, and letter names.

  (c) Beneath and between each pair of pitches, write **S** for same pitch, **W** for whole step, and **H** for half step. For skips, write **H** + **W**, **W** + **H**, or **W** + **W**.

Workspace

First half of the melody

Solfège syllables: m ___ ___ ___ ___ ___ ___ ___ ___ ___ ___ ___ ___

Scale-degree numbers: $\hat{3}$ ___ ___ ___ ___ ___ ___ ___ ___ ___ ___ ___ ___

Letter names: E ___ ___ ___ ___ ___ ___ ___ ___ ___ ___ ___ ___

Notation starting on E5:

Analysis:

5. Play your answer at the keyboard, and sing it in a comfortable vocal range with solfège syllables, scale-degree numbers, and letter names.

6. Play and sing again. This time, play the melody in both hands. Begin on E5 in the right hand and E3 in the left hand.

7. (a) Use your answers from question 4 to help you transpose the *second half* of the melodyto begin on the given pitch. Before each pitch you write, notate an accidental—♭, ♯, or ♮.

   (b) Play your answer at the keyboard, singing it with the same solfège syllables or scale-degree numbers as the original.

   (c) Play and sing again, this time doubling the melody in your left hand one octave lower.

8. Following the procedure from question 7, notate the *second half* of the melody on the following staff and perform it to check your work.

NAME ___________________________

Contextual Listening 1.4

In this CL exercise you will:

- Listen for the whole and half steps found in a Broadway melody
- Analyze melodic patterns to transpose the melody

Listen to part of a classic Broadway melody, and complete the following exercises.

1. (a) Analyze the whole and half steps. In the blanks beneath pitches 3-7, write **W** or **H**.

   (b) Use your analysis to write the correct accidental—♭, ♯, or ♮—before each pitch.

   (c) Compare your answer to what you heard by playing it at the keyboard.

2. (a) Use your answers from question 1 to help you transpose the melody to begin on the given pitch. Before each pitch you write, notate an accidental—♭, ♯, or ♮.

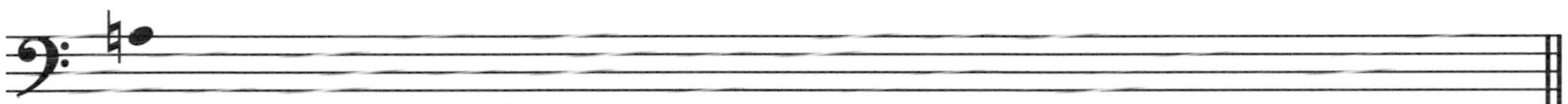

   (b) Compare what you wrote to the sound of the original by playing it at the keyboard.

Simple Meters

In this chapter you'll learn to:

- Identify the beat and the meter signature in simple meters
- Analyze and notate rhythm with beats and divided beats in simple meters
- Analyze and notate basic syncopations in simple meters
- Map pitches to notes, solfège syllables, scale-degree numbers, and letter names
- Notate a melody starting on various pitches

Dictation Strategies

When dictating rhythms, you may find it helpful to use shorthand as you take dictation. Here are some possible symbols:

/ slanted note slash that can be filled in later to form a solid note head ● or adapted to form an open note head 𝅝 and to which stems, beams, or dots can later be added

⁒ repeat previous pattern (may apply to a beat, a measure, etc.)

c 1 "copy measure 1 here" (e.g., when you hear that m. 3 is the same as m. 1)

𝄆 𝄇 draw traditional repeats and endings when appropriate

Preparatory Listening

Complete the *Try It* dictations to familiarize yourself with the following concepts and skills:

- Recognizing and notating single-line rhythmic patterns in simple meters
- Notating ties and dotted notes in single-line rhythmic patterns in simple meters

Try It

Listen to short rhythmic phrases that are played twice with a pause in between. Some dictations begin with an anacrusis. Occasional hints are provided to help orient you.

- Determine the pulse, then notate the rhythmic phrase on the staff provided with stems up and notes beamed to show beat grouping.
- Where bar lines do not appear, include them; always end with a double bar.
- If you are working by yourself, sing the rhythm with counting syllables.

NAME ____________________________

Quarter-Note Beat Unit (2/4, 4/4, and 3/4)

The first phrase is started for you.

1.

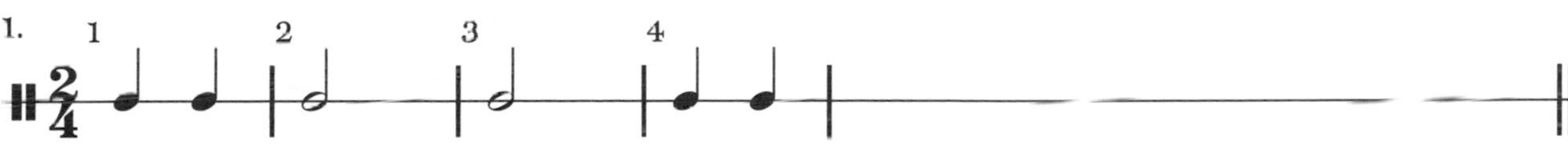

2.

3.

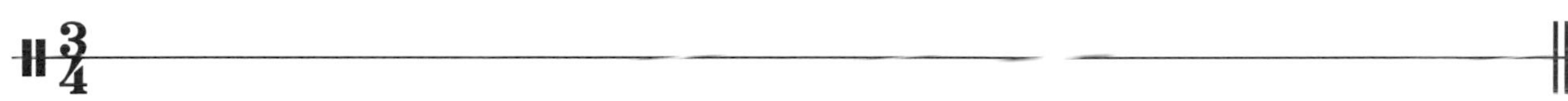

Quarter-Note Beat Unit (2/4, 4/4, and 3/4) with Anacrusis

Each of the following phrases begins with an anacrusis. The first phrase is started for you.

4.

5.

6.

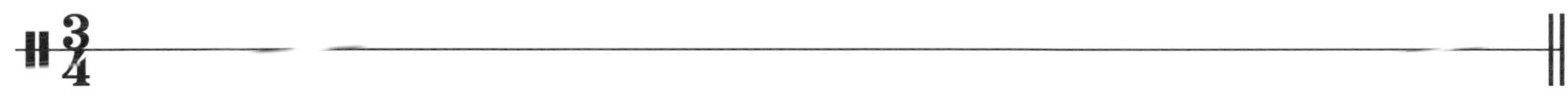

Quarter-Note Beat Unit (2/4, 4/4, and 3/4) with Beat Divisions

The shortest note value you will hear is the eighth note. Notate any syncopations with ties. Some dictation exercises begin with an anacrusis while others do not. The first phrase is started for you.

7.

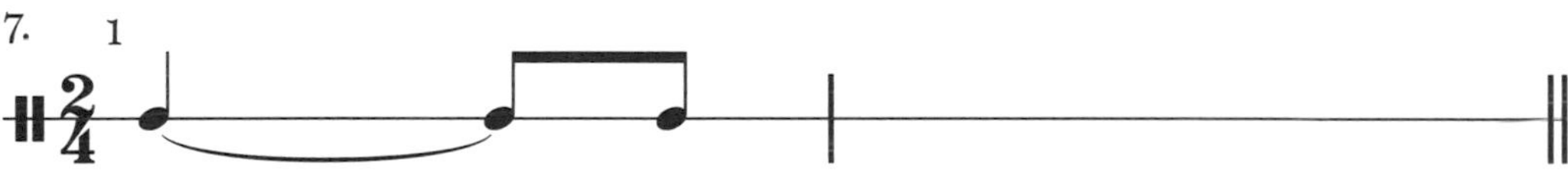

8.

9.

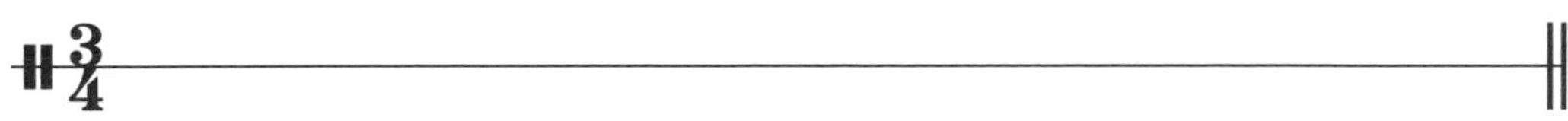

Notate any syncopations with full note values rather than with ties.

10.

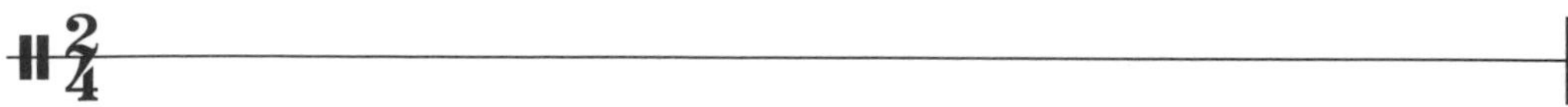

11.

12.

NAME ______________________

Contextual Listening

Because memorization is such a crucial step to taking dictation, consider the following strategies for notating musical excerpts:

- Take time to think about what you hear before starting your notation.
- Avoid an exclusively chronological listening of the excerpt. Instead, focus on how an excerpt both begins and concludes. If you know the last note but not those in the middle, write it down!
- Avoid the tendency to "give up" if you aren't sure about the music in the middle, and try to reorient yourself at the end. Eventually, you will be able to connect the beginning of the excerpt to its conclusion.
- If you get lost in an excerpt, try to invent a solution; you will find that your inventions are often quite similar to what really happens in the excerpt.
- When working alone, sing aloud with solfège syllables, scale-degrees numbers, and rhythm syllables. If not alone, sing silently, while imagining the association of sounds to syllables, and so on.
- Conduct as you listen to help stay on track.
- You may want to break the entire assignment into smaller, easier tasks—such as determining the meter, notating only the rhythm, or notating only the pitches.

Contextual Listening 2.1

In this CL exercise you will:

- Identify the beat and meter of a melody from a musical
- Notate the rhythm
- Map pitches to notes, solfège syllables, scale-degree numbers, and letter names, and then notate the melody
- Notate the melody in two different meters and clefs

Because this assignment is the first that requires you to notate both rhythm and pitch, it is presented in four steps that provide a strategy for how to divide a more comprehensive listening assignment into smaller, easier tasks.

Listen to an excerpt of a song from a musical, and complete the following exercises. The excerpt consists of two segments, each one seven pitches long.

Step 1: Determine the beats, beat groupings, and beat divisions.

1. Listen until you memorize segment 1.
2. While listening, tap the beat. Determine whether the beats group into measures of two, three, or four. The longest notes, pitches 7 and 14, occur on downbeats.
3. Practice the conducting pattern for the meter type you choose. Then conduct while singing the melody from memory on a neutral syllable, such as "du."
4. Which meter type(s) might work well—duple, triple, or quadruple?

Step 2: Notate the rhythm.

Use the workspace provided to capture the rhythm four different ways.

5. (a) While singing from memory and conducting, tap the beat divisions with your left hand. If necessary, choose a slower tempo. Notate the rhythm of the excerpt in simple quadruple meter. All the note heads should be placed on the line (*not* above or below) of the single-line staff with upward stems. Beam notes to show beat grouping.
   (b) Notate the same rhythm in a different simple quadruple meter.
   (c) Notate the same rhythm in simple duple meter.
   (d) Notate the same rhythm in a different simple duple meter.

Workspace

Step 3: Notate the pitches.

Use the workspace provided to capture the pitches of the melody.

Workspace

6. (a) Beginning on *do*, write the melody with solfège syllables.
   (b) Beginning on $\hat{1}$, write the melody with scale-degree numbers.
   (c) Beginning on C, write the melody with letter names.
   (d) Beginning on C3, notate the pitches of the melody. Write an appropriate clef and notate the melodic pitches using solid note *heads* only; don't worry about the rhythm.
   (e) Circle adjacent notes that make a half step.

Solfège syllables: d

Scale-degree numbers: $\hat{1}$

Letter names: C

Notation starting on C3:

NAME ______________________________

Step 4: Complete the notation.

7. Begin on C3 again, and notate both melody and rhythm in simple duple meter. Choose a clef appropriate to the melody's register. Include the meter signature and bar lines, and beam notes to show beat grouping.

8. Begin on C4 this time, and notate both the melody and rhythm in simple duple meter. Choose a clef appropriate to the melody's new register. Include the meter signature and bar lines, and beam notes to show beat grouping.

Sing-Check

Play *do* ($\hat{1}$) and sing the first melodic pitch with its solfège syllable or scale-degree number. Sing pitch 2, then check it by playing it. Continue until you finish the melody, always singing the pitch first, then checking it by playing.

NAME ______________________________

Contextual Listening 2.2

In this CL exercise you will:

- Notate the syncopated rhythm of a song from a musical
- Map pitches to notes, solfège syllables, scale-degree numbers, and letter names, then notate the melody

Listen to an excerpt of a song from a musical, and complete the following exercises. The excerpt begins on *sol* ($\hat{5}$).

1. (a) While listening, tap the beat with your foot and conduct in four. Memorize the melody.
   (b) Imagine the sound of the melody at a slower tempo. Tap the beat with your foot, tap beat divisions with your left hand, and conduct. Practice this until you can maintain a steady tempo.
   (c) Finally, sing the melody aloud while tapping the beats and beat divisions, and conducting. Gradually increase the tempo to meet or exceed that of the recording.

2. Use the workspace provided to capture the melody.
   (a) Notate the rhythm of the excerpt in common time ($\frac{4}{4}$); the first three notes are provided for you. Include the meter signature and bar lines. Beam notes to show beat grouping.
   (b) Below the rhythm staff, and under each note, continue writing the solfège syllables, scale-degree numbers, and note names of the entire melody.
   (c) The starting pitch is C3. On the staff, write an appropriate clef and notate the melodic pitches using solid note *heads* only; don't worry about the rhythm. For help, refer to your solfège syllables, scale-degree numbers, and letter names.
   (d) Combine your answers to notate both the pitches and rhythm of the excerpt. Choose a clef appropriate to the melody's register.

Workspace

Rhythm:

Solfège syllables: s
Scale-degree numbers: $\hat{5}$
Letter names: C

Notation starting on C3:

Pitches and rhythm combined:

NAME ____________________

Contextual Listening 2.3

In this CL exercise you will:

- Identify the beat and meter of a simple-meter excerpt
- Notate the rhythm
- Map pitches to notes, solfège syllables, scale-degree numbers, and letter names

Listen to an excerpt from a piano sonata, and complete the following exercises. The excerpt begins with a quarter-note anacrusis.

1. Use the workspace provided to capture the melody and analyze its construction.
   (a) Notate the rhythm of the upper part in simple quadruple meter on the single-line staff. Include the meter signature, quarter-note anacrusis, and bar lines. Beam notes to show beat grouping.
   (b) In the blanks provided, write the solfège syllables, scale-degree numbers, and letter names of the melody beginning on *sol* ($\hat{5}$) and G.
   (c) The starting pitch is G4. On the staff, write an appropriate clef and notate the melodic pitches using solid note *heads* only; don't worry about the rhythm. For help, refer to your solfège syllables, scale-degree numbers, and letters names.
   (d) Combine your answers to complete the notation of the pitches and rhythm of the melody. Write the appropriate clef and key signature.

Workspace

Rhythm:

Solfège syllables: s

Scale-degree numbers: $\hat{5}$

Letter names: G

Notation starting on G4:

Pitches and rhythm combined:

NAME ______________________

Contextual Listening 2.4

In this CL exercise you will:

- Notate the rhythm of a melody from an art song
- Map pitches to notes, solfège syllables, scale-degree numbers, and letter names
- Notate the melody in treble clef

Listen to an excerpt from an art song, and complete the following exercises. The excerpt begins with a one-beat anacrusis.

1. Use the workspace provided to capture the melody and analyze its construction.
   (a) Notate the rhythm of the melody on the single-line staff. The meter and first four notes are given for you. Choose a meter signature, and include bar lines (including one to show the anacrusis). Beam notes to show beat grouping.
   (b) In the blanks provided, write the solfège syllables, scale-degree numbers, and letter names of the melody beginning on *do* ($\hat{1}$).
   (c) The starting pitch is C4. On the staff, write an appropriate clef and notate the melodic pitches using solid note *heads* only; don't worry about the rhythm. For help, refer to your solfège syllables, scale-degree numbers, and letter names.
   (d) Combine your answers to complete the notation of the pitches and rhythm of the melody. Write the appropriate clef.

Workspace

Rhythm:

Solfège syllables: *d*

Scale-degree numbers: $\hat{1}$

Letter names: C

Notation starting on C4:

Pitches and rhythm combined:

Pitch Collections, Scales, and Major Keys

NAME ______________________

In this chapter you'll learn to:

- Recognize common pitch collections of the major scale and major keys
- Learn to relate notes, solfège syllables, scale-degree numbers, and letter names to major keys
- Notate simple-meter melodies in treble, bass, and alto clefs

Preparatory Listening

Complete the *Try It* dictations to familiarize yourself with the following concepts and skills:

- Recognizing and notating melodic patterns from the major pentachord
- Recognizing and notating formulaic rhythmic patterns in quadruple meter

Try It

Listen to short melodies that are played twice with a pause in between. Each dictation is preceded by two "count-off" measures to set the tempo and meter. The shortest note value is the sixteenth note. Occasional hints are provided to help orient you.

- Notate the pitches and rhythm for each example on the staff provided with notes beamed to show beat grouping.
- Where bar lines do not appear, include them; always end with a double bar.
- If you are working by yourself, sing the melody aloud with solfège syllables, scale-degree numbers, and/or letter names.

1.

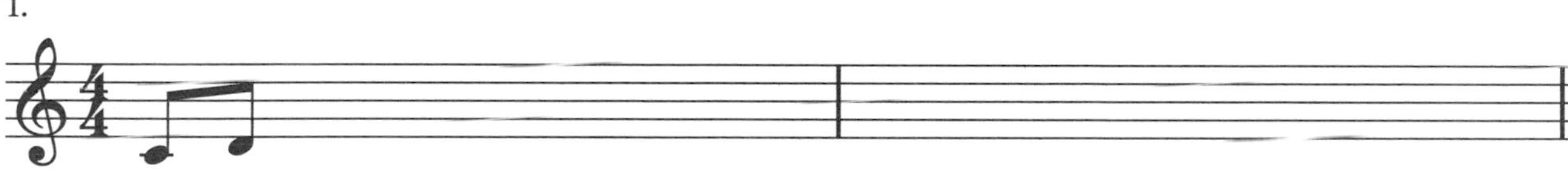

2.

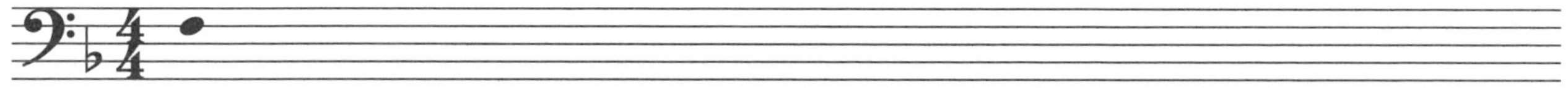

3.

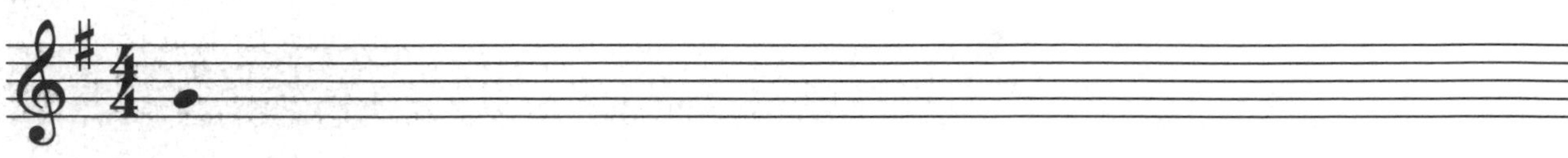

4.

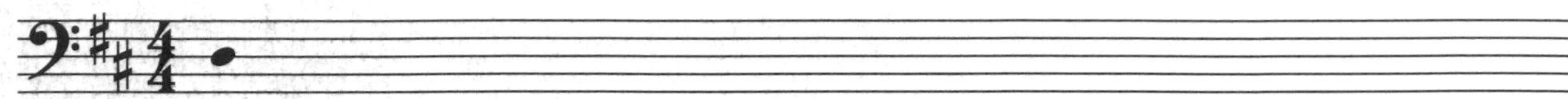

5.

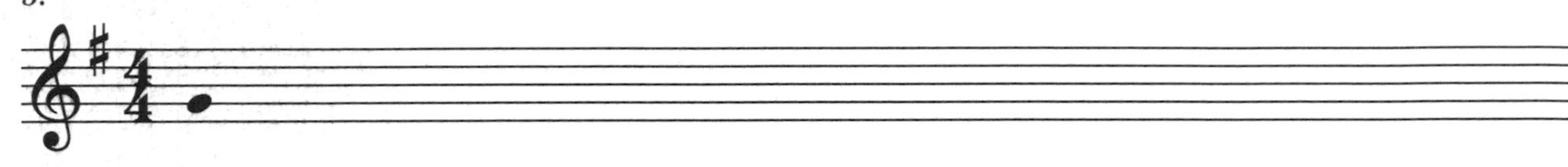

6.

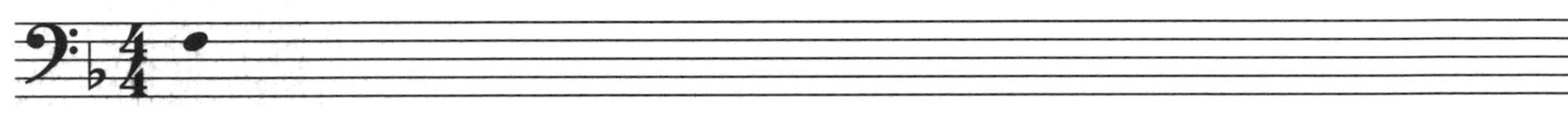

NAME ____________________

Contextual Listening 3.1

In this CL exercise you will:

- Identify the beat and meter of an excerpt
- Notate the rhythm
- Map pitches to notes, solfège syllables, and scale degree numbers, then notate the melody
- Notate the excerpt in two different keys and clefs

Listen to an excerpt from a familiar carol, and complete the following exercises.

1. Tap the beat with your foot, and tap beat divisions with your left hand. Then conduct while singing the melody from memory.
2. Use the workspace provided to capture the excerpt. Notate the rhythm on the single-line staff, with the quarter note as the beat unit. Both $\frac{2}{4}$ and $\frac{4}{4}$ are acceptable. The first three notes are indicated for you. Include the meter signature and bar lines. Beam notes to show beat grouping.
   (a) Below the rhythm staff, and under each note, write the solfège syllables or scale-degree numbers for the melody.
   (b) The starting pitch is D5. On the staff, write an appropriate clef and notate the melodic pitches using solid note *heads* only; don't worry about the rhythm. Use pitches of the D major scale.
   (c) Combine your answers to notate both the pitches and rhythm of the excerpt. Write a clef appropriate to the melody's register and include and key signature (or accidentals).

Workspace

Rhythm:

Solfège syllables: *d*

Scale-degree numbers: $\hat{1}$

Notation starting on D5:

Pitches and rhythm combined:

3. Refer to your notation to transpose the melody on the following staff.

4. From the melody's lowest pitch to its highest, which best describes its range?

   (a) *do* to *sol* ($\hat{1}$-$\hat{5}$) (b) *ti* to *la* ($\hat{7}$-$\hat{6}$) (c) *do* to *do* ($\hat{1}$-$\hat{1}$) (d) *sol* to *sol* ($\hat{5}$-$\hat{5}$)

5. Listen to the entire melody of this familiar carol (CL 3.1a), then sing with solfège syllables or scale-degree numbers. Conduct while you sing. Notate both the pitches and rhythm on the following staff.

Sing-Check

Play *do* ($\hat{1}$) and sing the first melodic pitch with its solfège syllable or scale-degree number. Sing pitch 2, then check it by playing it. Continue until you finish the melody, always singing the pitch first, then checking it by playing.

NAME ______________________________

Contextual Listening 3.4

In this CL exercise you will:

- Internalize beats and beat divisions at the same time
- Notate a simple-meter rhythm containing beats, beat divisions, doubled values of beats, and dotted-beat values
- Map pitches to notes, solfège syllables, and scale-degree numbers, then notate the melody
- Notate the melody in two different keys and clefs

Listen to an excerpt adapted from a work for piano, and complete the following exercises.

1. Tap the beat with your foot, and tap beat divisions with your left hand. Then conduct while singing the melody from memory.

2. From the melody's lowest pitch to its highest, which best describes its range?

   (a) *do* to *sol* ($\hat{1}$-$\hat{5}$) (b) *ti* to *la* ($\hat{7}$-$\hat{6}$) (c) *do* to *do* ($\hat{1}$-$\hat{1}$) (d) *sol* to *sol* ($\hat{5}$-$\hat{5}$)

3. Use the workspace provided to capture the excerpt.

   (a) Notate the rhythm on the single-line staff in simple duple meter, with the quarter note as the beat unit. Include the meter signature and bar lines. Beam notes to show beat grouping.

   (b) Below the rhythm staff, and under each note, write the solfège syllables or scale-degree numbers for the melody. Begin on *do* ($\hat{1}$).

   (c) The starting and ending pitch is E4. On the staff, notate the melodic pitches using solid note *heads*; don't worry about the rhythm. Use the appropriate clef and accidentals. Use the pitches of the E major scale.

   (d) Combine your answers to notate both the pitches and rhythm of the excerpt. Choose a clef appropriate to the melody's register.

Workspace

Rhythm:

Solfège syllables: *d*
Scale-degree numbers: $\hat{1}$

Solfège syllables:
Scale-degree numbers:

Notation starting on E4:

Pitches and rhythm combined:

4. Refer to your notation to transpose the melody on the following staff.

NAME ______________________________

Contextual Listening 3.5

In this CL exercise you will:

- Internalize beats and beat divisions
- Notate the syncopated rhythm in cut time
- Map pitches to notes, solfège syllables, and scale-degree numbers, then notate the melody
- Notate the melody in two different keys, clefs, and meters

Listen to an excerpt adapted from a keyboard composition, and complete the following exercises.

1. Tap the beat with your foot, and tap beat divisions with your left hand. Then conduct while singing the melody from memory.
2. At the beginning of the melody, which of the following rhythmic elements is featured?

   (a) anacrusis (b) syncopation (c) rest (d) dotted-note values

3. From the melody's lowest pitch to its highest, which best describes its range?

   (a) *do* to *sol* ($\hat{1}$-$\hat{5}$) (b) *ti* to *la* ($\hat{7}$-$\hat{6}$) (c) *do* to *do* ($\hat{1}$-$\hat{1}$) (d) *sol* to *sol* ($\hat{5}$-$\hat{5}$)

4. Use the workspace provided to capture the excerpt.

   (a) Notate the rhythm on the single-line staff in cut time, with the half note as the beat unit. Include the meter signature and bar lines. Beam notes to show beat grouping.

   (b) Renotate the rhythm in $\frac{2}{4}$, with the quarter note as the beat.

   (c) Below the rhythm staff, and under each note, write the solfège syllables or scale-degree numbers for the melody. Begin on *do* ($\hat{1}$).

   (d) The starting pitch is F3. On the staff, write an appropriate clef and notate the melodic pitches using solid note *heads*; don't worry about the rhythm. Use pitches of the F major scale.

   (e) Combine your answers to notate both the pitches and rhythm of the excerpt in cut time.

Workspace

Rhythm:

Solfège syllables: *d*
Scale-degree numbers: $\hat{1}$

Solfège syllables:
Scale-degree numbers:

Rhythm in $\frac{2}{4}$:

Notation starting on F3:

Pitches and rhythm combined:

5. Refer to your notation to transpose the melody on the following staff.

Compound Meters

NAME ______________________

In this chapter you'll learn to:

- Identify the beat and meter of musical excerpts
- Differentiate aurally between simple and compound meters
- Notate beats and beat divisions in compound meter
- Map pitches to notes, solfège syllables, and scale-degree numbers

Preparatory Listening

Complete the *Try It* dictations to familiarize yourself with the following concepts and skills:

- Recognizing and notating single-line rhythmic patterns in compound meters
- Recognizing and notating melodic and rhythmic patterns in a variety compound meters

Try It

Listen to short rhythmic phrases that are played twice with a pause in between. Some dictations begin with an anacrusis. The shortest note value is the eighth note. Occasional hints are provided to help orient you.

- Determine the pulse, then notate the rhythmic phrase on the staff provided with stems up and notes beamed to show beat grouping.
- Where bar lines do not appear, include them; always end with a double bar.
- If you are working by yourself, sing the rhythm with counting syllables.

Dotted-Quarter-Note Beat Unit ($\frac{6}{8}$, $\frac{12}{8}$, and $\frac{9}{8}$)

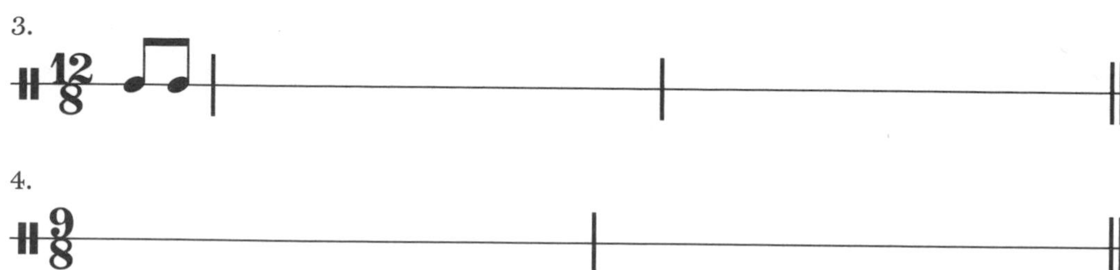

Each melody below is preceded by two "count-off" measures to set the tempo and meter. The starting pitches are given. Notate the pitches and rhythm of each melody.

5.

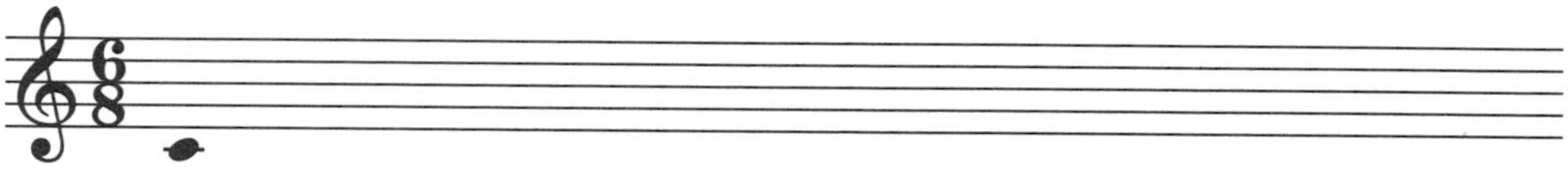

6.

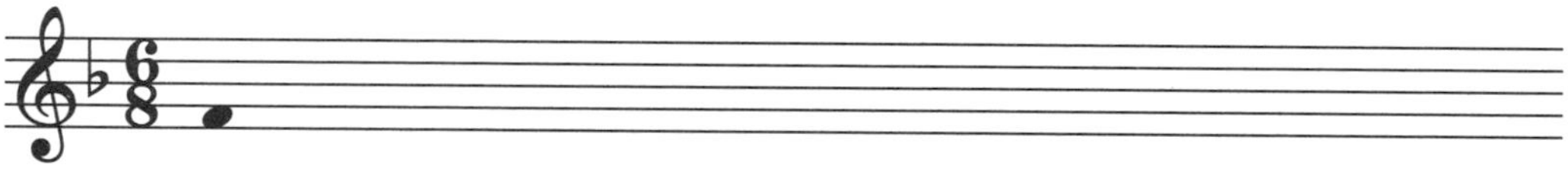

7.

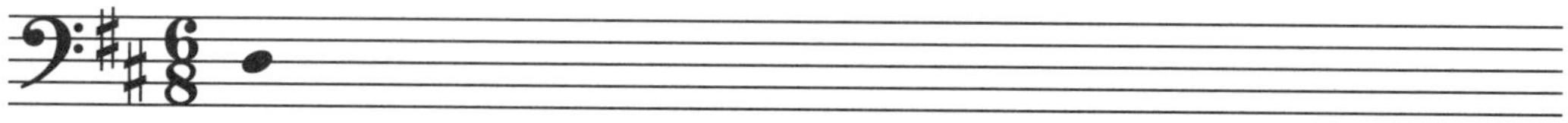

8.

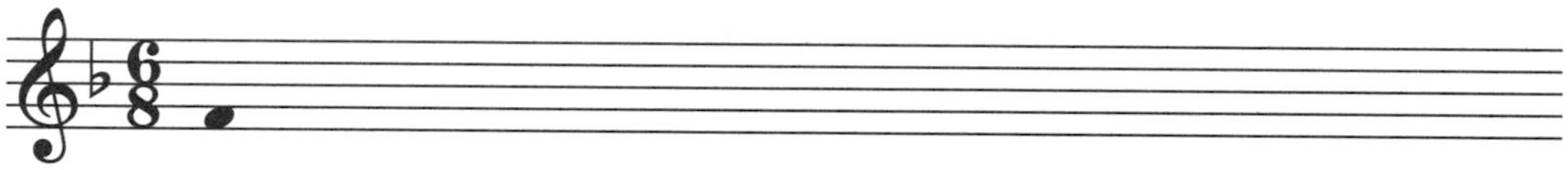

9.

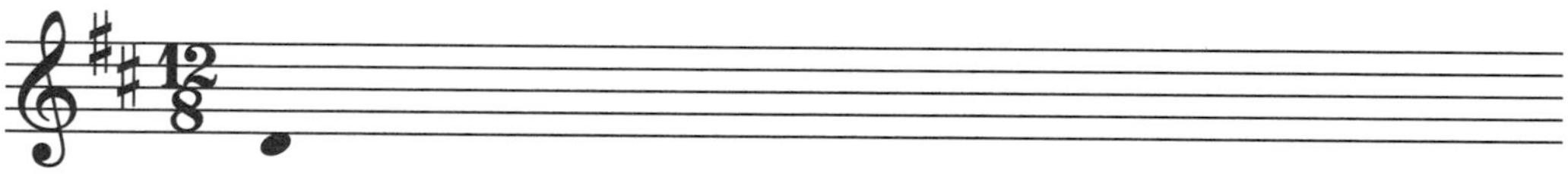

10.

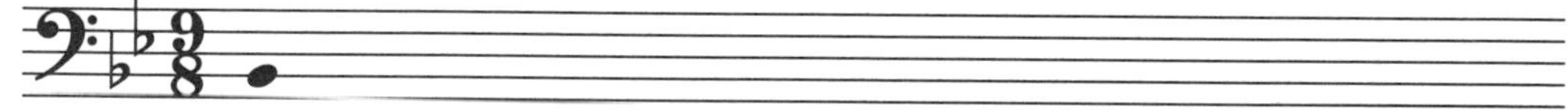

NAME ______________________________

Workspace

Rhythm:

Solfège syllables:

Scale-degree numbers:

Solfège syllables:

Scale-degree numbers:

Notation:

Rhythm:

Bass:

Solfège syllables:

Scale-degree numbers:

Solfège syllables:

Scale-degree numbers:

3. Refer to your notation to help you transpose the notation on the following staves.

NAME ______________________________

Contextual Listening 4.3

In this CL exercise you will:

- Apply shortcuts while notating repeated rhythmic patterns
- Map pitches to notes, solfège syllables, and scale-degree numbers, then notate the melody
- Transpose the melody to a different key and clef

Listen to an excerpt based on a sea chantey, and complete the following exercises. The excerpt consists of four segments, each one is two measures long.

1. From its lowest pitch to its highest, which is the range of the melody?

   (a) *do* to *sol* ($\hat{1}$-$\hat{5}$) (b) *la* to *la* ($\hat{6}$-$\hat{6}$) (c) *do* to *do* ($\hat{1}$-$\hat{1}$) (d) *sol* to *sol* ($\hat{5}$-$\hat{5}$)

2. Use the workspace provided to capture the excerpt.

   (a) Notate the rhythm of the excerpt in **C**, with the quarter note as the beat unit. Include the meter signature and bar lines. Because several measures are rhythmically identical to the first, notate the rhythm once, then use shorthand to indicate "This measure is the same." Here are three ways: write "c 1-2" (meaning "copy mm. 1-2"); write repeat signs that enclose the repeated music; draw arrows from the original segment to the copy of that segment.

   (b) "Outlining" a melody can help you grasp additional details during each hearing. Later you can fill in the gaps. Below each rhythm staff, and under *only the first and third beats*, write the solfège syllables or scale-degree numbers for the melody.

   (c) Referring to your answers, fill in the missing information to complete the notation of all of the pitches and rhythm of the melody in F major. Write the appropriate clef and key signature (or accidentals).

NAME ______________________________

Workspace

Rhythm:

Solfège syllables:

Scale-degree numbers:

Solfège syllables:

Scale-degree numbers:

Notation:

3. Refer to your notation to transpose the excerpt on the following staves.

NAME ______________________

Contextual Listening 4.4

In this CL exercise you will:

- Notate the rhythm of a movie theme in compound meter
- Map pitches to notes, solfège syllables, and scale-degree numbers, then notate the melody
- Transpose the melody to a different key and clef

Listen to the excerpt from a movie theme, and complete the following exercises.

1. Melodic pitches 1-4 make which tetrachord?

   (a) major (b) minor (c) Phrygian (d) harmonic

2. Use the workspace provided to capture the excerpt.

   (a) Notate the rhythm of the melody and bass line in compound duple meter. Choose a meter signature, and include bar lines. Beam notes to show beat grouping.

   (b) Below each rhythm staff, and under each note, write the solfège syllables or scale-degree numbers for the melody and bass line. Begin on *sol* ($\hat{5}$) for the melody and *do* ($\hat{1}$) for the bass.

   (c) Combine your answers to complete the notation of the pitches and rhythm of *only* the melody in B♭ major. The starting pitch is F4. Write the appropriate clef and key signature (or accidentals).

NAME ____________________

Workspace

Rhythm:

Melody:

Solfège syllables: *s*

Scale-degree numbers: $\hat{5}$

Solfège syllables:

Scale-degree numbers:

Notation:

Rhythm:

Bass:

Solfège syllables: *d*

Scale-degree numbers: $\hat{1}$

Solfège syllables:

Scale-degree numbers:

3. Refer to your notation to transpose the melody to the clef and key indicated in the following staves.

CHAPTER 5

Minor Keys and the Diatonic Modes

NAME ______________________________

In this chapter you'll learn to:

- Recognize pitch collections in minor keys and the diatonic modes
- Map pitches to notes, solfège syllables, and scale-degree numbers
- Notate minor and modal melodies in simple and compound meters
- Transpose melodies to different keys and clefs

Preparatory Listening

Complete the *Try It* dictations to familiarize yourself with the following concepts and skills:

- Recognizing and notating common melodic patterns occurring within minor scales
- Recognizing and notating common rhythmic patterns in simple quadruple meter

Try It

Listen to short melodies that are played twice with a pause in between. Each dictation is preceded by two "count-off" measures to set the tempo and meter. The shortest note value is the sixteenth note. Occasional hints are provided to help orient you.

- Notate the pitches and rhythm for each example on the staff provided, with notes beamed to show beat grouping.
- Include bar lines; always end with a double bar.
- If you are working by yourself, sing the melody aloud with solfège syllables, scale-degree numbers, and/or letter names.

1.

2.

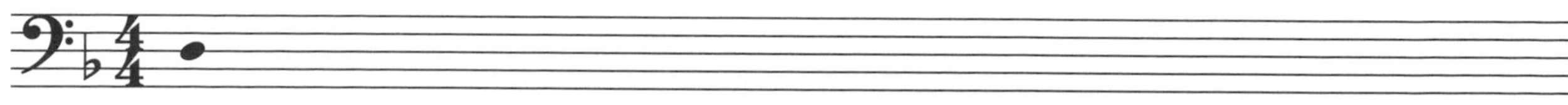

NAME ______________________________

3.

4.

5.

6.

NAME ______________________

Contextual Listening 5.1

In this CL exercise you will:

- Notate the rhythm of a melody from a work for piano
- Map pitches to notes, solfège syllables, and scale-degree numbers, then notate the melody
- Transpose the melody to a different key and clef

Listen to an excerpt from a work for piano, and complete the following exercises.

1. On which scale is the melody based?

   (a) major (b) harmonic minor

   (c) natural (descending melodic) minor (d) ascending melodic minor

2. From the melody's lowest pitch to its highest, which best describes its range?

   (a) *do* to *sol* ($\hat{1}$-$\hat{5}$) (b) *do* to *le* ($\hat{1}$-$\flat\hat{6}$) (c) *do* to *do* ($\hat{1}$-$\hat{1}$) (d) *sol* to *sol* ($\hat{5}$-$\hat{5}$)

3. Use the workspace provided to capture the excerpt.

   (a) Notate the rhythm of the melody on the single-line staff in compound duple meter. Choose a meter signature, and include bar lines. Beam notes to show beat grouping.

   (b) Below the rhythm staff, and under each note, write the solfège syllables or scale-degree numbers for the melody.

   (c) Combine your answers to complete the notation of the pitches and rhythm of the melody in G minor. Write the appropriate clef and key signature (or accidentals).

Workspace

Rhythm:

Melody: 

Solfège syllables:

Scale-degree numbers:

Notation:

4. Refer to your notation to transpose the melody to the clef and key indicated on the following staff.

NAME ______________________________

Contextual Listening 5.2

In this CL exercise you will:

- Identify the meter of a traditional melody and notate its rhythm
- Identify the key or mode
- Map pitches to notes, solfège syllables, and scale-degree numbers, then notate the excerpt

Listen to this excerpt from a folk song, and complete the following exercises.

1. Assume the melody ends on *do* ($\hat{1}$). From the melody's lowest pitch to its highest, which best describes its range?

   (a) *do* to *sol* ($\hat{1}$-$\hat{5}$) (b) *do* to *la* ($\hat{1}$-$\hat{6}$) (c) *do* to *do* ($\hat{1}$-$\hat{1}$) (d) *sol* to *sol* ($\hat{5}$-$\hat{5}$)

2. On which scale is the melody based?

   (a) harmonic minor (b) ascending melodic minor

   (c) Dorian mode (d) Mixolydian mode

3. At the beginning of the melody, which rhythmic feature is heard?

   (a) syncopation (b) rubato (uneven tempo)

   (c) dotted-note values (d) anacrusis

4. Which is the meter of this excerpt?

   (a) $\frac{2}{4}$ (b) $\frac{3}{4}$ (c) $\frac{4}{4}$ (d) $\frac{6}{8}$

5. Use the workspace provided to capture the excerpt.

   (a) Notate the rhythm on the single-line staff. Write the meter signature, and include bar lines. Beam notes to show beat grouping.

   (b) Below each rhythm staff, and under each note, write the solfège syllables or scale-degree numbers for the melody.

   (c) Combine your answers to complete the notation of the pitches and rhythm of the melody. The starting pitch is G4 and the ending pitch is E4. Write the appropriate clef and key signature (or accidentals).

Workspace

Rhythm:

Melody:

Solfège syllables:
Scale-degree numbers:

Notation:

NAME ____________________

Contextual Listening 5.4

In this CL exercise you will:

- Notate the rhythm of a compound-meter melody from an art song
- Identify the scale type and range
- Map pitches to notes, solfège syllables, and scale-degree numbers, then notate the melody
- Transpose the melody to a different key and clef

1. On which scale is the melody based?

   (a) major
   (b) harmonic minor
   (c) natural (descending melodic) minor
   (d) ascending melodic minor

2. Use the workspace provided to capture the excerpt.

   (a) Notate the rhythm of the melody in compound duple meter on the single-line staves. Write the meter signature, and include bar lines. Beam notes to show beat grouping.

   (b) Below each rhythm staff, and under each note, write the solfège syllables or scale-degree numbers for the melody. Then, using dotted half notes, notate the first bass pitch in each measure.

   (c) Combine your answers to complete the notation of the pitches and rhythm of the melody and downbeat bass notes. The starting pitches are C♯4 (melody) and C♯2 (bass). Write the appropriate clef and key signature (or accidentals).

Workspace

Rhythm:

Melody:

Solfège syllables:

Scale-degree numbers:

Solfège syllables:

Scale-degree numbers:

Notation:

Rhythm:

Bass:

Solfège syllables:

Scale-degree numbers:

Solfège syllables:

Scale-degree numbers:

3. Refer to your notation to transpose the melody to the clef and key indicated on the following staves.

NAME ______________________

Contextual Listening 5.5

In this CL exercise you will:

- Identify the scale or mode of a work for keyboard
- Notate the rhythm in simple meter
- Map pitches to notes, solfège syllables, and scale-degree numbers, then notate the melody

Listen to this excerpt from a work for keyboard, and complete the following exercises.

1. At the beginning, the melody is based on which scale or mode?

   (a) harmonic minor (b) natural minor (descending melodic)

   (c) Dorian mode (d) Lydian mode

2. The initial rhythm of the bass (lowest-sounding) line is best represented by which of the following?

   (a)  (b) 

   (c)  (d) 

3. Which are the last two pitches of the bass line?

   (a) *ti* to *do* ($\hat{7}$–$\hat{1}$) (b) *re* to *do* ($\hat{2}$–$\hat{1}$) (c) *fa* to *do* ($\hat{4}$–$\hat{1}$) (d) *sol* to *do* ($\hat{5}$–$\hat{1}$)

4. From the melody's lowest pitch to its highest, which best describes its range?

   (a) *do* to *sol* ($\hat{1}$–$\hat{5}$) (b) *do* to *la* ($\hat{1}$–$\hat{6}$) (c) *do* to *do* ($\hat{1}$–$\hat{1}$) (d) *sol* to *sol* ($\hat{5}$–$\hat{5}$)

5. Use the workspace provided to capture the excerpt.

   (a) Notate the rhythm of the melody in simple triple meter on the single-line staff, with the quarter note as the beat unit. Include the meter signature and bar lines.

   (b) Below each rhythm staff, and under each note, write the solfège syllables or scale-degree numbers for the melody.

   (c) Combine your answers to complete the notation of the pitches and rhythm of the melody beginning on E4. Write the appropriate clef and key signature (or accidentals).

Workspace

Rhythm:

Melody: 

Solfège syllables:

Scale-degree numbers:

Notation:

Intervals

NAME ______________________________

In this chapter you'll learn to:

- Isolate and identify motivic intervals in the context of major and minor keys
- Map pitches to notes, solfège syllables, and scale-degree numbers
- Notate rhythms in simple and compound meter
- Transpose melodies to different keys and clefs

Preparatory Listening

Complete the *Try It* dictations to familiarize yourself with the following concepts and skills:

- Recognizing and notating common intervallic patterns occurring within the major scale
- Recognizing and notating common rhythmic patterns in a variety of meters

Try It

Listen to short melodies that are played twice with a pause in between. Each dictation emphasizes a particular interval and is preceded by two "count-off" measures to set the tempo; a melody that begins on the given pitch follows.

- Notate the pitches and rhythm of each example on the staff provided, with notes beamed to show beat grouping.
- Include bar lines; always end with a double bar.
- If you are working by yourself, sing the melody aloud with solfège syllables, scale-degree numbers, and/or letter names.

NAME ____________________

1.

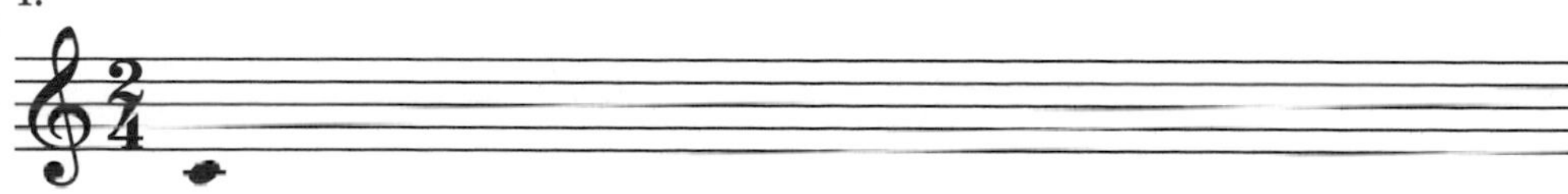

2.

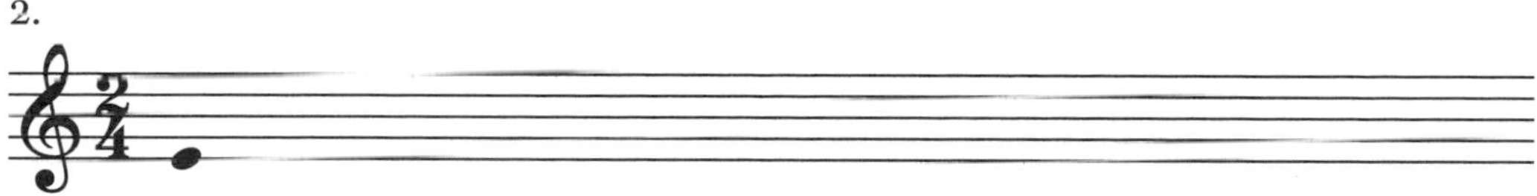

3.

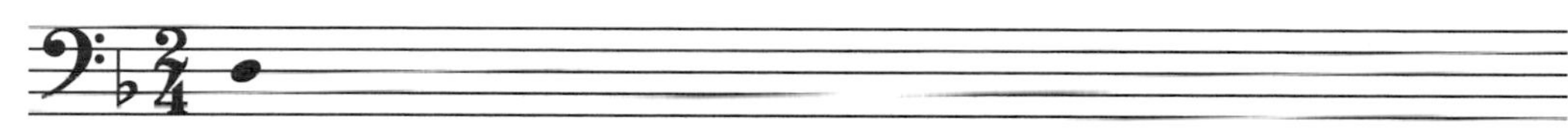

4.

5.

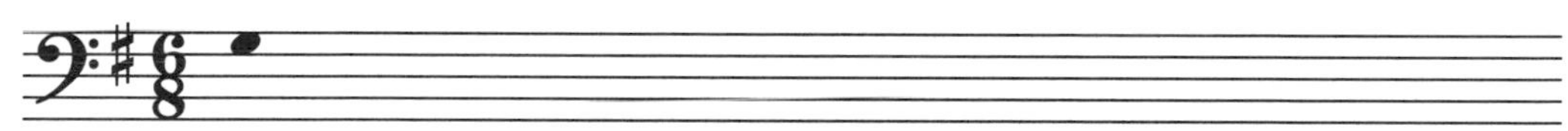

6.

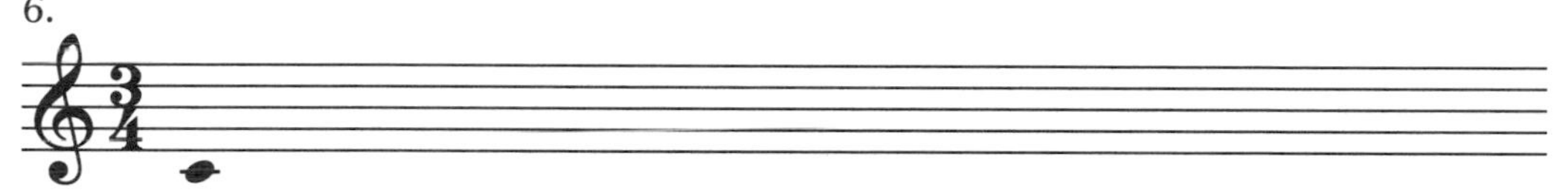

7.

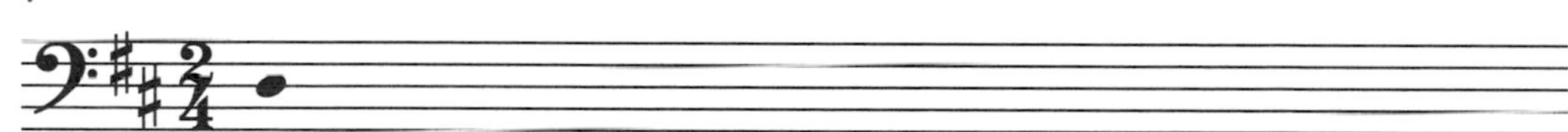

8.

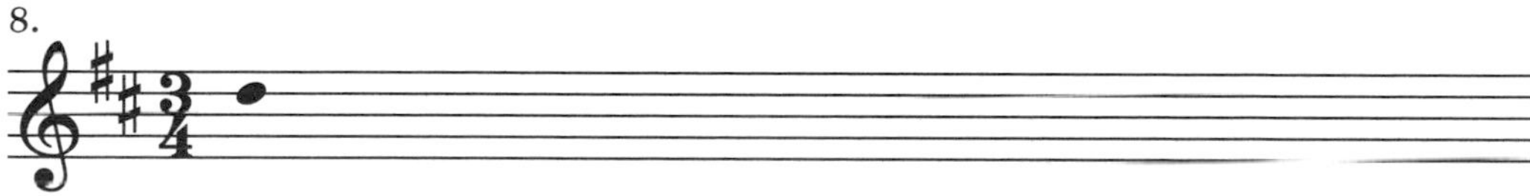

9.

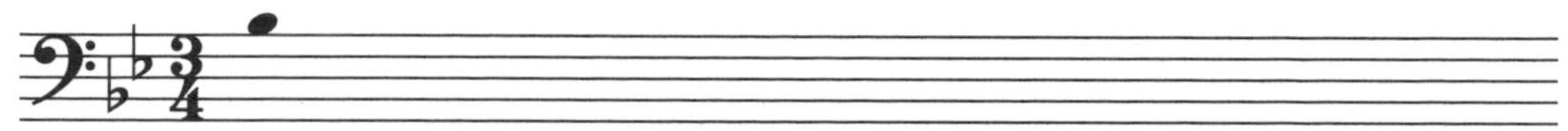

10.

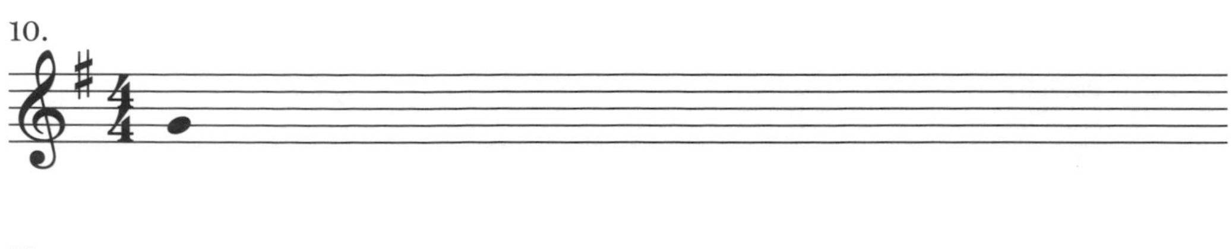

11.

NAME ______________________________

Contextual Listening 6.1

In this CL exercise you will:

- Notate the rhythm of the melody and bass line from a piano work
- Map pitches to notes, solfège syllables, and scale-degree numbers, then notate the melody
- Identify the melodic range

Listen to an excerpt from a piano work, and complete the following exercises.

1. Which of these represents the meter of this excerpt?
   (a) simple duple (b) simple quadruple
   (c) compound duple (d) compound triple
2. On which scale are the melody and bass parts based?
   (a) ascending melodic minor (b) natural minor (descending melodic)
   (c) harmonic minor (d) major
3. From the melody's lowest pitch to its highest, which describes its range?
   (a) *do* to *sol* ($\hat{1}$-$\hat{5}$) (b) *ti* to *la* ($\hat{7}$-$\hat{6}$) (c) *do* to *do* ($\hat{1}$-$\hat{1}$) (d) *sol* to *sol* ($\hat{5}$-$\hat{5}$)
4. Which are the solfège syllables or scale-degree numbers for melodic pitches 6-7?
   (a) *do* to *sol* ($\hat{1}$-$\hat{5}$) (b) *re* to *sol* ($\hat{2}$-$\hat{5}$) (c) *ti* to *fa* ($\hat{7}$-$\hat{4}$) (d) *re* to *la* ($\hat{2}$-$\hat{6}$)
5. What is the interval between melodic pitches 6 and 7?
   (a) P4 (b) P5 (c) M6 (d) d5
6. Use the workspace provided to capture the excerpt.
   (a) Notate the rhythm of the melody and bass parts on the single-line staves. Refer to your answer to question 1, and choose a meter signature. Include bar lines, and beam notes to show beat grouping.
   (b) Below the rhythm staff, and under each note, write the solfège syllables or scale-degree numbers for the melody and bass. Begin the melody on *mi* ($\hat{3}$) and the bass on *do* ($\hat{1}$).
   (c) Combine your answers to complete the notation of the pitches and rhythm of the excerpt. Begin the melody on G♯4 and the bass on E3. Write the appropriate clef, key signature, and meter signature. Be sure to vertically align the pitches that sound together.

Workspace

Rhythm:

Melody:

Solfège syllables: *m*

Scale-degree numbers: $\hat{3}$

Notation:

Rhythm:

Bass:

Solfège syllables: *d*

Scale-degree numbers: $\hat{1}$

NAME ____________________

Contextual Listening 6.2

In this CL exercise you will:

- Notate the rhythm appearing in the highest and lowest parts of a string quartet movement
- Identify harmonic and melodic intervals
- Map pitches to notes, solfège syllables, and scale-degree numbers, then notate the pitches of the melody

Listen to an excerpt from a string quartet (in which only three instruments play), then complete the following exercises.

1. On which scale is this music based?

   (a) major (b) natural minor (descending melodic)

   (c) ascending melodic minor (d) Phrygian

2. At the beginning, the two highest parts form which type of interval?

   (a) consonant (b) dissonant

3. At the beginning, which is the interval that the two highest parts form?

   (a) unisons throughout (b) thirds throughout

   (c) thirds changing to sixths (d) sixths changing to thirds

4. At the beginning of the lowest part, which is the melodic interval played?

   (a) M3 (b) P5 (c) M6 (d) P8

5. At the end of the excerpt, the lower part's last two pitches create which melodic interval?

   (a) m2 (b) M2 (c) P4 (d) P5

6. The excerpt concludes with which harmonic interval?

   (a) m3 (b) M3 (c) P5 (d) P8

7. Use the workspace provided to capture the excerpt.

   (a) Notate the rhythm of the highest and lowest parts on the single-line staves in simple quadruple meter. Choose a meter signature, and include bar lines. Beam notes to show beat grouping.

   (b) Below each rhythm staff, and under each note, write the solfège syllables or scale-degree numbers for the highest and lowest parts. Begin the highest part on *sol* ($\hat{5}$) and the lowest part on *do* ($\hat{1}$).

   (c) Combine your answers to complete the notation of the pitches and rhythm of the highest and lowest parts. The clefs, key signatures, and first notes are provided. Notate the lowest part even when the instrument changes. Write the appropriate meter signature and vertically align pitches that sound simultaneously.

Workspace

Rhythm:

Highest part: ‖

Solfège syllables: *s*

Scale-degree numbers: $\hat{5}$

‖

Solfège syllables:

Scale-degree numbers:

Notation:

Rhythm:

Lowest part: ‖

Solfège syllables: *d*

Scale-degree numbers: $\hat{1}$

‖

Solfège syllables:

Scale-degree numbers:

NAME ______________________

Contextual Listening 6.3

In this CL exercise you will:

- Notate the rhythm of a melody from an accompanied song
- Identify important harmonic and melodic intervals
- Map pitches to notes, solfège syllables, and scale-degree numbers, then notate the melody and bass

Listen to an excerpt from an art song, and complete the following exercises.

1. On which scale or mode is the singer's melody based?

   (a) ascending melodic minor (b) natural minor (descending melodic)

   (c) harmonic minor (d) Phrygian

2. What are the first three harmonic intervals between the voice and the lowest piano pitch?

   (a) m3-P4-m3 (b) P4-P5-P4 (c) P5-m6-P5 (d) P8-M7-P8

3. Use the workspace provided to capture the excerpt.

   (a) Notate the singer's rhythm in simple duple meter. The rhythm for the lowest part (piano) is provided. Choose a meter signature, and include bar lines. Beam notes to show beat grouping.

   (b) Below each rhythm staff, and under each note, write the solfège syllables or scale-degree numbers for the singer's melody and the lowest pitches of the piano part. Begin both parts on *do* ($\hat{1}$).

   (c) Combine your answers to complete the notation of the singer's melody and the lowest part (piano). The clefs, key signatures, and first notes are provided. Choose a meter signature, and include bar lines. Beam notes to show beat grouping.

Workspace

Rhythm:

Melody:

Solfège syllables: *d*

Scale-degree numbers: $\hat{1}$

Solfège syllables:

Scale-degree numbers:

Notation:

Rhythm:

Lowest part:

Solfège syllables: *d*

Scale-degree numbers: $\hat{1}$

Solfège syllables:

Scale-degree numbers:

NAME ______________________________

Contextual Listening 6.4

In this CL exercise you will:

- Identify the meter of an opera chorus excerpt and notate the rhythm of its melody
- Identify important rhythmic and intervallic motives
- Map pitches to notes, solfège syllables, and scale-degree numbers, then notate the melody
- Transpose the melody to a different key

Listen to an excerpt from an opera and complete the following exercises. The melody consists of two segments, each one eight pitches long.

1. Which is the meter signature of this excerpt?

   (a) $\frac{2}{4}$ (b) $\frac{3}{4}$ (c) $\frac{4}{4}$ (d) $\frac{6}{8}$

2. Melodic pitches 1–2 create which pitch interval?

   (a) m3 (b) M3 (c) P4 (d) P5

3. Melodic pitches 6–7 create which pitch interval?

   (a) m3 (b) M3 (c) P4 (d) P5

4. At the beginning, the melody is doubled at which interval?

   (a) third (b) fourth (c) sixth (d) octave

5. Segment 2 begins with which rhythmic feature(s)?

   (a) dotted notes (b) syncopation (c) anacrusis (d) rubato

6. The final note in the vocal parts creates which harmonic interval?

   (a) third (b) fourth (c) sixth (d) octave

7. Which describes the relationship between the vocal melody and the higher part of the accompaniment?

   (a) The accompaniment doubles the vocal melody.

   (b) The accompaniment imitates the vocal melody.

   (c) The accompaniment embellishes the vocal melody.

   (d) The accompaniment moves in contrary motion to the vocal melody.

8. Use the workspace provided to capture the excerpt.

   (a) Notate the rhythm of the vocal melody on the single-line staves. Choose a meter signature, and include bar lines. Beam notes to show beat grouping.

   (b) Below each rhythm staff, and under each note, write the solfège syllables or scale-degree numbers for the melody.

   (c) Combine your answers to complete the notation of the pitches and rhythm of the melody beginning on F♯4. Write the appropriate clef, key signature, and meter signature.

Workspace

Rhythm:

Vocal melody:

Solfège syllables:

Scale-degree numbers:

Solfège syllables:

Scale-degree numbers:

Notation:

9. Refer to your notation to transpose the melody to begin on E♭4. Use the appropriate clef and key signature.

CHAPTER 7

Triads

NAME ______________________________

In this chapter you'll learn to:

- Identify triadic constructions and patterns in melodic contexts
- Map pitches to notes, solfège syllables, and scale-degree numbers
- Transpose melodies to different keys and clefs
- Visualize correct rhythmic notation in context

Preparatory Listening

Complete the *Try It* dictations to familiarize yourself with the following concepts and skills:

- Recognizing and notating common melodic patterns occurring within the major scale
- Recognizing and notating common rhythmic patterns in simple meters

Try It

Listen to short melodies that are played twice with a pause in between. Each example outlines a triad and is preceded by two "count-off" measures to set the tempo and meter; a melody that begins on the given pitch follows.

- Notate the pitches and rhythm for each example on the staff provided with notes beamed to show beat grouping.
- Include bar lines; always end with a double bar.
- If you are working by yourself, sing the melody aloud with solfège syllables, scale-degree numbers, and/or letter names.

3.
4.
5.
6.
7.
8.

NAME ______________________________

Contextual Listening 7.1

In this CL exercise you will:

- Identify the meter of a work for keyboard and notate its rhythm
- Identify the quality of triads in a harmonic context

Listen to an excerpt from a keyboard work, and complete the following exercises.

1. Which is the meter signature of this excerpt?

   (a) $\frac{2}{4}$ (b) $\frac{3}{4}$ (c) $\frac{4}{4}$ (d) $\frac{6}{8}$

2. Use the workspace provided to identify triad types.

   (a) Notate the rhythm of the melody on the single-line staff. Write the meter signature, and include bar lines. Beam notes to show beat grouping.

   (b) Below the rhythm staff, indicate the triad quality on the downbeat of each measure using the abbreviations M, m, d, and A.

Workspace

Rhythm:

Melody:

Triad qualities:

Triad qualities:

NAME ______________________

Contextual Listening 7.2

In this CL exercise you will:

- Identify the meter of a work for piano and notate its rhythm
- Identify important harmonic and melodic intervals
- Identify a melodic segments as a triad type
- Map pitches to notes, solfège syllables, and scale-degree numbers, then notate the melody

Listen to an excerpt from a keyboard work, and complete the following exercises.

1. Which is the meter signature of this excerpt?

   (a) $\frac{2}{2}$ (b) $\frac{3}{4}$ (c) $\frac{6}{8}$ (d) $\frac{9}{8}$

2. At the beginning, which rhythmic feature is heard?

   (a) anacrusis (b) syncopation (c) rubato (d) dotted notes

3. On which scale or mode is this melody based?

   (a) major (b) natural minor (descending melodic)
   (c) Dorian (d) Phrygian

4. Throughout the excerpt, the melody is doubled at which interval?

   (a) m3 (b) P5 (c) M6 (d) P8

5. Use the workspace provided to capture the excerpt.

   (a) Notate the rhythm of the excerpt on the single-line staff. Write the meter signature, and include bar lines. Beam notes to show beat grouping.

   (b) Below the rhythm staff, and under each note, write the solfège syllables or scale-degree numbers for the melody starting on the tonic pitch.

   (c) Combine your answers to complete the notation of the pitches and rhythm of the melody beginning on C4. Write the appropriate clef, key signature, and meter signature.

Workspace

Rhythm:

Solfège syllables:

Scale-degree numbers:

Notation:

6. At the beginning of the melody, which type of triad is arpeggiated?

   (a) major (b) minor (c) augmented (d) diminished

7. The largest skips in the melody are which interval?

   (a) m3 (b) M3 (c) P4 (d) P5

NAME ___________________________________

Contextual Listening 7.3

In this CL exercise you will:

- Identify the meter and key or mode of a well-known spiritual
- Visualize the correct rhythmic notation
- Map pitches to notes, solfège syllables, and scale-degree numbers, then notate the melody
- Transpose the excerpt to a different key and clef

Listen to an excerpt from a spiritual, and complete the following exercises.

1. The excerpt begins and ends on which pitch?

   (a) mediant (b) subdominant (c) dominant (d) tonic

2. At the beginning, the rhythm is notated as in which of the following examples?

3. Use the workspace provided to capture the excerpt.

   (a) Transfer the rhythm of the excerpt from question 2 onto the single-line staff. Include a meter signature and bar lines, and beam notes to show beat grouping.

   (b) Below the rhythm staff, and under each note, write the solfège syllables or scale-degree numbers for the melody.

   (c) Combine your answers to complete the notation of the pitches and rhythm of the melody beginning on E4. Write the appropriate clef, key signature, and meter signature.

Workspace

Rhythm:

Solfège syllables:
Scale-degree numbers:

Solfège syllables:
Scale-degree numbers:

Notation:

4. Refer to your notation to transpose the melody to begin on B♭2. Use the appropriate clef, key signature, and meter signature.

5. This melody is based on arpeggiations of what quality of triad?
   (a) major (b) minor (c) diminished (d) augmented

6. Melodic pitch 3 is which type of embellishing tone?
   (a) neighbor tone (note above or below a single pitch of the triad)
   (b) passing tone (note between two different pitches of the triad)

7. From the melody's lowest pitch to its highest, which describes its range?
   (a) *do* to *sol* ($\hat{1}$-$\hat{5}$) (b) *ti* to *la* ($\hat{7}$-$\hat{6}$) (c) *do* to *do* ($\hat{1}$-$\hat{1}$) (d) *sol* to *sol* ($\hat{5}$-$\hat{5}$)

NAME ____________________

Contextual Listening 7.4

In this CL exercise you will:

- Identify the meter of a work for piano and notate its rhythm
- Map pitches to notes, solfège syllables, and scale-degree numbers, then notate the outer parts
- Identify intervals, tetrachords, and triad types

Listen to an excerpt from a piano work, and complete the following exercises.

1. Which is the meter signature of this excerpt?

   (a) $\frac{2}{2}$ (b) $\frac{3}{4}$ (c) $\frac{6}{8}$ (d) $\frac{9}{8}$

2. On which scale or mode is this excerpt based?

   (a) major
   (b) natural minor (descending melodic)
   (c) Dorian
   (d) Lydian

3. Use the workspace provided to capture the excerpt.

   (a) Notate the rhythm of both parts on the single-line staves. Write the meter signature from question 1, and include bar lines. Beam notes to show beat grouping.

   (b) Below each rhythm staff, and under each note, write the solfège syllables or scale-degree numbers for the melody and bass. Begin both parts on the tonic pitch.

   (c) Combine your answers to complete the notation of the pitches and rhythm of the excerpt. Begin on C4 (melody) and C3 (bass). Write the appropriate clefs, key signature, and meter signature.

Workspace

Rhythm:

Melody:

Solfège syllables:

Scale-degree numbers:

Solfège syllables:

Scale-degree numbers:

Notation:

Rhythm:

Bass:

Solfège syllables:

Scale-degree numbers:

Solfège syllables:

Scale-degree numbers:

4. At the beginning of the melody, which type of triad is arpeggiated?
   (a) major (b) minor (c) augmented (d) diminished
5. The melody concludes with which melodic pattern?
   (a) harmonic tetrachord (b) minor tetrachord
   (c) major pentachord (d) minor pentachord
6. At the end, the melody is doubled using which interval?
   (a) thirds (b) fourths (c) fifths (d) sixths
7. The largest skip in the melody is which interval?
   (a) m3 (b) P4 (c) P5 (d) P8

NAME ______________________________

Contextual Listening 7.5

In this CL exercise you will:

- Notate the rhythm of both parts of a work for piano
- Map pitches to notes, solfège syllables, and scale-degree numbers, then notate the outer parts
- Identify intervals, tetrachords, and triad types appearing in the work

Listen to an excerpt from a piano piece, and complete the following exercises.

1. Use the workspace provided to capture the excerpt.
   (a) Notate the rhythm of both parts in simple duple meter on the single-line staves. The shortest note value is the sixteenth note. Choose a meter signature, and include bar lines. Beam notes to show beat grouping.
   (b) Below each rhythm staff, and under each note, write the solfège syllables or scale-degree numbers for both parts. Begin the melody on the dominant pitch and the lowest part on the tonic pitch.
   (c) Combine your answers to complete the notation of the pitches and rhythm of the excerpt. Begin on C5 (melody) and F4 (lowest part). Write the appropriate clefs, key signature, and meter signature.

Workspace

Rhythm:

Melody:

Solfège syllables:

Scale-degree numbers:

Solfège syllables:

Scale-degree numbers:

Notation:

Rhythm:

Lowest part:

Solfège syllables:

Scale-degree numbers:

Solfège syllables:

Scale-degree numbers:

2. Which is the quality of the first triad?

   (a) major (b) minor (c) augmented (d) diminished

3. When the bass note changes, which is the quality of the triad?

   (a) major (b) minor (c) augmented (d) diminished

4. Which are the harmonic intervals in measures 1-3 in the accompaniment (lowest part)?

   (a) P5-P5 (b) M3-P5 (c) P4-P8 (d) m6-P8

5. The excerpt concludes with which harmonic interval?

   (a) M3 (b) P5 (c) M6 (d) P8

6. From the melody's lowest pitch to its highest, which describes its range?

   (a) *do* to *sol* ($\hat{1}$-$\hat{5}$) (b) *ti* to *la* ($\hat{7}$-$\hat{6}$) (c) *do* to *do* ($\hat{1}$-$\hat{1}$) (d) *sol* to *sol* ($\hat{5}$-$\hat{5}$)

CHAPTER 8

Seventh Chords

NAME ______________________

In this chapter you'll learn to:

- Identify seventh-chord constructions in melodic contexts
- Apply chord symbols to seventh-chord types
- Map pitches to notes, solfège syllables, and scale-degree numbers
- Visualize correct rhythmic notation in context
- Transpose melodies to different keys and clefs

Preparatory Listening

Complete the *Try It* dictations to familiarize yourself with the following concepts and skills:

- Recognizing and notating diatonic seventh chords that occur within major and minor scales
- Recognizing and notating common rhythmic patterns in compound duple meter

Try It

Listen to short melodies that are played twice with a pause in between. Each example outlines a seventh chord and is preceded by two "count-off" measures to set the tempo and meter; a melody that begins on the given pitch follows.

- Notate the pitches and rhythm for each example on the staff provided with notes beamed to show beat grouping.
- Include bar lines; always end with a double bar.
- If you are working by yourself, sing the melody aloud with solfège syllables, scale-degree numbers, and/or letter names.

1.

2.

3.
4.
5.
6.
7.
8.
9.
10.

NAME ______________________

Contextual Listening 8.1

In this CL exercise you will:

- Notate the rhythm of a jazz standard
- Map pitches to notes, solfège syllables, and scale-degree numbers, then notate the melody and bass line
- Identify intervals and tetrachords
- Apply chord symbols to seventh-chord types

Listen to an excerpt from a 1920s jazz standard, and complete the following exercises.

1. Use the workspace provided to capture the excerpt.

   (a) Notate the rhythm of the melody and bass on the single-line staves. At the beginning the bass moves in half notes. Choose a meter signature, and include bar lines.

   (b) Below each rhythm staff, and under each note, write the solfège syllables or scale-degree numbers for the melody and bass. Begin the melody on *do* ($\hat{1}$) and the bass on *re* ($\hat{2}$).

   (c) Combine your answers to complete the notation of the pitches and rhythm of the excerpt. Begin the melody on A♭4 and the bass line on B♭2. Write the appropriate clefs, key signature, and meter signature.

   (d) Above the grand staff, write the seventh chords with popular-music chord symbols (e.g., Cmaj7, E♭dim7, G7, etc.). There are two chords in all but the last two measures.

Workspace

Rhythm:

Melody:

Solfège syllables: *d*

Scale-degree numbers: $\hat{1}$

Solfège syllables:

Scale-degree numbers:

Notation:

Chord symbols:

Rhythm:

Bass:

Solfège syllables: *r*

Scale-degree numbers: $\hat{2}$

Solfège syllables:

Scale-degree numbers:

2. Melodic pitches 1-2 create which interval?
   (a) m3 (b) M3 (c) P4 (d) P5

3. The melody concludes with which melodic pattern?
   (a) major pentachord (b) major tetrachord
   (c) minor pentachord (d) minor tetrachord

NAME ______________________________

4. The last two melodic pitches create which interval?

(a) P5 (b) m6 (c) M6 (d) P8

5. The last two bass pitches make which interval?

(a) P8 (b) M6 (c) m6 (d) P4

Contextual Listening 8.2

In this CL exercise you will:

- Notate the rhythm of both parts of a work for piano
- Identify intervals, pitch collections, triad types
- Map pitches to notes, solfège syllables, and scale-degree numbers, then notate the entire excerpt
- Transpose the excerpt's melody to a different key and clef

Listen to an excerpt from a keyboard sonata, and complete the following exercises.

1. At the beginning, which rhythmic feature occurs?

   (a) anacrusis (b) syncopation (c) rubato (d) dotted notes

The melody is divided into four segments, each one four beats long. The first three segments begin with arpeggiated triads.

2. In melodic pitches 1-4, which is the quality and inversion of the arpeggiated triad?

   (a) major, first inversion (b) major, second inversion
   (c) minor, first inversion (d) minor, second inversion

3. In segment 2, which is the quality of the arpeggiated triad?

   (a) major (b) minor (c) augmented (d) diminished

4. In segment 3, which Roman numeral represents the arpeggiated triad?

   (a) I (b) ii (c) IV (d) V

5. The melody concludes with which pattern?

   (a) minor pentachord (b) minor triad
   (c) major pentachord (d) major triad

6. Which best describes the contour of the entire melodic line?

   (a) conjunct (b) disjunct (c) mostly conjunct (d) mostly disjunct

7. Use the workspace provided to capture the excerpt.

   (a) Notate the rhythm of the melody on the single-line staves in simple duple meter. The shortest note value is the sixteenth note. Include bar lines, and beam notes to show beat grouping.

   (b) Below each rhythm staff, and under each note, write the solfège syllables or scale-degree numbers for the melody. Begin the melody on the dominant pitch.

   (c) Combine your answers to complete the notation of the pitches and rhythm of the melody. Begin the melody on D4. Write the appropriate clef, key signature, and meter signature.

NAME ______________________________

Workspace

Rhythm:

Melody:

Solfège syllables:

Scale-degree numbers:

Solfège syllables:

Scale-degree numbers:

Notation:

8. Refer to your notation to transpose the melody to the key of B♭ major. The starting pitch is F2. Write the appropriate clef, key signature, and meter signature.

NAME ______________________________

Contextual Listening 8.3

In this CL exercise you will:

- Notate the rhythm of a violin melody from a chamber work
- Map pitches to notes, solfège syllables, and scale-degree numbers, then notate the melody
- Identify the work's triad and seventh-chord types in context

Listen to an excerpt from a chamber work, and complete the following exercises.

1. Use the workspace provided to capture the excerpt.
   (a) Notate the rhythm of the violin melody on the single-line staves in simple quadruple meter. The shortest note value is the sixteenth note. Write the appropriate meter signature, and include bar lines. Beam notes to show beat grouping.
   (b) Below the rhythm staves, and under each note, write the solfège syllables or scale-degree numbers for the violin melody. Begin on *sol* ($\hat{5}$).
   (c) Combine your answers to complete the notation of the pitches and rhythm of the violin melody beginning on G5. Use the appropriate clef, key signature, and meter signature.

Workspace

Rhythm:

Melody: 

Solfège syllables: s

Scale-degree numbers: $\hat{5}$

Solfège syllables:

Scale-degree numbers:

Notation:

2. The following rhythm indicates when the excerpt's harmonies change. In each blank, write the quality of the chord in that measure. For triads, write the abbreviations M, m, A, and d; for seventh chords, write MM, Mm, mm, dm, and dd. (Measure 5 includes a pedal tone, which is not part of the chord.)

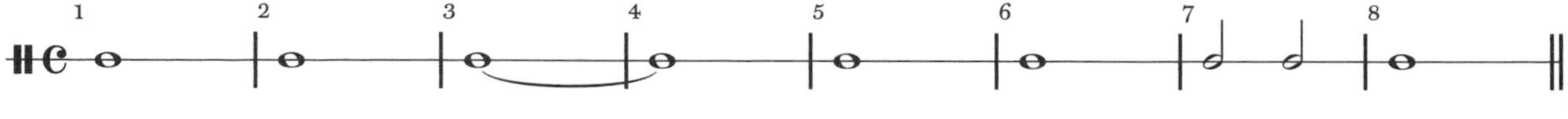

NAME ______________________________

Contextual Listening 8.4

In this CL exercise you will:

- Visualize the notation of an important rhythmic motive from a chamber-work melody and notate its rhythm
- Map pitches to notes, solfège syllables, and scale-degree numbers, then notate the melody
- Transpose the excerpt's melody to a different key and clef
- Identify triads by type, function, and Roman numeral

Listen to an excerpt from a chamber work, and complete the following exercises.

1. At the beginning, the violin's anacrusis is represented by which rhythm?

   (a)  (b) 

   (c)  (d) 

2. The violin melody begins with a triad arpeggio of which quality?

   (a) major (b) minor (c) augmented (d) diminished

3. Use the workspace provided to capture the excerpt.

   (a) Notate the rhythm of the violin melody on the single-line staves in simple quadruple meter. The shortest note value is the sixteenth note. Choose a meter signature, and include bar lines.

   (b) Below the rhythm staves, and under each note, write the solfège syllables or scale-degree numbers for the violin melody. Begin on *sol* ($\hat{5}$).

   (c) Combine your answers to complete the notation of the pitches and rhythm of the violin melody beginning on B♭4. Write the appropriate clef, key signature, and meter signature.

Workspace

Rhythm:

Melody:

Solfège syllables: *s*

Scale-degree numbers: $\hat{5}$

Solfège syllables:

Scale-degree numbers:

Notation:

4. Refer to your notation to transpose the melody to the key of G major. The starting pitch is D3. Use the appropriate clef and key signature.

5. The piano's first arpeggiated triad is which of the following chords? (This triad begins at the same time as the violin's third pitch.)

   (a) tonic (b) supertonic (c) subdominant (d) dominant

6. The piano's second arpeggiated triad is which of the following chords?

   (a) I (b) ii (c) IV (d) V

7. The violin's last two pitches create which interval?

   (a) M3 (b) P4 (c) P5 (d) M6

8. The piano's last two triad arpeggios are of which qualities? (These occur during the violin's last seven pitches.)

   (a) major, minor (b) major, diminished

   (c) minor, minor (d) minor, diminished

9. From the violin's lowest pitch to its highest, which of the following best describes its range?

   (a) *do* to *sol* ($\hat{1}$-$\hat{5}$) (b) *ti* to *la* ($\hat{7}$-$\hat{6}$) (c) *do* to *do* ($\hat{1}$-$\hat{1}$) (d) *sol* to *sol* ($\hat{5}$-$\hat{5}$)

Note-to-Note Counterpoint

NAME ______________________

In this chapter you'll learn to:

- Map pitches to notes, solfège syllables, and scale-degree numbers in note-to-note counterpoint
- Identify two-part contours and types of motion
- Identify harmonic intervals in a two-part contrapuntal texture
- Transpose note-to-note counterpoint to different keys and clefs

Preparatory Listening

Complete the *Try It* dictations to familiarize yourself with the following concepts and skills:

- Recognizing different types of motion in two-part, note-to-note counterpoint
- Notating two parts in note-to-note counterpoint

Try It

Listen to contrapuntal excerpts that are played twice with a pause in between. Each example is preceded by two "count-off" measures to set the tempo; a two-part excerpt beginning on the given pitches follows.

- Notate the pitches using whole notes only.
- Divide each dictation into two halves separated by a bar line; always end with a double bar.
- If you are working by yourself, sing each part aloud with solfège syllables, scale-degree numbers, and/or letter names.

1.

2.

3.
4.
5.
6.
7.
8.

NAME ______________________

Contextual Listening 9.1

In this CL exercise you will:

- Identify the meter of a two-part work for piano, and notate the rhythm of both parts
- Map pitches to notes, solfège syllables, and scale-degree numbers, then notate the entire excerpt
- Identify the scale type and the melodic intervals
- Identify harmonic intervals between parts

Listen to an excerpt of an adapted piano sonata, and complete the following exercises. Because the tempo is quick, memorize what you hear and play it back slowly in your imagination.

1. Which is the meter signature of this excerpt?
   (a) $\substack{6\\8}$ (b) $\substack{9\\8}$ (c) $\substack{2\\4}$ (d) $\substack{4\\4}$
2. On which scale is the excerpt based?
   (a) ascending melodic minor (b) natural minor (descending melodic)
   (c) harmonic minor (d) major
3. Pitches 2–3 create which melodic interval?
   (a) M3 (b) P4 (c) P5 (d) M6
4. The last two pitches in the bass create which melodic interval?
   (a) m2 (b) M2 (c) P4 (d) P5
5. The excerpt concludes with which harmonic interval?
   (a) P8 (b) P5 (c) M3 (d) m3
6. From the melody's lowest pitch to its highest, which best describes its range?
   (a) *do* to *sol* ($\hat{1}$-$\hat{5}$) (b) *ti* to *la* ($\hat{7}$-$\hat{6}$) (c) *do* to *do* ($\hat{1}$-$\hat{1}$) (d) *sol* to *la* ($\hat{5}$-$\hat{6}$)
7. Use the workspace provided to capture the excerpt.
   (a) Notate the rhythm of the melody and bass on the single-line staves in compound duple meter. The initial four notes are an anacrusis to the first complete measure. Choose a meter signature, and include bar lines. Beam notes to show beat grouping.
   (b) Below each rhythm staff, and under each note, write the solfège syllables or scale-degree numbers for the melody and bass. Begin the melody on *sol* ($\hat{5}$) and the bass on *mi* ($\hat{3}$).
   (c) Combine your answers to complete the notation of the pitches and rhythm of the excerpt. Begin the melody on D4 and the bass on B2. Use the appropriate clefs, key signature, and meter signature.
   (d) Between the five-line staves, write harmonic interval numbers between the two parts. Notice the three places in the excerpt that are not note-to-note counterpoint.
   (e) Circle the dissonant interval (not allowed in strict note-to-note counterpoint).

Workspace

Rhythm:

Melody:

Solfège syllables: *s*

Scale-degree numbers: $\hat{5}$

Notation:

Rhythm:

Bass:

Solfège syllables: *m*

Scale-degree numbers: $\hat{3}$

8. Examine the harmonic interval types in your answer to question 7. Which type of consonance occurs more often?

   (a) imperfect (b) perfect

9. Melodic pitches 3-5 and 9-11 and their counterpoint feature all of the following except which of these?

   (a) conjunct motion in each part
   (b) contrary motion between parts
   (c) cross relation between parts
   (d) voice exchange between parts

NAME ______________________________

Contextual Listening 9.2

In this CL exercise you will:

- Notate the rhythm of a two-part excerpt from a string quartet
- Map pitches to notes, solfège syllables, and scale-degree numbers, then notate the entire excerpt
- Determine the scale or mode
- Identify melodic intervals and the harmonic intervals between parts
- Identify types of contrapuntal motion

Listen to an excerpt from a string quartet, and complete the following exercises. The excerpt consists of four phrases; each begins with an anacrusis, and is eight notes long.

1. Use the workspace provided to capture the excerpt.
   (a) Notate the rhythm of the upper and lower parts on the single-line staves. The shortest note value is the half note. Choose a meter signature, and includes bar lines.
   (b) Below each rhythm staff and under each note, write the solfège syllables or scale-degree numbers for the upper and lower parts. Begin on *do* ($\hat{1}$) for both parts.
   (c) Combine your answers to complete the notation of the pitches and rhythm of the excerpt. Begin the upper part on F4 and the lower part on F3. Use the appropriate clefs, key signature, and meter signature.
   (d) Between the five-line staves, write harmonic intervals.

Workspace

Rhythm:

Upper part: 𝄃

Solfège syllables: *d*

Scale-degree numbers: $\hat{1}$

𝄃

Solfège syllables:

Scale-degree numbers:

Notation:

Rhythm:

Lower part: 𝄃

Solfège syllables: *d*

Scale-degree numbers: $\hat{1}$

𝄃

Solfège syllables:

Scale-degree numbers:

2. Which harmonic interval types are heard most frequently in this excerpt?
   (a) thirds and fifths
   (b) thirds and sixths
   (c) fifths and octaves
   (d) sixths and octaves
3. The first three pitches of the lower part outline which type of triad?
   (a) major (b) minor (c) augmented (d) diminished
4. Between the first two harmonic pitches, which type of motion occurs?
   (a) contrary (b) oblique (c) similar (d) parallel

NAME ______________________________

5. Phrase 1's last two harmonic pitches (pitches 7–8) create which type of motion?

   (a) contrary (b) oblique (c) similar (d) parallel

6. During all of phrase 2, which best describes the types of motion that occur?

   (a) parallel throughout (b) parallel, then contrary

   (c) contrary, then parallel (d) oblique, then contrary

7. Phrase 3's first two harmonic pitches create which type of motion?

   (a) contrary (b) oblique (c) similar (d) parallel

8. In phrase 4, between pitches 3 and 4, which unusual succession of harmonic intervals occurs?

   (a) PU-PU (b) P4-P4 (c) P5-P5 (d) P8-P8

9. The excerpt's melodic high point occurs at the end of which phrase?

   (a) 1 (b) 2 (c) 3 (d) 4

10. The excerpt concludes with which harmonic intervals?

    (a) m3-M6 (b) M3-m6 (c) P5-P8 (d) M10-P8

11. On which scale or mode is the excerpt based?

    (a) major (b) natural minor (descending melodic)

    (c) Dorian (d) Lydian

12. Refer to your answers from previous questions to transpose the upper and lower parts to begin on C4 and C3, respectively. Be sure to include any appropriate accidental(s).

NAME ______________________________

Contextual Listening 9.3

In this CL exercise you will:

- Identify the meter of a two-part choral work
- Notate the rhythm of both parts
- Identify the scale or mode, as well as triadic segments
- Identify types of contrapuntal motion
- Map pitches to notes, solfège syllables, and scale-degree numbers, then notate the entire excerpt

Listen to an excerpt from a choral work, here sung in two voice parts. There are six segments in the excerpt, each separated from the next by a rest.

1. Which is the meter signature of this excerpt?

   (a) $\frac{3}{4}$ (b) $\frac{4}{4}$ (c) $\frac{6}{8}$ (d) $\frac{9}{8}$

2. On which scale or mode is the entire excerpt based?

   (a) major (b) natural minor (descending melodic)

   (c) Dorian (d) Lydian

3. Segments 3 and 4 consist entirely of which type of motion?

   (a) contrary (b) oblique (c) similar (d) parallel

4. At the beginning of segment 5 ("folget meiner leichten Spur"), which type of motion occurs?

   (a) contrary (b) oblique (c) similar (d) parallel

5. During segment 5, the higher part contains two arpeggiated triads. What are their qualities?

   (a) minor, minor (b) major, minor (c) major, major (d) diminished, major

6. At the beginning of the last segment, the higher part arpeggiates which type of triad?

   (a) major (b) minor (c) augmented (d) diminished

7. In the last segment, which best describes the types of motion that occur?

   (a) parallel throughout (b) contrary throughout

   (c) parallel, then contrary (d) oblique, then parallel

8. The excerpt concludes with which harmonic intervals?

   (a) m3-M6 (b) M3-m6 (c) P4-M6 (d) A4-m6

9. The end of segment 6 is like the end of which earlier segment?

   (a) 1 (b) 2 (c) 3 (d) 4

10. Which is the better description of the counterpoint in this excerpt?

    (a) entirely first species (b) mostly first species

11. Use the workspace provided to capture the excerpt.

    (a) Notate the rhythm of both parts on the single-line staves. Refer to your answer to question 1 to help you. Choose a meter signature, and include bar lines. Beam notes to show beat grouping.

(b) Below each rhythm staff, and under each note, write the solfège syllables or scale-degree numbers for the upper and lower parts. Begin both parts on the dominant pitch. Note that the seventh pitch in the upper part is a lowered note: *te* ($\flat\hat{7}$).

(c) Combine your answers to complete the notation of the pitches and rhythm of the excerpt. Begin both parts on B4 and indicate the lowered note with an accidental. Use the appropriate clefs, key signature, and meter signature.

(d) Between the five-line staves, write harmonic interval numbers where simultaneous pitches occur.

Workspace

Rhythm:

Upper part:

Solfège syllables:

Scale-degree numbers:

Solfège syllables:

Scale-degree numbers:

Notation:

Rhythm:

Lower part:

Solfège syllables:

Scale-degree numbers:

Solfège syllables:

Scale-degree numbers:

12. Which two harmonic intervals are heard most frequently in this excerpt?

    (a) thirds and fifths
    (b) thirds and sixths
    (c) fifths and sixths
    (d) sixths and octaves

13. Refer to your notation to transpose the excerpt to D major, this time for *men's* voices. Write the appropriate clefs, key signature, meter signature, and accidentals.

NAME ___________________________

Contextual Listening 9.4

In this CL exercise you will:

- Notate the rhythm of a keyboard work
- Map pitches to notes, solfège syllables, and scale-degree numbers, then notate the melody and bass line
- Identify the scale or mode
- Identify types of contrapuntal motion
- Identify harmonic intervals between parts

Listen to an excerpt from a keyboard work, and complete the following exercises.

1. On which scale or mode is this music based?

   (a) major (b) Lydian mode

   (c) ascending melodic minor (d) harmonic minor

2. The melody's first two pitches create which type of motion with the bass?

   (a) parallel (b) similar (c) oblique (d) contrary

3. In measures 3-4 in the melody, three arpeggiated triads descend by step. Which chords are arpeggiated?

   (a) iv-III-ii° (b) iii-ii-I (c) ii-I-vii° (d) I-VII-VI

4. Near the end of the excerpt, the bass line descends by step. Which harmonic interval sounds on each beat?

   (a) fifth (b) sixth (c) octave (d) tenth

5. Use the workspace provided to capture the excerpt.

   (a) Notate the rhythm of both parts on the single-line staves in simple quadruple meter. The value of the first pitch is an eighth note. Choose a meter signature, and include bar lines. Beam notes to show beat grouping.

   (b) Below each rhythm staff, and under each note, write the solfège syllables or scale-degree numbers for the melody and bass. Begin the melody on the dominant pitch, and the bass on the tonic pitch.

   (c) Combine your answers to complete the notation of the pitches and rhythm of the excerpt. Begin on F5 (melody) and B♭2 (bass). Use the appropriate clefs, key signature, and meter signature.

Workspace

Rhythm:

Melody:

Solfège syllables:

Scale-degree numbers:

Solfège syllables:

Scale-degree numbers:

Notation:

Rhythm:

Bass:

Solfège syllables:

Scale-degree numbers:

Solfège syllables:

Scale-degree numbers:

6. Refer to your notation. Coinciding with the pitches of the melody, 2, 6, 8, 12, 14, and 18, the recurring harmonic interval is which of the following?

   (a) 5 (b) 6 (c) 7 (d) 10

Melodic/Rhythmic Embellishment in Two-Part Counterpoint

NAME ______________________________

In this chapter you'll learn to:

- Map pitches to notes, solfège syllables, and scale-degree numbers in embellished two-voice counterpoint
- Convert notation in simple meter to compound meter
- Identify two-part contours and types of motion
- Identify harmonic intervals in a two-part contrapuntal texture
- Identify types of melodic embellishment
- Transpose melodies to different keys and clefs

Preparatory Listening

Complete the *Try It* dictations to familiarize yourself with the following concepts and skills:

- Recognizing different types of melodic and rhythmic embellishments in two-part counterpoint
- Notating both parts in embellished note-to-note counterpoint

Try It

Listen to contrapuntal excerpts that are played twice with a pause in between. Each example is preceded by two "count-off" measures to set the tempo; a two-part excerpt beginning on the given pitches follows.

- Notate the pitches using whole notes, half notes, quarter notes, and eighth notes.
- Divide each dictation into two halves separated by a bar line; always end with a double bar.
- If you are working by yourself, sing each part aloud with solfège syllables, scale-degree numbers, and/or letter names.

1.

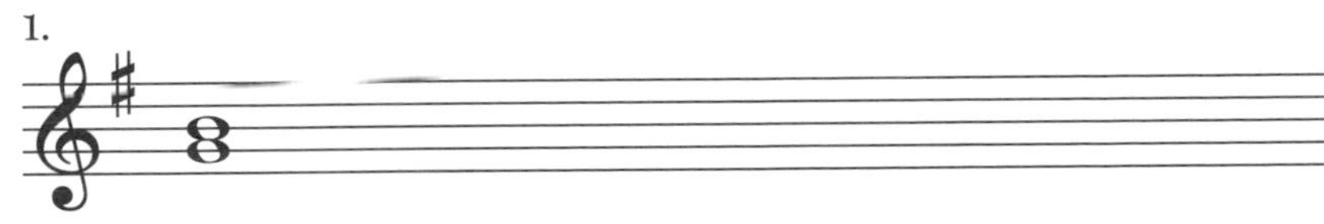

2.
3.
4.
5.
6.
7.
8.

NAME ______________________________

Contextual Listening 10.1

In this CL exercise you will:

- Listen to the rhythm of an art song's piano accompaniment in simple meter and then convert it to compound meter

Listen to an excerpt from an art song, and complete the following exercises.

1. On the single-line staves, notate the rhythm of the accompaniment (left hand/right hand) for the first measure in a *simple* meter. Choose a meter signature, include bar lines, and beam notes to show beat grouping given your choice of meter.

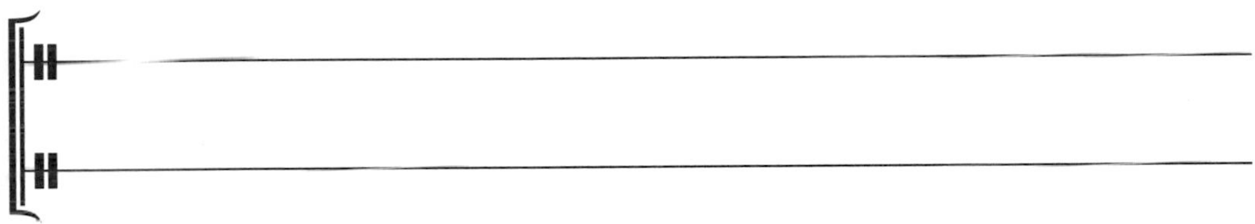

2. On the single-line staves, notate the rhythm of the accompaniment (left hand/right hand) for the first measure in a *compound* meter. Choose a meter signature, include bar lines, and beam notes to show beat grouping given your choice of meter.

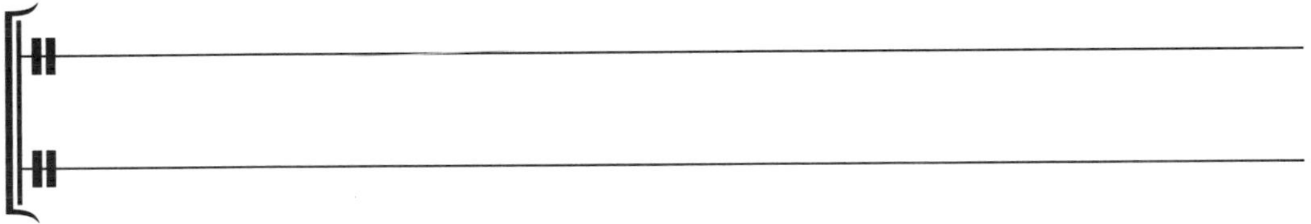

NAME ______________________

Contextual Listening 10.2

In this CL exercise you will:

- Identify the meter of a two-part work for piano and notate the rhythm of both parts
- Map pitches to notes, solfège syllables, and scale-degree numbers, then notate the entire excerpt
- Identify harmonic intervals between parts
- Identify melodic embellishments between parts

Listen to an excerpt from a cantata, and complete the following exercises.

1. Which is the meter signature of this excerpt?

   (a) $\frac{2}{4}$ (b) $\frac{3}{4}$ (c) $\frac{6}{8}$ (d) $\frac{9}{8}$

2. Which is the bass line's first melodic interval?

   (a) m3 (b) m6 (c) P5 (d) P8

3. Which is the melody's first melodic interval?

   (a) m2 (b) M2 (c) M3 (d) P5

4. The two parts begin with which harmonic interval?

   (a) M3 (b) P5 (c) M6 (d) P8

5. The two parts end with which harmonic interval?

   (a) M3 (b) P5 (c) M6 (d) P8

6. Use the workspace provided to capture the excerpt.

   (a) Notate the rhythm of both parts on the single-line staves. Choose a meter signature, and include bar lines. Beam notes to show beat grouping.

   (b) Below each rhythm staff, and under each note, write the solfège syllables or scale-degree numbers for the melody and bass line.

   (c) Combine your answers to complete the notation of the pitches and rhythm of both parts. Begin on C4 (melody) and C3 (bass). Write the appropriate clef, key signature, and meter signature.

   (d) Between the five-line staves, write the harmonic interval numbers between the voices. Circle each dissonant interval, and label its function using the abbreviations N (neighbor) and P (passing tone).

NAME ______________________________

Workspace

Rhythm:

Melody: ‖

Solfège syllables:

Scale-degree numbers:

Notation:

Rhythm:

Bass: ‖

Solfège syllables:

Scale-degree numbers:

6. Refer to your notation to transpose the excerpt so that it begins on C5 (melody) and F3 (bass). Write the appropriate clefs, key signature, and meter signature.

Diatonic Harmony and Tonicization

Soprano and Bass Lines in Eighteenth-Century Style

NAME ______________________

In this chapter you'll learn to:

- Determine the solfège syllables or scale-degree numbers in two-part textures
- Classify cadences as conclusive or inconclusive
- Identify intervals between melodic notes
- Recognize different types of contrapuntal motion
- Notate the outer parts of eighteenth-century chorales

Preparatory Listening

Complete the *Try It* dictations to familiarize yourself with the following concepts and skills:

- Determining the solfège syllables or scale-degree numbers for the melody and bass of two-voice contrapuntal frameworks
- Converting solfège syllables or scale-degree numbers to pitches and notating them on the grand staff

Try It

Listen to two-part dictations that are played once each. The key signature, meter signature, and first bass pitch are given.

- Focus on the bass line first, and notate its pitches.
- Notate the soprano line next; determine the starting pitch from your earlier work.
- Add bar lines including the double bar at the end.
- If you are working by yourself, sing each part aloud with solfège syllables, scale-degree numbers, and/or letter names.

3.
4.
5.
6.
7.
8.
9.
10.

Contextual Listening 11.1

In this CL exercise you will:

- Write the rhythm of the melody and bass from a chorale
- Determine the solfège syllables or scale-degree numbers of the melody and bass, and convert this to notation on the staff
- Classify cadences as conclusive or inconclusive
- Identify harmonic intervals between the parts
- Identify the scale type

Listening Strategy

Typically, *inconclusive cadences* end with *sol* ($\hat{5}$) in the bass. These are called half cadences. The melody at the cadence of inconclusive phrases often falls *mi-re* ($\hat{3}$-$\hat{2}$) or *do-ti* ($\hat{1}$-$\hat{7}$). Sometimes it is important to distinguish between the harmonic and melodic conclusions of a phrase. The harmonic conclusion occurs at the moment of bass resolution. The melodic conclusion may occur later—after dissonances, such as suspensions or retardations, have been resolved.

Listen to the melody and bass of a four-measure phrase from a chorale, and complete the following exercises.

1. Use the workspace provided to capture the excerpt.
   (a) Notate the rhythm of the melody and bass in simple triple meter on the single-line staves. The shortest note value you will hear is the quarter note. The final pitch is sustained for about twice its notated duration. Write a quarter note with a fermata above it. Choose a meter signature, and include bar lines.
   (b) Below each rhythm staff, and under each note, write the solfège syllables or scale-degree numbers for the melody and bass. Begin both parts on *do* ($\hat{1}$).
   (c) Combine your answers to complete the notation of the pitches and rhythm of the melody and bass beginning on G4 and G2 respectively. Write the appropriate clefs, key signature (and any accidentals), and meter signature.
   (d) Write the harmonic interval numbers between the treble and bass staves.

Workspace

Rhythm:

Melody:

Solfège syllables:
Scale-degree numbers:

Notation:

Rhythm:

Bass:

Solfège syllables:
Scale-degree numbers:

2. In the bass line, pitches 1-2 create which melodic interval?
   (a) P4 (b) P5 (c) M6 (d) P8
3. In the bass line, pitches 6-7 create which melodic interval?
   (a) M3 (b) P4 (c) d5 (d) P5
4. The phrase ends with which type of cadence?
   (a) conclusive (b) inconclusive
5. The pitches of the melody belong to which of the following patterns?
   (a) major tetrachord (b) minor tetrachord
   (c) major pentachord (d) minor pentachord
6. The pitches of the bass line belong to which of the following scales?
   (a) major (b) natural minor (descending melodic)
   (c) ascending melodic minor (d) harmonic minor

NAME ______________________

Contextual Listening 11.2

In this CL exercise you will:

- Write the rhythm of the melody and bass from a chorale
- Determine the solfège syllables or scale-degree numbers of the melody and bass, and convert this to notation on the staff
- Classify cadences as conclusive or inconclusive
- Identify harmonic intervals between the parts
- Identify types of contrapuntal motion
- Identify the scale type

Listen to the melody and bass of two phrases from a chorale (each phrase is two measures long), and complete the following exercises.

1. Use the workspace provided to capture the excerpt.
   (a) Notate the rhythm of the melody and bass in common time on the single-line staves. The shortest note value you will hear is the eighth note. The final pitch of each phrase is sustained longer than its notated duration; write a half note with a fermata above it. Choose a meter signature, and include bar lines.
   (b) Below each rhythm staff, and under each note, write the solfège syllables or scale-degree numbers for both parts. Begin the melody on *sol* ($\hat{5}$) and the bass line on *do* ($\hat{1}$).
   (c) Combine your answers to complete the notation of the pitches and rhythm of the melody and bass beginning on G4 and C4 respectively. Write the appropriate clefs, key signature (and any accidentals), meter signature, and beam notes to show beat grouping.
   (d) Write the harmonic interval numbers between the treble and bass staves.

Workspace

Rhythm:

Melody: 𝄃

Solfège syllables:
Scale-degree numbers:

Notation:

Rhythm:

Bass: 𝄃

Solfège syllables:
Scale-degree numbers:

2. In the melody, pitches 1-2 create which melodic interval?
   (a) m3 (b) P4 (c) P5 (d) m6
3. In phrase 1, harmonic pitches 3-5 produce which type of motion?
   (a) contrary (b) oblique (c) similar (d) parallel
4. Phrase 1 ends with which type of cadence?
   (a) conclusive (b) inconclusive
5. In phrase 2, harmonic pitches 1-2 produce which type of motion?
   (a) contrary (b) oblique (c) similar (d) parallel
6. The last two harmonic pitches produce which type of motion?
   (a) contrary (b) oblique (c) similar (d) parallel
7. In the bass line, the last two pitches create which melodic interval?
   (a) M3 (b) P4 (c) d5 (d) P5
8. Phrase 2 ends with which type of cadence?
   (a) conclusive (b) inconclusive
9. In phrase 2, the pitches of the bass line belong to which of the following scales?
   (a) major (b) natural minor (descending melodic)
   (c) ascending melodic minor (d) harmonic minor

During phrase 1, how are the melody and bass parts related?

NAME ______________________________

Contextual Listening 11.3

In this CL exercise you will:

- Write the rhythm of the melody and bass from a chorale
- Determine the solfège syllables or scale-degree numbers of the melody and bass of a chorale, and convert this to notation on the staff
- Classify cadences as conclusive or inconclusive
- Identify harmonic intervals between the parts
- Identify types of contrapuntal motion
- Identify the scale type

Listen to the melody and bass of two phrases from a chorale (each phrase is two measures long), and complete the following exercises.

1. Use the workspace provided to capture the excerpt.
   (a) Notate the rhythm of the melody and bass in common time on the single-line staves. Begin with a quarter-note anacrusis. For the final pitch of each phrase, write a quarter note with a fermata above it.
   (b) Below each rhythm staff, and under each note, write the solfège syllables or scale-degree numbers for the melody and bass. Begin both parts on *do* ($\hat{1}$).
   (c) Combine your answers to complete the notation of the pitches and rhythm of the melody and bass beginning on F4 and F3 respectively. Write the appropriate clefs, key signature, meter signature, and beam notes to show beat grouping.
   (d) Write the harmonic interval numbers between the treble and bass staves.

Workspace

Rhythm:

Melody:

Solfège syllables:
Scale-degree numbers:

Notation:

Rhythm:

Bass:

Solfège syllables:
Scale-degree numbers:

2. In the melody, pitches 1-2 create which melodic interval?
   (a) m3 (b) P4 (c) P5 (d) m6
3. In phrase 1, harmonic pitches 1-2 produce which type of motion?
   (a) contrary (b) oblique (c) similar (d) parallel
4. Phrase 1 ends with which type of cadence?
   (a) conclusive (b) inconclusive
5. In phrase 2, harmonic pitches 1-4 produce which type of motion?
   (a) contrary (b) oblique (c) similar (d) parallel
6. The last two harmonic pitches produce which type of motion?
   (a) contrary (b) oblique (c) similar (d) parallel
7. In the bass, the last two pitches create which melodic interval?
   (a) M3 (b) P4 (c) d5 (d) P5
8. Phrase 2 ends with which type of cadence?
   (a) conclusive (b) inconclusive
9. All the pitches belong to which of the following scales?
   (a) major (b) natural minor (descending melodic)
   (c) ascending melodic minor (d) harmonic minor

Contextual Listening 11.4

In this CL exercise you will:

- Write the rhythm of the melody and bass from a chorale
- Determine the solfège syllables or scale-degree numbers of the melody and bass, and convert this to notation on the staff
- Classify cadences as conclusive or inconclusive
- Identify harmonic intervals between the parts
- Identify types of contrapuntal motion
- Identify the scale type

Listen to the melody and bass of a two-phrase chorale, and complete the following exercises.

1. Use the workspace provided to capture the excerpt.
   (a) Notate the rhythm of the melody and bass in common time on the single-line staves. Begin with a quarter-note anacrusis. The eleventh pitch and the final pitch mark the end of their respective phrases. For each, write a quarter note with a fermata above it.
   (b) Below each rhythm staff, and under each note, write the solfège syllables or scale-degree numbers for the melody and bass. Begin both parts on *do* ($\hat{1}$).
   (c) Combine your answers to complete the notation of the pitches and rhythm of the melody and bass beginning on A4 and A2 respectively. Write the appropriate clefs, key signature (and any accidentals), meter signature, and beam notes to show beat grouping.
   (d) Write the harmonic interval numbers between the treble and bass staves.
2. In the melody, pitches 1–2 create which melodic interval?
   (a) M2 (b) m3 (c) M3 (d) P4
3. In phrase 2, the bass line's largest leaps create which interval?
   (a) P4 (b) P5 (c) m6 (d) M6
4. Phrase 1 ends with which type of cadence?
   (a) conclusive (b) inconclusive
5. Phrase 2 ends with which type of cadence?
   (a) conclusive (b) inconclusive

Workspace

Rhythm:

Melody:

Solfège syllables:

Scale-degree numbers:

Solfège syllables:

Scale-degree numbers:

Notation:

Rhythm:

Bass:

Solfège syllables:

Scale-degree numbers:

Solfège syllables:

Scale-degree numbers:

6. The pitches of the melody belong to which of the following patterns?

   (a) major tetrachord (b) minor tetrachord

   (c) major pentachord (d) minor pentachord

7. The pitches of phrase 2 belong to which of the following scales?

   (a) major (b) natural minor (descending melodic)

   (c) ascending melodic minor (d) harmonic minor

The Basic Phrase in SATB Style

NAME ______________________________

In this chapter you'll learn to:

- Identify the meter of excerpts in various genres
- Determine melodic lines using solfège syllables or scale-degree numbers
- Notate melodies, bass lines, and piano accompaniments
- Describe cadences as conclusive and inconclusive and identify them by type
- Recognize a cadential extension
- Identify harmonies by Roman numeral function
- Arrange an excerpt for saxophone quartet

Preparatory Listening

Complete the *Try It* dictations to familiarize yourself with the following concepts and skills:

- Determining the solfège syllables or scale-degree numbers for the melody and bass of two-voice tonic-dominant frameworks
- Converting solfège syllables or scale-degree numbers to pitches and notating them on the staff

Try It

Listen to two-part dictations that are played once each. The key signature, meter signature, and first bass pitch are given. Each example is preceded by two "count-off" measures to set the tempo; a two-part excerpt beginning on the given pitches follows.

- Listen to the dictation and memorize the bass line.
- Focus on the bass line first, and notate its pitches.
- Notate the soprano line next.
- Add bar lines including the double bar at the end.
- If you are working by yourself, sing each part aloud with solfège syllables, scale-degree numbers, and/or letter names.

1.
2.
3.
4.
5.
6.
7.

NAME ______________________________

Contextual Listening 12.1

In this CL exercise you will:

- Identify the meter of a melody
- Determine the solfège syllables or scale-degree numbers and convert to notation on the staff
- Identify cadences and label chords with Roman numerals
- Identify phrases and determine the relationships to other phrases
- Write a transposition for B♭ clarinet

Listen to two phrases of a clarinet solo from a twentieth-century ballet, and complete the following exercises.

Listening Strategies

- Listen for *do* ($\hat{1}$) to occur in the bass of *conclusive* cadences. Often the last two bass pitches will be *sol-do* ($\hat{5}$-$\hat{1}$), which supports the progression V(7)-I. Any V(7)-I cadence is an authentic cadence.
- In conclusive cadences, the melody often ends with *mi-re-do* ($\hat{3}$-$\hat{2}$-$\hat{1}$) or *ti-do* ($\hat{7}$-$\hat{1}$). When V(7)-I authentic cadences end with *do* ($\hat{1}$) in both the bass and soprano, the cadence is a perfect authentic cadence (PAC). Listen to the example and focus just on the melody.
- Does the V chord contain *fa* ($\hat{4}$)? If so, the chord is V^7.

Expansions at the end of a phrase are known as cadential extensions.

1. Pitches 1-2 form which melodic interval?

   (a) M3 (b) P4 (c) P5 (d) M6

2. Which of these represents the meter of this excerpt?

   (a) compound duple (b) compound quadruple

   (c) simple triple (d) simple quadruple

3. At the first cadence (just before the return of the opening melodic idea), which triad is arpeggiated?

   (a) tonic (b) supertonic (c) subdominant (d) dominant

4. The melody ends on which scale degree?

   (a) $\hat{1}$ (b) $\hat{2}$ (c) $\hat{3}$ (d) $\hat{5}$

5. At the end of the excerpt, which harmony is implied?

   (a) I (b) ii (c) V (d) vi

6. The implied cadences are best described by which of the following pairs? Listen for the melodic pitch at each cadence. Conclusive cadences end on *do* ($\hat{1}$), while inconclusive cadences often end on *re* ($\hat{2}$), *ti* ($\hat{7}$), or *sol* ($\hat{5}$).

First cadence	*Second cadence*
(a) inconclusive	inconclusive
(b) inconclusive	conclusive
(c) conclusive	conclusive
(d) conclusive	inconclusive

7. Phrase 1 concludes with which type of cadence?

   (a) half (b) imperfect authentic (c) perfect authentic

8. Phrase 2 concludes with which type of cadence?

   (a) half (b) imperfect authentic (c) perfect authentic

9. The melody of the excerpt spans the range of which interval?

   (a) P5 (b) M6 (c) M7 (d) P8

10. From the melody's lowest pitch to its highest, which best describes its range?

    (a) *do* to *sol* ($\hat{1}$-$\hat{5}$) (b) *ti* to *la* ($\hat{7}$-$\hat{6}$) (c) *do* to *do* ($\hat{1}$-$\hat{1}$) (d) *sol* to *sol* ($\hat{5}$-$\hat{5}$)

11. Use the workspace provided to capture the excerpt.

    (a) Notate the rhythm of the melody on the single-line staff beginning with a half-note anacrusis. Choose a meter signature, and include bar lines. Beam notes to show beat grouping.

    (b) Below each rhythm staff, and under each note, write the solfège syllables or scale-degree numbers for the melody beginning on *sol* ($\hat{5}$).

    (c) Combine your answers to complete the notation of the pitches and rhythm of the melody beginning on D♭4. Write the appropriate clef, key signature, and meter signature.

NAME ______________________________

Workspace

Rhythm:

Melody:

Solfège syllables:

Scale-degree numbers:

Solfège syllables:

Scale-degree numbers:

Notation:

12. You notated the melody in concert pitch. Now, transpose it up a M2 to create a B♭ clarinet part. Write the new key signature, and refer to the answers from previous exercises to help you. If possible, perform the untransposed version on piano, along with the transposed version on B♭ clarinet.

NAME ______________________________

Contextual Listening 12.2

In this CL exercise you will:

- Identify the meter of an excerpt from a piano work
- Determine the solfège syllables or scale-degree numbers of the melody and bass, and convert this to notation on the staff
- Identify cadences by type and label chords with Roman numerals

Listen to a phrase from a work for piano, and complete the following exercises. Concentrate on the bass line and general musical features initially, then on the melody.

1. Which of these represents the meter of this excerpt?
   (a) compound triple (b) compound quadruple
   (c) simple triple (d) simple quadruple
2. The melodic pitches belong to which of the following scales?
   (a) natural minor (descending melodic) (b) harmonic minor
   (c) ascending melodic minor (d) major
3. The bass line ends on which scale degree?
   (a) $\hat{1}$ (b) $\hat{2}$ (c) $\hat{3}$ (d) $\hat{5}$ (e) $\hat{6}$
4. The excerpt concludes with which type of cadence?
   (a) imperfect authentic (b) perfect authentic (c) half
5. All of the skips in the melody are of which generic interval type?
   (a) seconds (b) thirds (c) fifths (d) sixths
6. Use the workspace provided to capture the excerpt.
   (a) Notate the rhythm of the melody and bass line on the single-line staves in common time. The shortest note value you will hear is the sixteenth note. Include bar lines and beam notes to show beat grouping. The first measure is provided for you.
   (b) Below each rhythm staff, and under each note, write the solfège syllables or scale-degree numbers for both parts. The first measure is provided for you.
   (c) Combine your answers to complete the notation of the pitches and rhythm of both parts. The first measure is provided for you.

NAME ______________________________

Workspace

Rhythm:

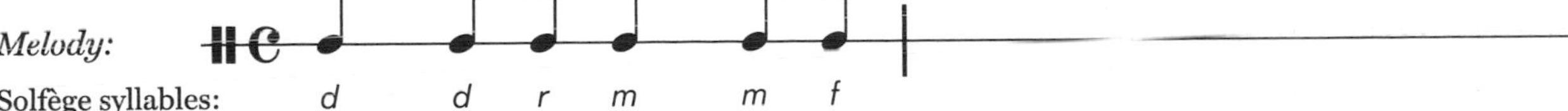

Solfège syllables: *d d r m m f*

Scale-degree numbers: $\hat{1}$ $\hat{1}$ $\hat{2}$ $\hat{3}$ $\hat{3}$ $\hat{4}$

Solfège syllables:

Scale-degree numbers:

Notation:

Rhythm:

Bass:

Solfège syllables: *d*

Scale-degree numbers: $\hat{1}$

Solfège syllables:

Scale-degree numbers:

NAME ______________________

Contextual Listening 12.3

In this CL exercise you will:

- Identify the meter of an art song
- Determine the solfège syllables or scale-degree numbers of the melody and bass
- Identify chord types
- Notate the melody, bass line, and accompaniment

Listen to an excerpt from an art song, and complete the following exercises.

1. Which of these represents the meter of this excerpt?

   (a) compound duple (b) compound triple

   (c) simple triple (d) simple quadruple

2. At the beginning, which rhythmic feature is heard?

   (a) anacrusis (b) syncopation

   (c) triplets in the accompaniment (d) augmentation of the vocal melody in the bass

3. The vocal melody's pitches 1-5 outline which type of chord?

   (a) minor triad (b) major triad (c) mm7 (d) MM7 (e) Mm7

4. At the end of the vocal line, which rhythmic device occurs?

   (a) anacrusis (b) duplets (c) triplets (d) syncopation

5. From the vocal melody's lowest pitch to its highest, which best describes its range?

   (a) *do* to *sol* ($\hat{1}$-$\hat{5}$) (b) *ti* to *sol* ($\hat{7}$-$\hat{5}$) (c) *do* to *do* ($\hat{1}$-$\hat{1}$) (d) *sol* to *sol* ($\hat{5}$-$\hat{5}$)

6. Use the workspace provided to capture the excerpt.

   (a) Notate the rhythm of the vocal melody and bass line in common time on the single-line staves. The first downbeat occurs when the piano accompaniment begins. Include bar lines (including one to show the anacrusis), and beam notes to show beat grouping.

   (b) Below each rhythm staff, and under each note, write the solfège syllables or scale-degree numbers for the melody and bass line. Begin the melody on *mi* ($\hat{3}$) and the bass line on *do* ($\hat{1}$).

   (c) Combine your answers to complete the notation of the pitches and rhythm of the vocal melody (top treble-clef staff) and bass line (bass-clef staff) beginning on C5 and A♭2 respectively. Write the appropriate clefs, key signature, and meter signature. Beam notes to show beat grouping.

   (d) Beneath each bass pitch, write the quality and inversion of the chord in the accompaniment; for example, Mm7 first, M root, and so on.

   (e) Write the pitches and rhythm of the accompaniment on the middle staff.

7. The excerpt ends with which type of cadence?

   (a) half (b) imperfect authentic (c) perfect authentic

NAME ______________________________

Workspace

Rhythm:

Melody:

Solfège syllables:

Scale-degree numbers:

Solfège syllables:

Scale-degree numbers:

Notation:

Rhythm:

Bass:

Solfège syllables:

Scale-degree numbers:

Solfège syllables:

Scale-degree numbers:

8. On your own staff paper, arrange this excerpt for saxophone quartet. Write the appropriate clefs, key signatures, and meter signature. Keep the same concert key and pitches, but transpose the soprano saxophone part up a M2, the alto saxophone part up a M6, the tenor saxophone part up a M2 plus one octave, and the baritone saxophone part up a M6 plus one octave. Refer to your previous answers for help.

Contextual Listening 12.4

In this CL exercise you will:

- Identify the meter of an excerpt from a concerto grosso
- Determine the solfège syllables or scale-degree numbers of the melody and bass, and convert this to notation on the staff
- Identify chords with Roman numerals
- Identify cadences and label chords with Roman numerals

Listen to an excerpt from a piece for string orchestra and continuo, and complete the following exercises.

1. Which of these represents the meter of this excerpt?
   (a) simple triple (b) simple quadruple
   (c) compound duple (d) compound triple
2. Melodic pitches 1-2 create which interval?
   (a) M2 (b) m2 (c) M3 (d) m3
3. Which are the first two chords of the excerpt?
   (a) V-I (b) V7-I (c) I-V (d) I-V7
4. The bass line ends on which scale degree?
   (a) $\hat{1}$ (b) $\hat{2}$ (c) $\hat{3}$ (d) $\hat{5}$ (e) $\hat{6}$
5. The melody ends on which scale degree?
   (a) $\hat{1}$ (b) $\hat{2}$ (c) $\hat{3}$ (d) $\hat{5}$ (e) $\hat{6}$
6. The excerpt concludes with which type of cadence?
   (a) half (b) imperfect authentic (c) perfect authentic
7. Which are the last two chords of the excerpt?
   (a) V-I (b) V7-I (c) I-V (d) I-V7
8. Use the workspace provided to capture the excerpt.
   (a) Notate the rhythm of the melody and bass line in common time on the single-line staves. Omit any ornaments. Include bar lines, and beam notes to show beat grouping.
   (b) Below each rhythm staff, and under each note, write the solfège syllables or scale-degree numbers for the melody and bass line. Omit any ornaments
   (c) Combine your answers to complete the notation of the pitches and rhythm of the melody and bass line beginning on F5 and F3 respectively. Write the appropriate clefs, key signature, and meter signature, and vertically align pitches that sound together.

NAME ______________________________

Workspace

Rhythm:

Melody: 𝄆 ______________________________

Solfège syllables:

Scale-degree numbers:

Notation:

Rhythm:

Bass: 𝄆 ______________________________

Solfège syllables:

Scale-degree numbers:

CHAPTER 13

Dominant Sevenths, the Predominant Area, and Melody Harmonization

In this chapter you'll learn to:

- Identify the meter of excerpts from an art song, a string quartet, a symphony, and a work for piano
- Identify cadences by type
- Describe the relationships between phrases
- Identify harmonic progressions
- Notate the outer parts of works in varying textures
- Perform various transpositions

Preparatory Listening

Complete the *Try It* dictations to familiarize yourself with the following concepts and skills:

- Determining the solfège syllables or scale-degree numbers for the soprano and bass in model SATB phrases
- Associating solfège syllables or scale-degree numbers with dominant sevenths and chords of the predominant area
- Converting solfège syllables and scale-degree numbers to pitches and notating them on the staff
- Applying Roman numerals to basic phrase models

Try It

Listen to model SATB progressions that are played once each. The key signature, meter signature, and first bass pitch are given.

- Focus on the bass line first, and notate its pitches.
- Beneath the bass pitches, write Roman numerals that represent the harmony; if more than one chord seems possible, write all the possibilities and choose the correct one after additional hearings.
- Focus last on the soprano, determining the starting pitch by comparing it to the first bass pitch, then notate the entire soprano line.
- Add bar lines including the double bar at the end.
- If you are working by yourself, sing each part aloud with solfège syllables, scale-degree numbers, and/or letter names.

NAME ______________________________

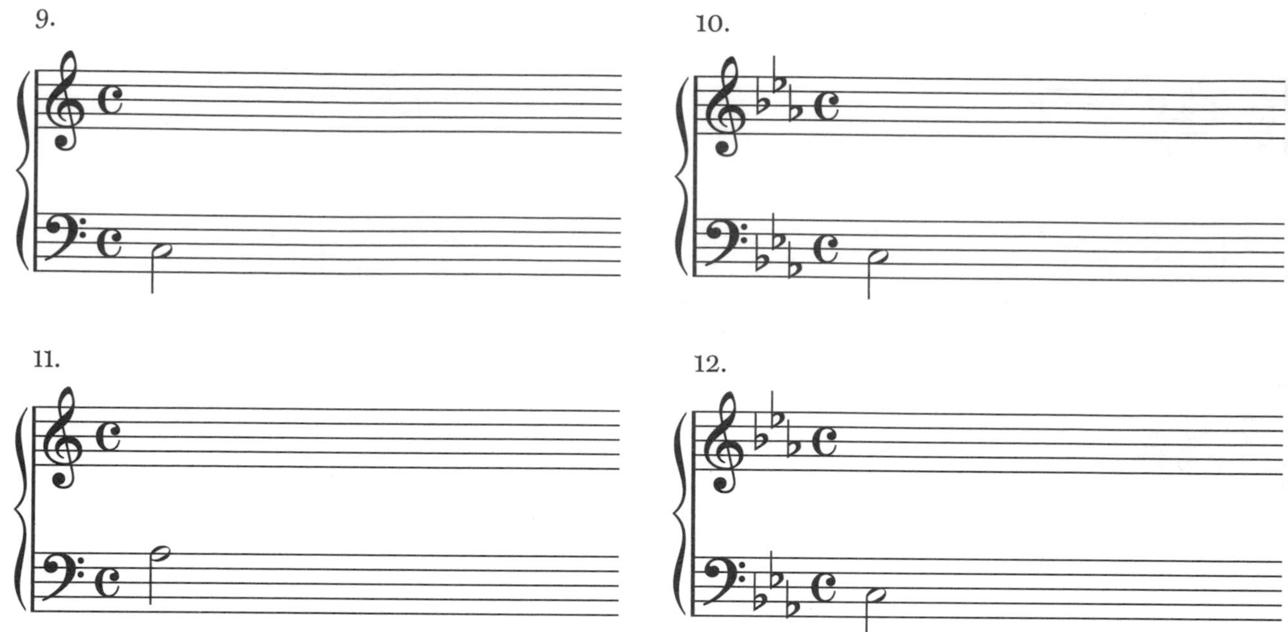
9.
10.
11.
12.

NAME ______________________________

Contextual Listening 13.1

In this CL exercise you will:

- Identify the meter of an excerpt from an art song
- Describe the harmonic intervals of an accompaniment
- Indicate the range of the melody
- Notate the melody
- Transcribe the work for string quartet

Listen to an excerpt from an art song, and complete the following exercises.

1. Which is the meter signature of this excerpt?
   (a) simple duple (b) simple triple
   (c) compound duple (d) compound triple

2. In the piano introduction, which best describes the harmonic intervals?
   (a) parallel thirds throughout
   (b) parallel sixths throughout
   (c) parallel thirds, then alternating sixths and thirds
   (d) parallel sixths, then alternating thirds and sixths

3. On which scale is the melody based?
   (a) major (b) natural minor (descending melodic)
   (c) harmonic minor (d) ascending melodic minor

4. Use the workspace provided to capture the excerpt.
   (a) Notate the rhythm of the vocal line (which begins in measure 5) on the single-line staff; pitch 1 of the melody is an eighth note. Choose a meter signature, and include bar lines.
   (b) Below each rhythm staff, and under each note, write the solfège syllables or scale-degree numbers for the vocal melody.
   (c) Combine your answers to complete the notation of the pitches and rhythm of the vocal melody beginning on A4. Write the appropriate clef, key signature, and meter signature.

Workspace

Rhythm:

Melody:

Solfège syllables:
Scale-degree numbers:

Solfège syllables:
Scale-degree numbers:

Solfège syllables:
Scale-degree numbers:

Notation:

5. From the melody's lowest pitch to its highest, which of the following describes its range?

   (a) *do* to *sol* ($\hat{1}$-$\hat{5}$) (b) *te* to *le* ($\flat\hat{7}$-$\flat\hat{6}$) (c) *do* to *do* ($\hat{1}$-$\hat{1}$) (d) *sol* to *sol* ($\hat{5}$-$\hat{5}$)

6. Notate the pitches and rhythm of the melody and accompaniment on your own staff paper.

7. On your own staff paper, transcribe the first phrase of the song (ending with the words "O sweet content!") for string quartet. Assign the melody to the first violin, the moving parts of the accompaniment to the second violin and viola, and the bass part to the cello. Transpose the song to G minor. Write the appropriate clefs, key signature, and meter signature.

NAME ________________________________

Contextual Listening 13.2

In this CL exercise you will:

- Identify the meter of a string quartet adapted for piano
- Identify cadences by type
- Determine consonant and dissonant harmonic intervals
- Notate the melody and bass line

Listen to an excerpt from a string quartet (during which only two instruments play), and complete the following exercises.

1. Which of these represents the meter of this excerpt?

   (a) simple duple   (b) simple triple

   (c) compound duple   (d) compound triple

2. Which rhythmic device is featured at the beginning?

   (a) anacrusis   (b) sycopation

   (c) triplets in the accompaniment   (d) *ritardando*

3. Use the workspace provided to capture the excerpt.

   (a) Notate the rhythm of both parts on the single-line staves. Choose a meter signature, and include bar lines.

   (b) Below each rhythm staff, and under each note, write the solfège syllables or scale-degree numbers for both parts. Begin the melody on *sol* ($\hat{5}$) and the bass on *do* ($\hat{1}$).

   (c) Combine your answers to complete the notation of the pitches and rhythm of both parts beginning on A3 and D3 respectively. Write the appropriate clefs, key signature, and meter signature. Beam notes to show beat grouping. Vertically align pitches that sound simultaneously.

   (d) Write the harmonic interval numbers between the treble and bass staves.

Workspace

Rhythm:

Melody:

Solfège syllables:

Scale-degree numbers:

Solfège syllables:

Scale-degree numbers:

Solfège syllables:

Scale-degree numbers:

Notation:

NAME ______________________________

Rhythm:

Bass:  ______________________________

Solfège syllables:

Scale-degree numbers:

 ______________________________

Solfège syllables:

Scale-degree numbers:

‖ ______________________________

Solfège syllables:

Scale-degree numbers:

4. Refer to your analysis of harmonic intervals.
   (a) Which type of harmonic interval occurs more often?
      (1) dissonant (2, 4, 7) (2) consonant (3, 5, 6, 8)
   (b) Which consonant harmonic interval occurs more than any other?
      (1) 3 (2) 5 (3) 6 (4) 8

5. The cadences are of which type(s)?

	First cadence	*Second cadence*
(a)	half	half
(b)	half	perfect authentic
(c)	perfect authentic	half
(d)	perfect authentic	perfect authentic

6. How does phrase 2 relate to phrase 1?
   (a) same beginning, same conclusion
   (b) same beginning, different conclusion
   (c) different beginning, same conclusion
   (d) different beginning, different conclusion

NAME ______________________________

Contextual Listening 13.3

In this CL exercise you will:

- Identify the meter of an excerpt from a symphony
- Identify nonchord tones
- Identify cadences by type
- Notate the melody and bass line
- Supply Roman numerals
- Transpose the melody

Listen to an excerpt from a symphony, and complete the following exercises.

1. Which of these represents the meter of this excerpt?
   (a) simple triple (b) simple quadruple
   (c) compound duple (d) compound triple

2. Use the workspace provided to capture the excerpt.
   (a) Notate the rhythm of the melody (clarinet 1) and bass line (bassoon 2) on the single-line staves. Choose a meter signature, and include bar lines.
   (b) Below each rhythm staff, and under each note, write the solfège syllables or scale-degree numbers for the melody and the bass line.
   (c) Combine your answers to complete the notation of the pitches and rhythm of the melody and bass line beginning on C5 and C3 respectively. Write the appropriate clefs, key signature, and meter signature. Beam notes to show beat grouping.
   (d) Beneath each bass pitch notate the correct Roman numeral. (The scale degree of the bass pitch is often the root of the chord above it. When the bass has $\hat{3}$, the chord is usually I^6.)

NAME ___________________________

Workspace

Rhythm:

Melody: ‖

Solfège syllables:

Scale-degree numbers:

Notation:

Rhythm:

Bass: ‖

Solfège syllables:

Scale-degree numbers:

3. Melodic pitches 2–3 are which embellishing tones?
   (a) accented passing tones (b) unaccented passing tones
   (c) upper neighbor tones (d) double neighbor tone

4. Transpose the melody from CL 13.3 up a M2 to create a B♭ clarinet part. Write the appropriate clef, key signature, and meter signature.

5. The excerpt concludes with which type of cadence?
   (a) perfect authentic (b) imperfect authentic (c) half

NAME ______________________________

Contextual Listening 13.4

In this CL exercise you will:

- Identify the meter of a work for piano
- Identify harmonic intervals between the melody and bass line
- Notate the melody and bass line
- Identify harmonic progressions
- Describe the counterpoint and type of motion between the melody and bass line
- Describe the relationship between phrases
- Transpose the melody and bass line

Listen to an excerpt of a work for piano, and complete the following exercises.

1. Which is the meter signature of this excerpt?

   (a) $\frac{2}{4}$ (b) $\frac{3}{4}$ (c) $\frac{6}{8}$ (d) $\frac{9}{8}$

2. Use the workspace provided to capture the excerpt.

   (a) Notate the rhythm of the melody and bass line on the single-line staves. Begin with an eighth-note anacrusis. Choose a meter signature, and include bar lines (including one to show the anacrusis). Beam notes to show beat grouping.

   (b) Below each rhythm staff, and under each note, write the solfège syllables or scale-degree numbers for both parts. Begin the melody on the dominant pitch and the bass line on the tonic pitch.

   (c) Combine your answers to complete the notation of the pitches and rhythm of both parts beginning on D4 and G3 respectively. Write the appropriate clefs, key signature, and meter signature.

   (d) For phrase 1 only, write the harmonic interval numbers between the treble and bass staves.

NAME ______________________________

Workspace

Rhythm:

Melody: ||

Solfège syllables:

Scale-degree numbers:

||

Solfège syllables:

Scale-degree numbers:

Notation:

Rhythm:

Bass: ||

Solfège syllables:

Scale-degree numbers:

||

Solfège syllables:

Scale-degree numbers:

3. In phrase 1, which best describes the counterpoint between the outer parts?
   (a) mostly first species (1:1)
   (b) mostly second species (2:1)
   (c) first species (1:1), then second species (2:1)
   (d) second species (2:1), then first species (1:1)

4. Chords 1-3 are best represented by which progression? Listen to bass pitches 1-3, and compare them with the bass lines implied by each possible answer.

   (a) i-V7-i (b) i-V^{6}_{5}-i (c) I-V^{4}_{3}-I^{6} (d) I-V^{4}_{2}-I^{6}

5. At the beginning of phrase 2, which type of motion occurs between the outer parts?

   (a) similar (b) parallel (c) oblique (d) contrary

6. The end of the melody is based on which scale?

   (a) major (b) natural minor (descending melodic)

   (c) ascending melodic minor (d) harmonic minor

7. The first and last cadences are of which type(s)?

   (a) HC, HC (b) HC, PAC (c) PAC, HC (d) PAC, PAC

8. How does the melody of phrase 3 relate to that of phrase 1?

   (a) same beginning, same conclusion

   (b) same beginning, different conclusion

   (c) different beginning, same conclusion

   (d) different beginning, different conclusion

9. Melodic pitches 1-14 embellish a triad. Subtract the pitches that don't belong to the triad and notate the triad's outline on the following staff. For help, refer to your answer to question 2.

10. Transpose the excerpt to B minor. Write the appropriate clef and key signature.

Expanding the Tonic and Dominant Areas

NAME ______________________

In this chapter you'll learn to:

- Identify the meter of excerpts from string quartets and a piano work
- Associate cadence types with particular solfège syllables or scale-degree numbers
- Associate common bass patterns with their equivalent harmonic progressions
- Understand cadences as conclusive or inconclusive
- Describe the texture of a musical excerpt

Preparatory Listening

Complete the *Try It* dictations to familiarize yourself with the following concepts and skills:

- Determining the solfège syllables or scale-degree numbers for the soprano and bass in model SATB phrases
- Associating solfège syllables or scale-degree numbers with dominant sevenths and chords that expand the tonic and predominant areas
- Converting solfège syllables and scale-degree numbers to pitches and notating them on the staff
- Applying Roman numerals to basic phrase models

Try It

Listen to model SATB progressions that are played once each. The key signature, meter signature, and first bass pitch are given.

- Focus on the bass line first, and notate its pitches.
- Beneath the bass pitches, write Roman numerals that represent the harmony; if more than one chord seems possible, write all the possibilities and choose the correct one after additional hearings.
- Focus last on the soprano, determining the starting pitch by comparing it to the first bass pitch, then notate the entire soprano line.
- Add bar lines including the double bar at the end.
- If you are working by yourself, sing each part aloud with solfège syllables, scale-degree numbers, and/or letter names.

1.
2.
3.
4.
5.
6.
7.
8.
9.
10.

NAME ______________________

Contextual Listening 14.2

In this CL exercise you will:

- Identify the meter of an excerpt from a piano work
- Describe cadences as either conclusive or inconclusive
- Focus on the solfège syllables or scale-degree numbers that conclude phrases to determine cadence types
- Determine harmonic progressions from cues provided by bass line solfège syllables or scale-degree numbers
- Notate the doubled melody

The following exercises, based on an excerpt from a piano work, are divided in two parts that may be assigned separately. Listen to the excerpt, then complete the part(s) assigned.

Part A

1. Which of these represents the meter of this excerpt?
   (a) simple duple (b) simple triple
   (c) compound duple (d) compound triple
2. The opening melody arpeggiates which type of chord?
   (a) major triad (b) minor triad
   (c) dominant seventh (d) diminished seventh
3. At the first cadence (just before the return of the opening melodic idea), the bass line ends on which scale degree?
   (a) $\hat{1}$ (b) $\hat{2}$ (c) $\hat{3}$ (d) $\hat{5}$ (e) $\hat{6}$
4. At the first cadence, the melody ends on which scale degree?
   (a) $\hat{1}$ (b) $\hat{2}$ (c) $\hat{3}$ (d) $\hat{5}$ (e) $\hat{6}$
5. The bass line ends (the whole excerpt) on which scale degree?
   (a) $\hat{1}$ (b) $\hat{2}$ (c) $\hat{3}$ (d) $\hat{5}$ (e) $\hat{6}$
6. The melody concludes on which scale degree?
   (a) $\hat{1}$ (b) $\hat{2}$ (c) $\hat{3}$ (d) $\hat{5}$ (e) $\hat{6}$
7. The cadences are best described by which of the following pairs?

	First cadence	*Second cadence*
(a)	inconclusive	inconclusive
(b)	inconclusive	conclusive
(c)	conclusive	conclusive
(d)	conclusive	inconclusive

8. Phrase 1 concludes with which type of cadence?
   (a) half (b) imperfect authentic (c) perfect authentic

9. Phrase 2 concludes with which type of cadence?

   (a) half (b) imperfect authentic (c) perfect authentic

10. At the beginning of phrase 2, the melody arpeggiates which type of chord?

   (a) major triad (b) minor triad

   (c) dominant seventh (d) diminished seventh

11. Compared with the beginning of phrase 1, the beginning of phrase 2 is transposed in which way?

   (a) down a second (b) down a third (c) up a second (d) up a third

12. Use the workspace provided to capture the excerpt.

   (a) Notate the rhythm of melodic pitches 1-10 on the single-line staff. Choose a meter signature, and include bar lines. Beam notes to show beat grouping.

   (b) Below the rhythm staff, and under each note, write the solfège syllables or scale-degree numbers for melodic pitches 1-10.

   (c) Combine your answers to complete the notation of the pitches and rhythm of melodic pitches 1-10. The melody is doubled in octaves; notate the octaves using both staves. Write the appropriate clefs, key signature, and meter signature. Begin on A3 and A2 respectively.

Workspace

Rhythm:

Melody:

Solfège syllables:

Scale-degree numbers:

Notation:

Part B

Before proceeding, review these listening strategies.

Bass line	*Probable harmonization*
fa-mi ($\hat{4}$-$\hat{3}$)	Write V^4_2-I^6.
ti-do ($\hat{7}$-$\hat{1}$)	Write V^6-I and listen for *fa* ($\hat{4}$). If you hear *fa* ($\hat{4}$), write V^6_5-I. (The harmonization vii°-I is unlikely; composers seldom wrote root-position diminished triads outside the descending-fifth progression.) Listen also for chord quality: V^6_5 is a dominant seventh with *fa* ($\hat{4}$); V^6 is a major triad without *fa* ($\hat{4}$).

NAME ______________________________

NAME ______________________

Contextual Listening 15.1

In this CL exercise you will:

- Identify the type of nonchord tones found in the melody and bass of a chorale
- Identify the scale or mode
- Describe the relationships between phrases
- Notate the melody and bass line

Listen to the melody and bass of four phrases from a chorale (each phrase is two measures), and complete the following exercises.

1. On which scale or mode is the excerpt based?

   (a) major (b) minor (c) Dorian (d) Lydian

2. Use the workspace provided to capture the excerpt.

   (a) Notate the rhythm of both parts on the single-line staves in common time. The first pitch in the melody is a quarter note. Write the meter signature, and include bar lines. Beam notes to show beat grouping. Place a fermata above the last half note of each phrase.

   (b) Below each rhythm staff, and under each note, write the solfège syllables or scale-degree numbers for both parts.

   (c) Combine your answers to complete the notation of the pitches and rhythm of the melody and bass. The first phrase is notated for you.

   (d) Continue to write harmonic interval numbers between the treble and bass staves for phrases 2-4.

3. Each time the harmonic interval is 4, which type of dissonance occurs?

   (a) passing tone (b) neighboring tone (c) suspension

4. Phrase 1 concludes with which type of cadence?

   (a) half (b) imperfect authentic (c) perfect authentic (d) plagal

5. Phrase 2 features which type of suspension?

   (a) 2-3 (b) 4-3 (c) 7-6 (d) 9-8

Embellishing Tones in Four Voices

NAME ____________

In this chapter you'll learn to:

- Understand embellishing tones in excerpts for unaccompanied choir; an art song; and strings and continuo
- Associate cadence types with specific solfège syllables or scale-degree numbers
- Aurally reduce embellished textures to simpler outlines
- Associate bass lines with typical harmonic progressions
- Employ shortcuts when notating melodic lines

Preparatory Listening

Complete the *Try It* dictations to familiarize yourself with the following concepts and skills:

- Determining the solfège syllables or scale-degree numbers for the soprano and bass in model SATB phrases
- Associating solfège syllables or scale-degree numbers with embellishing tones in four voices
- Converting solfège syllables and scale-degree numbers to pitches and notating them on the staff
- Applying Roman numerals to basic phrase models

Try It

Listen to embellished SATB progressions, some of which are drawn from Chapter 15; each is played once. The key signature, meter signature, and first bass pitch are given.

- Focus on the bass line first, and notate its pitches.
- Beneath the bass pitches, write Roman numerals that represent the harmony; if more than one chord seems possible, write all the possibilities and choose the correct one after additional hearings.
- Focus last on the soprano, determining the starting pitch by comparing it to the first bass pitch, then notate the entire soprano line.
- Add bar lines including the double bar at the end.
- Circle and identify all embellishing tones using abbreviations (e.g., P, N, S 4–3, etc.).
- If you are working by yourself, sing each part aloud with solfège syllables, scale-degree numbers, and/or letter names

1.
2.
3.
4.
5.
6.
7.
8.
9.

NAME ______________________________

Contextual Listening 16.1

In this CL exercise you will:

- Identify the meter of a work for unaccompanied choir
- Identify nonchord tones by type
- Identify cadences by type
- Identify chord qualities
- Notate the melody and bass line

Listen to an excerpt from an unaccompanied SATB choral work, and complete the following exercises. CL 16.1 is an *a cappella* version; CL 16.1a is a recording of a piano reduction.

1. Which is the meter signature of this excerpt?

   (a) $\frac{3}{4}$ (b) $\frac{4}{4}$ (c) $\frac{6}{8}$ (d) $\frac{9}{8}$

2. Chords 1-2 are of which qualities?

   (a) MM7, major triad (b) Mm7, major triad (c) mm7, major triad

   (d) MM7, minor triad (e) Mm7, minor triad

3. Melodic pitches 1-5 outline which type of chord?

   (a) major triad (b) minor triad (c) MM7 (d) Mm7

4. Measure 3, beat 1 features which type of suspension?

   (a) 9-8 (b) 7-6 (c) 4-3 (d) 2-3

5. The second-to-last melodic pitch is which type of embellishment?

   (a) passing tone (b) incomplete neighbor tone

   (c) consonant skip (d) anticipation

6. The excerpt ends with which type of cadence?

   (a) half (b) imperfect authentic (c) perfect authentic (d) deceptive

7. Use the workspace provided to capture the excerpt.

   (a) Notate the rhythm of the melody and bass on the single-line staves. Choose a meter signature (refer to question 1), and include bar lines.

   (b) Below each rhythm staff, and under each note, write the solfège syllables or scale-degree numbers for the melody and bass beginning on *sol* ($\hat{5}$) in both parts.

   (c) Combine your answers to complete the notation of the pitches and rhythm of the melody and bass. Begin on G4 and G3 respectively. Follow the stem-direction conventions for SATB notation.

Workspace

Rhythm:

Melody:

Solfège syllables:

Scale-degree numbers:

Notation:

Rhythm:

Bass:

Solfège syllables:

Scale-degree numbers:

NAME ______________________________

Contextual Listening 16.2

In this CL exercise you will:

- Focus on the solfège syllables or scale-degree numbers that conclude phrases to determine cadence types
- Identify cadences by type
- Identify harmonic progressions
- Employ shortcuts to simplify and capture melodic lines
- Notate the melody and bass line

Listen to the piano introduction to an art song, and complete the following exercises. Listen to the entire excerpt with a broad perspective, then focus on the details.

1. Which of the following pairs best describes the order of the cadences of this excerpt?

   (a) inconclusive; inconclusive (b) inconclusive; conclusive

   (c) conclusive; conclusive (d) conclusive; inconclusive

2. At the first cadence (before the return of the opening melody), the bass ends on which scale degree?

   (a) $\hat{1}$ (b) $\hat{2}$ (c) $\hat{3}$ (d) $\hat{5}$ (e) $\hat{6}$

3. At the first cadence, the melody ends on which scale degree?

   (a) $\hat{1}$ (b) $\hat{2}$ (c) $\hat{3}$ (d) $\hat{5}$ (e) $\hat{6}$

4. Phrase 1 concludes with which type of cadence?

   (a) half (b) imperfect authentic (c) perfect authentic (d) deceptive

5. On which scale degree does the bass line end?

   (a) $\hat{1}$ (b) $\hat{2}$ (c) $\hat{3}$ (d) $\hat{5}$ (e) $\hat{6}$

6. On which scale degree does the melody end?

   (a) $\hat{1}$ (b) $\hat{2}$ (c) $\hat{3}$ (d) $\hat{5}$ (e) $\hat{6}$

7. Phrase 2 concludes with which type of cadence?

   (a) half (b) imperfect authentic (c) perfect authentic (d) deceptive

8. In phrase 2, bass pitches 3-4 are harmonized by which of the following?

   (a) V-V7 (b) V-V^{6}_{5} (c) $V^{6-\,\overset{7}{5}}_{4-3}$ (d) ii^{6}-V^{6-5}_{4-3}-I

9. The last two chords of the excerpt represent which harmonic progression? Listen to the bass pitches, which in this case are also the roots of their respective chords.

   (a) I-I (b) IV-I (c) V7-I (d) I-IV (e) I-V7

10. The final melodic rhythm is best notated by which of the following?

In the remaining exercises, you will simplify the melody to reveal the counterpoint between the outer voices.

Listening Strategies

- Listen first for the simple patterns on which the melody is based. Then think about how the patterns have been embellished (e.g., neighbor tone, chromatic passing tone, grace notes). Doing this allows you to remember additional details each time you listen.
- Because phrase 2 begins like phrase 1, indicate this fact with a shortcut. For example, write c 1 in measure 5 ("copy measure 1 here"). Use the extra time to figure out the more difficult areas of the dictation.

11. Use the workspace provided to capture the excerpt.
    (a) Notate the rhythm of the melody and bass on the single-line staves in $\frac{4}{4}$. Write the meter signature, and include bar lines.
    (b) Determine the melodic outline. Conduct in four as you listen. In each measure, determine the melodic pitch that sounds on beats 1 and 3 (at each half note). Write the solfège syllables or scale-degree numbers of these pitches below the upper rhythm staff. Ignore the embellishing tones.
    (c) Below the lower rhythm staff, and under each note, write the solfège syllables or scale-degree numbers for the bass line.
    (d) Combine your answers to complete the notation of the pitches and rhythm of the melody (first and third beats only) and bass (complete). Begin on D4 and B♭2 respectively. Write the appropriate clefs, key signature, and meter signature.
    (e) Write harmonic interval numbers between the treble and bass staves.

NAME ________________________________

Workspace

Rhythm:

Melody:

Solfège syllables:

Scale-degree numbers:

Solfège syllables:

Scale-degree numbers:

Notation:

Rhythm:

Bass:

Solfège syllables:

Scale-degree numbers:

Solfège syllables:

Scale-degree numbers:

NAME ____________________

Contextual Listening 16.3

In this CL exercise you will:

- Determine the meter of a trio sonata
- Determine concluding solfège syllables or scale-degree numbers and identify cadences by type
- Identify harmonic progressions
- Identify the scale of the melody and bass line
- Notate the melody and bass line

Listen to a five-measure excerpt from a trio sonata, written for three stringed instruments and a continuo instrument that realizes harmonies from figured-bass notation.

1. Beginning with melodic pitch 8, which rhythmic feature is heard?

   (a) anacrusis (b) mixed beat division

   (c) syncopation (d) dotted rhythms

2. Use the workspace provided to capture the excerpt.

   (a) Notate the rhythm of the melody and bass on the single-line staves in common time. Write the meter signature, and include bar lines. Beam notes to show beat grouping.

   (b) Below each rhythm staff, and under each note, write the solfège syllables or scale-degree numbers for the melody and bass beginning on *sol* ($\hat{5}$) and *do* ($\hat{1}$).

   (c) Combine your answers to complete the notation of the pitches and rhythm of the melody and bass. Begin on G5 and C3 respectively. Write the appropriate clefs, key signature (and any accidentals), and meter signature.

3. The melodic pitches of the highest violin part belong to which of the following scales?

   (a) harmonic minor (b) natural minor (descending melodic)

   (c) Dorian (d) Phrygian

4. Bass pitches 1-7 are harmonized by which of the following progressions?

   (a) i-(i)-iv-V-i-V-i (b) i-(i)-iv-i-V-i-V

   (c) i-(i)-V6-i-V-i-V6 (d) i-(i)-V7-i-V-i-V7

5. From bass pitch 8 to the end of the bass line, all the pitches belong to which of the following scales?

   (a) harmonic minor (b) natural minor (descending melodic)

   (c) Dorian (d) Phrygian

NAME ____________________

Workspace

Rhythm:

Melody: ‖ ____________________

Solfège syllables:

Scale-degree numbers:

‖ ____________________

Solfège syllables:

Scale-degree numbers:

Notation:

Rhythm:

Bass: ‖ ____________________

Solfège syllables:

Scale-degree numbers:

‖ ____________________

Solfège syllables:

Scale-degree numbers:

6. Near the end of the bass line, which chord harmonizes *fa* ?
   (a) ii^{o6} (b) iv6 (c) V^4_2 (d) $ii^{\varnothing 6}_5$
7. The second-to-last chord is embellished with which type of suspension?
   (a) 9-8 (b) 7-6 (c) 6-5 (d) 4-3
8. The excerpt concludes with which type of cadence?
   (a) Phrygian (b) imperfect authentic
   (c) perfect authentic (d) deceptive

CHAPTER 17

The vii$^{\circ 6}$, vii$^{\circ 7}$, vii$^{\varnothing 7}$, and Other Voice-Leading Chords

In this chapter you'll learn to:

- Hear voice-leading chords in works for piano and accompanied voice
- Associate cadence types with particular solfège syllables or scale-degree numbers
- Describe the relationship between motivic statements
- Aurally reduce embellished textures to simpler outlines
- Identify common harmonic progressions involving voice-leading chords
- Identify the range of a melody

Preparatory Listening

Complete the *Try It* dictations to familiarize yourself with the following concepts and skills:

- Determining the solfège syllables or scale-degree numbers for the melody and bass in model SATB phrases
- Associating solfège syllables or scale-degree numbers with voice-leading chords
- Converting solfège syllables and scale-degree numbers to pitches and notating them on the staff
- Applying Roman numerals to basic phrase models

Try It

Listen to model SATB progressions that are played once each. The key signature, meter signature, and first bass pitch are given.

- Focus on the bass line first, and notate its pitches.
- Beneath the bass pitches, write Roman numerals that represent the harmony; if more than one chord seems possible, write all the possibilities and choose the correct one after additional hearings. Here, when scale degree $\hat{7}$ appears in the bass and descends to scale degree $\hat{6}$, the harmony will be (I^{4}_{2}). This is written in parentheses to indicate a passing function.
- Focus last on the soprano, determining the starting pitch by comparing it to the first bass pitch, then notate the entire soprano line.
- Add bar lines including the double bar at the end.
- If you are working by yourself, sing each part aloud with solfège syllables, scale-degree numbers, and/or letter names.

NAME ______________________________

Contextual Listening 17.3

In this CL exercise you will:

- Reduce an ornamented texture to its simple form
- Identify harmonic progressions
- Determine concluding solfège syllables or scale-degree numbers and identify cadences by type
- Notate a melody and bass line
- Identify the melodic range

Listen to an eight-measure phrase from a keyboard work, and complete the following exercises.

1. The initial melodic rhythm is best notated by which of the following?

Dictation strategy: When seventeenth- and eighteenth-century composers embellished a pitch with a neighbor tone, they wrote 𝆗 for "mordent" and 𝆘 for "inverted mordent." The mordent featured the upper neighbor tone (twice) and the inverted mordent the lower neighbor tone. Add these symbols to your list of dictation shortcuts.

2. Use the workspace provided to capture the excerpt.
   (a) Notate the rhythm of the melody on the single-line staff in $\frac{3}{4}$. Write the meter signature, and include bar lines. Beam notes to show beat grouping.
   (b) Below the rhythm staff, and under each note, write the solfège syllables or scale-degree numbers for the melody beginning on *sol* ($\hat{5}$). Leave out the embellishments.
   (c) Combine your answers to complete the notation of the pitches and rhythm of the melody. Begin on E5 and disregard the embellishments. Write the appropriate clef, key signature (and any accidentals), and meter signature. Beam notes to shown beat grouping.

3. The melodic pitches belong to which of the following scales?
   (a) major
   (b) harmonic minor
   (c) melodic minor
   (d) natural minor (descending melodic)

Workspace

Rhythm:

Melody: 𝄃

Solfège syllables:
Scale-degree numbers:

𝄃

Solfège syllables:
Scale-degree numbers:

Notation:

4. Melodic pitches 6-7 are harmonized with which chord? (This chord occurs on the downbeat of m. 3.)

   (a) i (b) iv (c) V (d) VI

5. Measure 5 includes which type of suspension?

   (a) 2-3 (b) 4-3 (c) 7-6 (d) 9-8

6. In measures 5-6, which is the chord progression?

   (a) vii°6-i (b) ii-i (c) V^6_4-i^6 (d) iv- i^6

7. The bass line begins on which pitch?

   (a) *do* ($\hat{1}$) (b) *me* ($\flat\hat{3}$) (c) *fa* ($\hat{4}$) (d) *sol* ($\hat{5}$)

8. The bass line ends on which pitch?

   (a) *do* ($\hat{1}$) (b) *me* ($\flat\hat{3}$) (c) *sol* ($\hat{5}$) (d) *ti* ($\hat{7}$)

9. From the melody's lowest pitch to its highest, which best describes its range?

   (a) *do* to *sol* ($\hat{1}$-$\hat{5}$) (b) *ti* to *le* ($\hat{7}$-$\flat\hat{6}$) (c) *do* to *do* ($\hat{1}$-$\hat{1}$) (d) *sol* to *sol* ($\hat{5}$-$\hat{5}$)

10. The excerpt concludes with which type of cadence?

    (a) Phrygian (b) imperfect authentic
    (c) perfect authentic (d) deceptive

11. On the downbeats of measures 3-6, which harmonic interval occurs between the outer voices?

    (a) 5 (b) 6 (c) 8 (d) 10

Phrase Structure and Motivic Analysis

NAME ______________________

In this chapter you'll learn to:

- Understand phrase structure in excerpts from a string quartet, a traditional song, and works for keyboard
- Identify cadences
- Identify motives, phrases, and subphrases
- Describe the relationship between phrases
- Identify phrase structures by name
- Draw diagrams to show the phrase structure
- Notate the initial motives of phrases

Preparatory Listening

Complete the *Try It* dictations to review the following concepts and skills:

- Determining the solfège syllables or scale-degree numbers for the soprano and bass in model SATB phrases
- Associating solfège syllables or scale-degree numbers to chords of the tonic and dominant areas, root progressions, and voice-leading chords
- Converting solfège syllables and scale-degree numbers to pitches and notating them on the staff
- Applying Roman numerals to basic phrase models

Try It

Listen to model SATB progressions drawn from previous chapters; each is played once. The key signature, meter signature, and first bass pitch are given.

- Focus on the bass line first, and notate its pitches.
- Beneath the bass pitches, write Roman numerals that represent the harmony; if more than one chord seems possible, write all the possibilities and choose the correct one after additional hearings. Here, when scale degree $\hat{7}$ appears in the bass and descends to scale degree $\hat{6}$, the harmony will be (I^4_2). This is written in parentheses to indicate a passing function.
- Focus last on the soprano, determining the starting pitch by comparing it to the first bass pitch, then notate the entire soprano line.

- Add bar lines including the double bar at the end.
- If you are working by yourself, sing each part aloud with solfège syllables, scale-degree numbers, and/or letter names.

NAME ______________________

9.

10.

11.

12.

Contextual Listening

Review the following concepts to help you successfully complete the Contextual Listening exercises in this and future chapters.

Motive and subphrase

Two small units of structure, **motive** and **subphrase**, are smaller than a phrase. Neither contains a cadence. A motive is the smallest recognizable musical idea (recall the four-note beginning of Beethoven's Fifth Symphony). Motives are characterized by their pitches, contours, and/or rhythms. Subphrases may consist of a motive or motives and are usually more substantial musical ideas.

Phrase and sentence

A **phrase** is the smallest musical idea that concludes with a cadence.

A **sentence** is a structure comprised of three units, often in the proportion 1:1:2. In a four-measure structure, the sentence might be 1 + 1 + 2 measures. In longer structures, the sentence may still follow the same proportion (e.g., 2 + 2 + 4). Unit 1 states an idea, which is repeated or varied in unit 2; unit 3, which may or may not be related to the original idea, leads to a cadence. (Recall the first phrase of Beethoven's Fifth Symphony.) Sentences may be independent structures (e.g., the opening of Beethoven's Piano Sonata in F Minor, Op. 2, No. 1) or part of a period structure.

Period

A **period** is typically a two-phrase harmonic structure: an inconclusive tonal motion followed by a conclusive one. The first phrase, the **antecedent**, initiates a harmonic motion that resolves in the second, the **consequent**. The antecedent usually cadences on V, and the consequent phrase usually reaches a perfect authentic cadence (PAC). Some theorists define the antecedent-consequent relationship strictly, reserving the term "period" for only those structures of HC-PAC. Others permit different weak-strong phrases (e.g., IAC-PAC).

A four-phrase period is a **double period**. A double period consists of four phrases in which the only PAC occurs at the end, following three inconclusive cadences.

Design

Design refers to the melody and rhythm of a musical passage. In a period, if the design at the beginning of each phrase is the same or similar, the phrases are **parallel**. If the design at the beginning of each phrase is different, the phrases are **contrasting**. Though the harmonic structure creates a period, it is the design that defines the *type* of period you hear. To determine the design of a double period, compare the beginning of the first antecedent phrase with that of the first consequent phrase (compare the design of phrase 1 with that of phrase 3).

Design is open to interpretation. It is more important to state musical reasons for your opinion of design than to argue in absolutes. Good reasons might include a statement such as "Phrase 2's design is similar to phrase 1's because it begins with similar pitches, rhythm, and harmonies."

Symmetry

If the number of antecedent phrases is the same as the number of consequent phrases, the period is symmetrical; otherwise, the period is asymmetrical. Symmetrical periods are far more common. Symmetry does *not* refer to the number of measures in a phrase; a symmetrical period might contain a five-measure antecedent followed by an eight-measure consequent.

An asymmetrical period might contain (a) two antecedents and one consequent phrase or (b) one antecedent and two consequent phrases, as shown next. To determine which case applies in a given passage, find the stronger of the two non-PAC cadences. This stronger cadence will mark the end of the antecedent phrase(s).

(a)	*Phrase 1*	*Phrase 2*	*Phrase 3*
	Antecedent 1	Antecedent 2	Consequent
	weakest cadence	stronger cadence	strongest cadence
	(e.g., a HC or an IAC)	(e.g., a chromaticized HC)	(PAC)
(b)	*Phrase 1*	*Phrase 2*	*Phrase 3*
	Antecedent 1	Consequent 1	Consequent 2
	strong cadence	weaker cadence	strongest cadence
	(e.g., a chromaticized HC)	(e.g., a HC or an IAC)	(PAC)

Though uncommon, it is possible to have an asymmetrical double period. To determine whether the structure is 1 + 3 or 3 + 1, answer this question: Of phrases 1-3, which has the strongest cadence? That cadence will mark the end of the antecedent phrase(s).

Phrase groups and independent phrases

Two or more phrases none of which end with a conclusive cadence constitute a **phrase group**. Phrase groups are often found between passages of more-stable music organized into periods. The phrases in a group may feature common motivic or thematic relationships, but none ends with a PAC.

Sometimes phrases do not belong to larger units of structure. A single phrase that concludes with a PAC is called an **independent phrase**. For example, Baroque music that is unrelated to dance often features a series of independent phrases, each of which cadences with a PAC in a related key.

Phrase-structure diagrams

The following diagram illustrates structural relationships, such as those between phrases in a period. When drawing phrase diagrams:

- Draw a curve to indicate a phrase or subphrase.
- Draw one or more curves above to demonstrate the hierarchy. Smaller units (like phrases) appear lower; larger units (like periods) appear higher.
- Place beneath the diagram the cadence labels (and later, the Roman numeral of the key in which a cadence occurs). Usually these are HC, PAC, and IAC.
- Place a lowercase letter to indicate the design above the middle of each phrase curve.

Variations

- Label antecedent and consequent phrases (if appropriate).
- When you determine the meter, label cadences with measure and beat numbers (e.g., HC 4.1 is a shortcut meaning that a half cadence occurs on beat 1 of m. 4).
- Abbreviate terms during real-time listening (e.g., || per is a shortcut for parallel period).
- One way to show variation of phrase design is to write **a–a′**, as illustrated next. Another way is **a**[1]–**a**[2].

Refer to these models when completing Contextual Listening assignments.

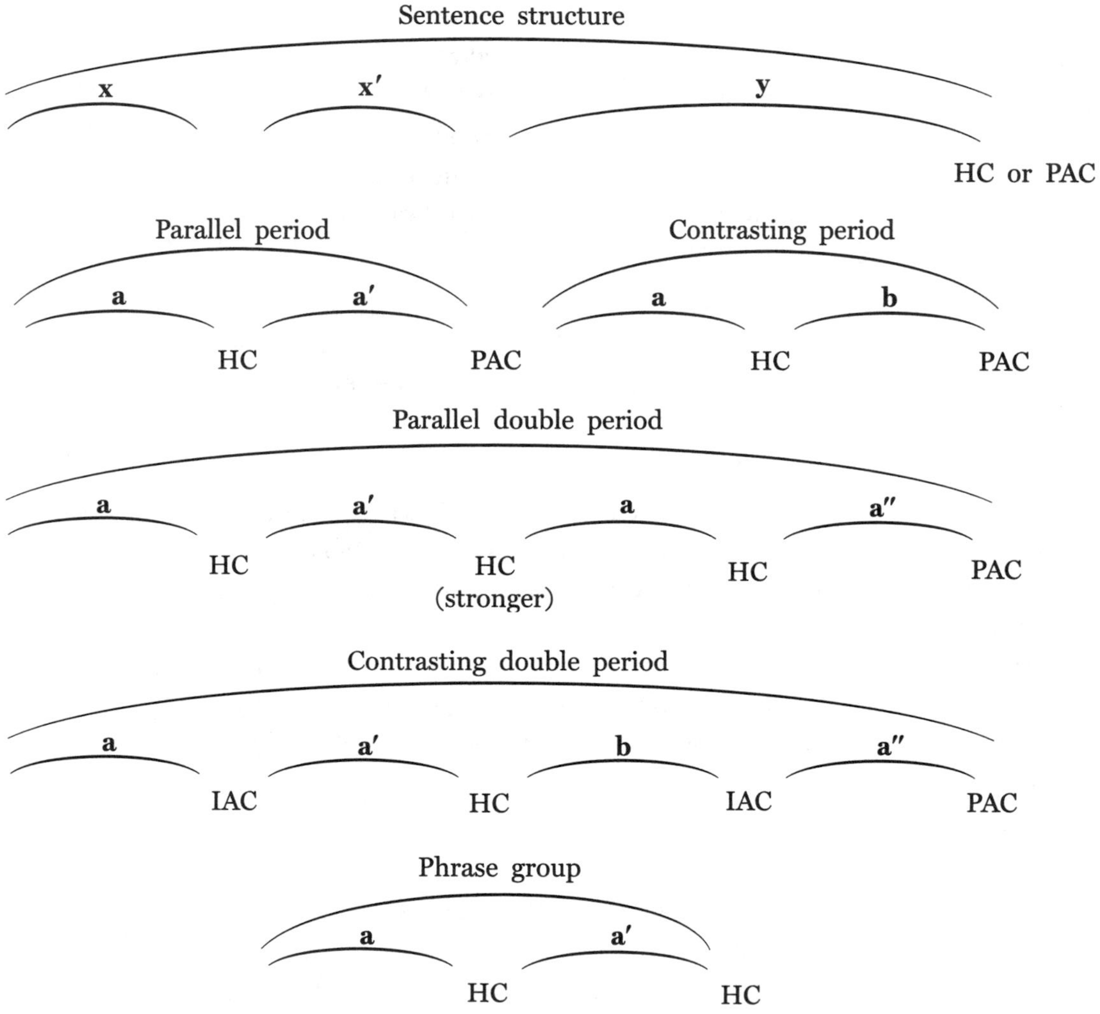

NAME ______________________________

Contextual Listening 18.5

In this CL exercise you will:

- Identify the relationship between phrases in an excerpt for string quartet
- Supply the solfège syllables or scale-degree numbers for the initial motive of the excerpt
- Identify cadences by name
- Identify the excerpt's phrase structure by name
- Draw a diagram of the phrase structure of the excerpt

Listen to an excerpt from a string quartet, and complete the following exercises.

1. Which of these represents the excerpt's design?

   (a) **a-a-a-a** (b) **a-a′-a-a′** (c) **a-b-a-a** (d) **a-b-a-b′**

2. Phrase 1's melody concludes on which pitch?

   (a) *do* ($\hat{1}$) (b) *re* ($\hat{2}$) (c) *mi* ($\hat{3}$) (d) *sol* ($\hat{5}$)

3. Phrase 2's melody concludes on which pitch?

   (a) *do* ($\hat{1}$) (b) *re* ($\hat{2}$) (c) *mi* ($\hat{3}$) (d) *sol* ($\hat{5}$)

4. Phrase 3's melody concludes on which pitch?

   (a) *do* ($\hat{1}$) (b) *re* ($\hat{2}$) (c) *mi* ($\hat{3}$) (d) *sol* ($\hat{5}$)

5. Phase 4's melody concludes on which pitch?

   (a) *do* ($\hat{1}$) (b) *re* ($\hat{2}$) (c) *mi* ($\hat{3}$) (d) *sol* ($\hat{5}$)

6. The cadences occur in which order? (Listen for the cadential bass pitches. Compare them with your answers to questions 2–5.)

   (a) HC-HC-HC-PAC (b) HC-IAC-HC-PAC

   (c) IAC-HC-IAC-PAC (d) IAC-IAC-IAC-PAC

7. Which of these represents the excerpt's phrase structure?

   (a) parallel period (b) contrasting period

   (c) parallel double period (d) contrasting double period

8. Draw a diagram of the phrase structure of the excerpt. Include labels for cadences, design, and the overall structure.

CL exercises 18.6 and 18.7 are works that you haven't encountered yet. Your teacher will probably assign each separately.

NAME ______________________

Contextual Listening 18.6

In this CL exercise you will:

- Identify the meter of an excerpt from a piano sonata
- Identify the relationship between phrases in the excerpt
- Notate initial motives of the phrases in the excerpt, and draw their contours
- Identify cadences by name
- Identify the excerpt's phrase structure by name
- Draw a diagram of the phrase structure of the excerpt

Listen to an excerpt from a piano sonata (performed on a fortepiano), and complete the following exercises.

1. Which of these represents the meter of this excerpt?
   (a) simple duple (b) simple triple
   (c) compound duple (d) compound triple

Exercises 2-5 refer only to phrase 1.

2. Use the workspace provided to capture the initial motive of phrase 1.
   (a) Notate the rhythm of phrase 1's initial motive on the single-line staff. Choose a meter signature, and include bar lines. Beam notes to show beat groupings.
   (b) Below the rhythm staff, and under each note, write the solfège syllables or scale-degree numbers for the initial motive of phrase 1.
   (c) Above the rhythm staff, draw the contour of the initial motive of phrase 1.
   (d) Combine your answers to complete the notation of the pitches and rhythm of phrase 1's initial motive beginning on B4. Write the appropriate clef, key signature, and meter signature.

Workspace

Rhythm:

Melody:

Solfège syllables:
Scale-degree numbers:

Notation:

NAME ______________________________

3. After the second varied statement of the motive (melodic pitches 9–18), why can there be no cadence?
   (a) There is no bass motion at the end.
   (b) There is a tonic pedal point.
   (c) There has been no harmonic motion.
   (d) All of the above.

4. Phrase 1 ends with which type of cadence?
   (a) half (b) imperfect authentic (c) perfect authentic (d) deceptive

5. Phrase 1 concludes with which type of cadential motion?
   (a) V–I (b) V^{4}_{2}–I^{6} (c) I–V (d) V^{6-5}_{4-3}

Exercises 6–11 refer only to phrase 2.

6. Phrase 2 is preceded with which of the following?
   (a) three-pitch lead-in (b) mixed beat division
   (c) rests in both voices (d) change of meter

7. Use the workspace provided to capture the initial motive of phrase 2.
   (a) Notate the rhythm of phrase 2's initial motive on the single-line staff. Choose a meter signature, and include bar lines. Beam notes to show beat grouping.
   (b) Below the rhythm staff, and under each note, write the solfège syllables or scale-degree numbers for the initial motive of phrase 2.
   (c) Above the rhythm staff, draw the contour of the initial motive of phrase 2.
   (d) Combine your answers to complete the notation of the pitches and rhythm of phrase 2's initial motive beginning on B4. Write the appropriate clef, key signature, and meter signature.

Workspace

Rhythm:

Melody:

Solfège syllables:

Scale-degree numbers:

Notation:

8. Phrase 2's cadence is embellished with which of the following?
   (a) 9–8 suspension (b) 7–8 retardation
   (c) 4–3 suspension (d) all of the previous

9. Which of these represents the design of phrases 1-2? (Refer to your notation of both phrases.)

   (a) **a-a**   (b) **a-a′**   (c) **a-b**

10. Phrases 1-2 form which larger unit of structure?

    (a) parallel period   (b) contrasting period

    (c) phrase group   (d) two independent phrases

11. Draw a diagram of the phrase structure for phrases 1-2. Include labels for cadences, design, and the overall structure.

NAME ____________________

Contextual Listening 18.7

In this CL exercise you will:

- Identify the meter of an excerpt from a piano sonata
- Identify the relationship between phrases in the excerpt
- Identify cadences by name
- Identify the excerpt's phrase structure by name
- Draw a diagram of the phrase structure of the excerpt

Listen to an excerpt from a piano sonata, and complete the following exercises.

1. Which of these represents the meter of this excerpt?

   (a) simple duple (b) simple triple

   (c) compound duple (d) compound triple

2. Given your choice of meter in question 1, phrase 1 lasts for how many measures?

   (a) two (b) four (c) six (d) eight

3. Phrase 1 ends with which type of cadence?

   (a) half (b) imperfect authentic (c) perfect authentic (d) deceptive

4. Phrase 2 lasts for how many measures?

   (a) two (b) four (c) six (d) eight

5. Phrase 2 ends with which type of cadence?

   (a) half (b) imperfect authentic (c) perfect authentic (d) deceptive

6. Phrase 3 lasts for how many measures?

   (a) two (b) four (c) six (d) eight

7. Phrase 3 ends with which type of cadence?

   (a) half (b) imperfect authentic (c) perfect authentic (d) deceptive

8. Given the answers to questions 3, 5, and 7, what do you expect to hear in measure 16?

9. What does occur in measure 16?

10. The last phrase ends with which type of cadence?

    (a) half (b) imperfect authentic (c) perfect authentic (d) deceptive

11. Draw a diagram of the phrase structure of the excerpt. Include labels for cadences, design, and the overall structure.

12. Given your answer to question 11, which is the number of antecedent and consequent phrases?

	Antecedent phrase(s)	*Consequent phrase(s)*
(a)	1	3
(b)	2	2
(c)	2	3
(d)	3	2

Diatonic Sequences

NAME ______________________

In this chapter you'll learn to:

- Aurally recognize diatonic harmonic and melodic sequences in a string quartet, traditional songs, and a trio sonata
- Determine the LIP (linear intervallic pattern) of a sequence
- Map the initial pattern of a sequence onto successive transpositions
- Aurally identify cadences and phrases
- Determine phrase structure in sequential passages

Preparatory Listening

Complete the *Try It* dictations to review the following concepts and skills:

- Determining the solfège syllables or scale-degree numbers for the soprano and bass in model SATB and keyboard-style phrases
- Associating solfège syllables or scale-degree numbers with diatonic sequences
- Converting solfège syllables and scale-degree numbers to pitches and notating them on the staff
- Applying Roman numerals to basic phrase models

Try It

Each of the following exercises presents a harmonic sequence—a succession of harmonies based on a root progression with a repeated intervallic pattern in an upper voice. Listen to model progressions in both SATB and keyboard style that are played once each. The key signature, meter signature, and first bass pitch are given.

- Focus on the bass line first, and notate its pitches.
- Beneath the bass pitches, write Roman numerals that represent the harmony; if more than one chord seems possible, write all the possibilities and choose the correct one after additional hearings.
- Focus last on the soprano, determining the starting pitch by comparing it to the first bass pitch, then notate the entire soprano line.
- The answers for some progressions are notated in SATB style; others are notated in keyboard style. Practice notating both styles or in the style indicted by your teacher.
- Add bar lines including the double bar at the end.

- If you are working by yourself, sing each part aloud with solfège syllables, scale-degree numbers, and/or letter names.

NAME ________________________________

6.

7.

8.

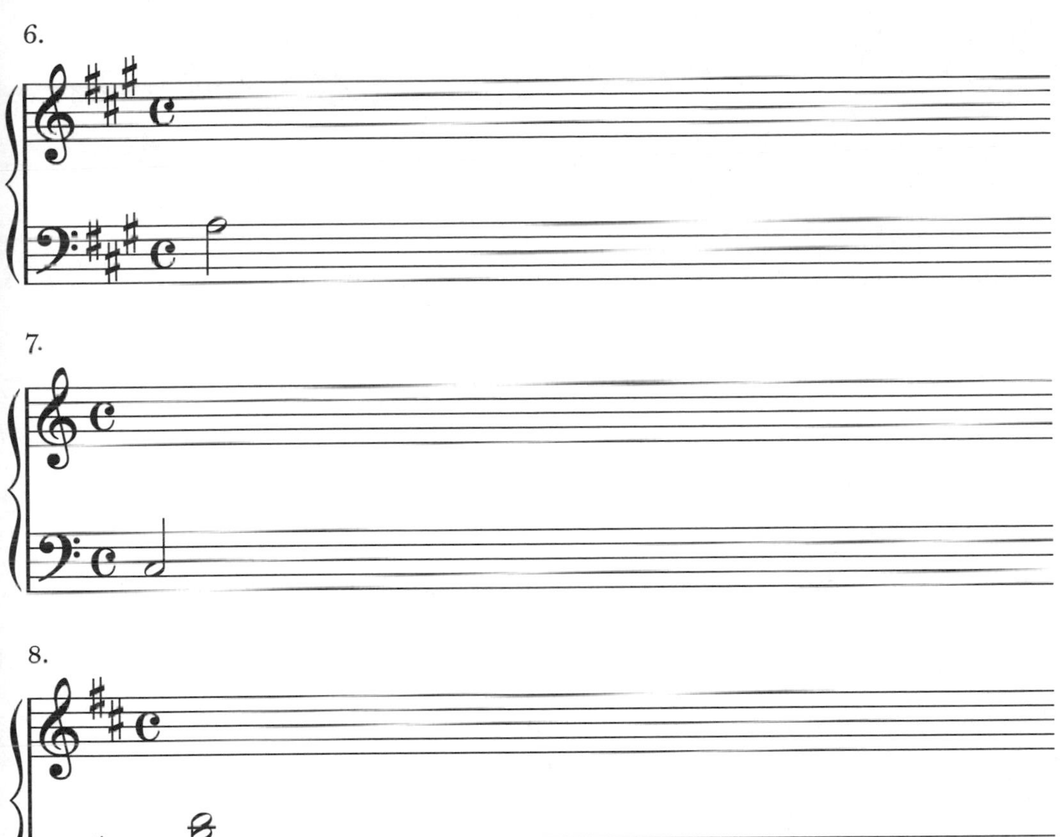

NAME ______________________________

Contextual Listening 19.1

In this CL exercise you will:

- Identify the meter of an excerpt from a string quartet
- Describe the compositional treatment of its main motive
- Determine the type of sequence
- Identify nonchord tones and $^6_4$ chord types
- Notate the soprano and bass and provide a Roman numeral analysis

Listen to an excerpt from a string quartet, and complete the following exercises.

1. Which of these represents the meter of this excerpt?

   (a) simple duple (b) simple triple

   (c) simple quadruple (d) compound triple

2. The violin melody begins with a five-pitch motive. Its development is best described by which of the following?

	First time	*Second time*	*Third time*
(a)	motive stated	exact repetition	transposed repetition
(b)	motive stated	exact repetition	varied repetition
(c)	motive stated	transposed repetition	transposed repetition
(d)	motive stated	transposed repetition	transposed and varied repetition

3. The excerpt contains a sequence that is both melodic and harmonic. Which is the name for this sequence?

   (a) ascending 5-6 (b) descending parallel $^6_3$

   (c) descending thirds (d) descending fifths

4. The excerpt concludes with which type of cadence?

   (a) half (b) imperfect authentic (c) perfect authentic (d) deceptive

5. The second-to-last melodic pitch is which of the following dissonant embellishing tones?

   (a) retardation (b) suspension (c) passing tone (d) appoggiatura

6. The second-to-last harmony is which type of $^6_4$ chord?

   (a) passing (b) neighboring (c) cadential (d) arpeggiated

7. Use the workspace provided to capture the excerpt.

   (a) Notate the rhythm of the melody and bass on the single-line staves. Choose a meter signature, and include bar lines. Beam notes to show beat grouping.

   (b) Below each rhythm staff, and under each note, write the solfège syllables or scale-degree numbers for the melody and bass. Begin the melody on *sol* ($\hat{5}$) and the bass on *do* ($\hat{1}$).

   (c) Combine your answers to complete the notation of the pitches and rhythm of the melody and bass. Begin on G4 and C4 respectively. Write the appropriate clefs, key signature, and meter signature.

NAME ______________________________

(d) Write Roman numerals beneath the bass pitches.

(e) Notate the inner two parts in measure 1.

(f) Next, notate the inner parts in measures 3–6. Refer to question 3 and notice that in a sequence, you need not hear everything in order to notate the parts correctly, only the initial pattern. Decide whether the sequence moves up or down and by what interval. Then apply that information to the initial pattern to help copy and transpose the pattern.

Workspace

Rhythm:

Melody:

Solfège syllables:

Scale-degree numbers:

Solfège syllables:

Scale-degree numbers:

Notation:

Rhythm:

Bass:

Solfège syllables:

Scale-degree numbers:

Solfège syllables:

Scale-degree numbers:

NAME ________________________________

Contextual Listening 19.2

In this CL exercise you will:

- Identify the meter of a choral work
- Identify cadences and phrase structure
- Determine the type of sequence
- Identify nonchord tones and $^6_4$ chord types
- Describe the relationship between phrases
- Notate the soprano and bass and provide a Roman numeral analysis

Listen to two phrases from a choral work, and complete the following exercises.

1. Which is the meter signature of this excerpt?
   (a) $^3_4$ (b) $^4_4$ (c) $^6_8$ (d) $^9_8$
2. Phrase 1 concludes with which type of cadence?
   (a) half (b) imperfect authentic (c) perfect authentic (d) deceptive
3. Phrase 2 concludes which type of cadence?
   (a) half (b) imperfect authentic (c) perfect authentic (d) deceptive
4. Each phrase contains how many subphrases?
   (a) one (b) two (c) three (d) four
5. Which statement about phrase 2 is false?
   (a) It is a varied repetition of phrase 1.
   (b) Its harmonic rhythm is faster than phrase 1's.
   (c) Its cadence differs from that of phrase 1.
   (d) Its sequence is chromaticized.
6. Phrases 1-2 create which larger structure?
   (a) parallel period (b) contrasting period
   (c) contrasting double period (d) phrase group
7. Diagram the phrase structure of the excerpt in the following space.

Exercises 8-18 focus on specific details of the excerpt.

8. During the words "in excelsis," which type of $^6_4$ chord occurs?
   Hint: Listen carefully to the outer voices.
   (a) passing (b) neighboring (c) cadential (d) arpeggiated
9. The final cadence features which type of suspension?
   (a) 2-3 (b) 4-3 (c) 7-6 (d) 9-8

NAME ______________________________

10. Bass pitches 1-2, 3-4, and 5-6 create which melodic interval?

(a) M2 (b) m3 (c) P4 (d) P5

11. Phrase 1 begins with which type of sequence?

(a) ascending 5-6
(b) descending parallel $^6_3$
(c) descending thirds
(d) descending fifths

12. From the end of phrase 1 ("Deo") to the beginning of phrase 2 ("Gloria"), which voice-leading error occurs?

(a) parallel octaves
(b) parallel fifths
(c) similar motion to an octave
(d) similar motion to a fifth

13. Use the workspace provided to capture the excerpt.

(a) Notate the rhythm of the melody and bass in common time on the single-line staves. Write the meter signature, and include bar lines.

(b) Below each rhythm staff, and under each note, write the solfège syllables or scale-degree numbers for the melody and bass. Begin the melody on *sol* ($\hat{5}$) and the bass on *do* ($\hat{1}$).

(c) Combine your answers to complete the notation of the pitches and rhythm of the melody and bass. Begin on D5 and G3 respectively. Write the appropriate clefs, key signature, and meter signature.

(d) Write Roman numerals beneath the bass pitches.

(e) Notate the two inner parts in measures 1-2.

(f) Next, notate the inner parts in measures 3-6. Refer to your notation and to question 11 for help.

Workspace

Rhythm:

Melody:

Solfège syllables:

Scale-degree numbers:

Solfège syllables:

Scale-degree numbers:

Solfège syllables:

Scale-degree numbers:

Notation:

NAME ______________________________

Rhythm:

Bass:

Solfège syllables:

Scale-degree numbers:

Solfège syllables:

Scale-degree numbers:

Solfège syllables:

Scale-degree numbers:

Contextual Listening 19.3

In this CL exercise you will:

- Identify the meter of a holiday song
- Identify cadences and phrase structure
- Identify nonchord tones
- Notate the soprano and bass and provide a Roman numeral analysis
- Determine the LIP (linear intervallic pattern)

Listen to a piano arrangement of a holiday song, and complete the following exercises.

1. Which is the meter signature of this excerpt?

   (a) $\frac{2}{4}$ (b) $\frac{3}{4}$ (c) $\frac{6}{8}$ (d) $\frac{9}{8}$

2. Phrase 1 concludes with which type of cadence?

   (a) half (b) imperfect authentic (c) perfect authentic (d) deceptive

3. Phrase 2 concludes with which type of cadence?

   (a) half (b) imperfect authentic (c) perfect authentic (d) deceptive

4. Phrases 1-2 create which larger structure?

   (a) parallel period (b) contrasting period
   (c) contrasting double period (d) phrase group

5. Diagram the phrase structure of the excerpt in the following space.

6. The bass line's chromatic pitch is which type of embellishing tone?

   (a) passing (b) neighbor (c) appoggiatura (d) anticipation

7. At the end of each phrase, the higher parts feature which parallel harmonic intervals?

   (a) thirds (b) fourths (c) fifths (d) sixths

8. Use the workspace provided to capture the excerpt.

   (a) Notate the rhythm of the melody and bass for phrase 1 in simple duple meter on the single-line staves. Write the meter signature, and include bar lines. Beam notes to show beat grouping.

   (b) Below each rhythm staff, and under each note, write the solfège syllables or scale-degree numbers for the melody and bass for phrase 1.

   (c) Combine your answers to complete the notation of the pitches and rhythm of the melody and bass for phrase 1. Begin on D5 and B♭2 respectively. Write the appropriate clefs, key signature, and meter signature.

   (d) Write Roman numerals beneath the bass pitches.

   (e) Write popular-music chord symbols above the melody.

NAME ________________________________

Workspace

Rhythm:

Melody:

Solfège syllables:
Scale-degree numbers:

Solfège syllables:
Scale-degree numbers:

Notation:

Rhythm:

Bass:

Solfège syllables:
Scale-degree numbers:

Solfège syllables:
Scale-degree numbers:

9. Circle the outer voices on beat 1 of measures 1-6, and write the interval between them in the blanks below.

_____ m. 1 _____ m. 2 _____ m. 3 _____ m. 4 _____ m. 5 _____ m. 6

10. Recall that linear intervallic patterns (LIPs) are recurring intervallic patterns between outer voices. In question 9, measures 1-2, 3-4, and 5-6 create interval pairs. Because the first and third pair are the same, you can assume they represent the LIP, and that the middle pair features a melodic variation. If the middle pair followed the LIP strictly, melodic pitch 12 would be which of the following?

    (a) *re* ($\hat{2}$) (b) *fa* ($\hat{4}$) (c) *sol* ($\hat{5}$) (d) *ti* ($\hat{7}$)

11. On which harmonic sequence is the excerpt based?

    (a) ascending 5-6 (b) descending thirds

    (c) descending fourths (d) descending fifths

NAME ______________________________

Contextual Listening 19.4

In this CL exercise you will:

- Notate the pitches of the outer parts from a work studied previously
- Write harmonic intervals between parts
- Determine the LIP (linear intervallic pattern)

Listen to an excerpt from a trio sonata that you studied in Chapter 16, and complete these additional exercises.

1. On the following grand staff, notate the pitches specified in parts (a) and (b) in the key of C minor. Write the key signature and include any accidentals; vertically align simultaneous pitches.
   (a) Beginning with *do* ($\hat{1}$), notate bass pitches 8–21.
   (b) Beginning with *le* ($\flat\hat{6}$), notate melodic pitches 8–15.

2. Write the harmonic intervals between the staves in question 1.
3. Judging from your answer to question 2, which linear intervallic patern (LIP) occurs?
   (a) 7-6 (b) 7-10 (c) 10-5 (d) 10-6
4. Look at the bass line in question 1. Which harmonic sequence is implied?
   (a) ascending 5-6 (b) descending parallel $^6_3$
   (c) descending thirds (d) descending fifths

CHAPTER 20

Secondary Dominant and Leading-Tone Chords to V

In this chapter you'll learn to:

- Aurally identify secondary dominant and leading-tone chords to V in excerpts from string quartets, a traditional song, and art songs
- Recognize these harmonies quickly by listening for the chromatic syllable *fi* ($\sharp\hat{4}$).
- Notate melodies and bass lines that outline these harmonies

---

Preparatory Listening

Complete the *Try It* dictations to review the following concepts and skills:

- Determining the solfège syllables or scale-degree numbers for the soprano and bass in model SATB phrases
- Associating solfège syllables or scale-degree numbers with secondary dominant and leading-tone chords to V
- Converting solfège syllables and scale-degree numbers to pitches and notating them on the staff
- Applying Roman numerals to show tonicizations

Try It

Listen to model SATB phrases that are played once each. The key signature, meter signature, and first bass pitch are given.

- Focus on the bass line first, and notate its pitches.
- Beneath the bass pitches, write Roman numerals that represent the harmony; if more than one chord seems possible, write all the possibilities and choose the correct one after additional hearings.
- Show the tonicization with a slash (e.g., V^6/V) or as indicated by your teacher.
- Focus last on the soprano, determining the starting pitch by comparing it to the first bass pitch, then notate the entire soprano line.
- Add bar lines including the double bar at the end.
- If you are working by yourself, sing each part aloud with solfège syllables, scale-degree numbers, and/or letter names.

NAME ______________________________

NAME ________________________________

Contextual Listening 20.1

In this CL exercise you will:

- Listen for the chromatic syllable *fi* ($\sharp\hat{4}$).
- Associate this syllable with a secondary harmony
- Distinguish between secondary dominants and secondary leading-tone chords

Focus your listening on the conclusion of this excerpt.

1. Which of the following is *fi* ($\sharp\hat{4}$)?
   (a) a melodic embellishment
   (b) a member of a chord that leads to V
2. The last three melodic pitches are which of the following?
   (a) *mi-do-sol* ($\hat{3}$-$\hat{1}$-$\hat{5}$) (b) *re-do-sol* ($\hat{2}$-$\hat{1}$-$\hat{5}$)
   (c) *do-mi-sol* ($\hat{1}$-$\hat{3}$-$\hat{5}$) (d) *ti-sol-sol* ($\hat{7}$-$\hat{5}$-$\hat{5}$)
3. The chord that harmonizes bass pitch *fi* ($\sharp\hat{4}$) is of which quality? (Consider your answer to question 2.)
   (a) MM7 (b) Mm7 (c) mm7 (d) dm7 (^{ø7})
4. Which chord harmonizes *fi* ($\sharp\hat{4}$)? (Consider your answer to question 3.)
   (a) I^7 (b) V^7/V (c) ii^7 (d) $vii^{ø7}/V$

NAME ______________________________

Contextual Listening 20.4

In this CL exercise you will:

- Listen for the chromatic syllable *fi* ($\sharp\hat{4}$).
- Associate this syllable with a common secondary harmony
- Notate the pitches of a melody and bass that outline a secondary harmony

The following exercises focus on the end of this excerpt.

1. On the following grand staff, write a treble and bass clef, and notate the key signature for A major.
2. Beginning with F♯5, notate the last seven melodic pitches ("blauen Augen seh'n").
3. Beginning with D3, notate the last five bass pitches. Vertically align pitches that sound simultaneously; ignore the octave doubling in the bass.

4. Which of the following is bass pitch *fi* ($\sharp\hat{4}$)?
   (a) a melodic embellishment
   (b) a member of a chord that leads to V
5. Bass pitch *fi* ($\sharp\hat{4}$) is harmonized with a chord of which quality?
   (a) M triad (b) m triad (c) Mm7 (d) dm7 (ø7)
6. Which chord harmonizes bass pitch *fi* ($\sharp\hat{4}$)? (Consider your answer to question 5.)
   (a) V^6/V (b) ii^6 (c) V^7 (d) $vii^{ø7}$/V

Contextual Listening 20.5

In this CL exercise you will:

- Identify cadences in an excerpt for piano and diagram its phrase structure
- Notate the melody and bass line
- Identify the harmonic interval of the left-hand accompaniment

Listen to an excerpt from a work for piano, and complete the following exercises.

1. Which is the most likely meter signature of this excerpt?

   (a) $\frac{2}{4}$ (b) $\frac{3}{4}$ (c) $\frac{6}{8}$ (d) $\frac{9}{8}$

2. At the beginning, the two lower parts make which harmonic interval?

   (a) thirds (b) fifths (c) sixths (d) octaves

3. Phrase 1 concludes with which type of cadence?

   (a) half (b) imperfect authentic (c) perfect authentic (d) deceptive

4. Phrase 2 concludes with which type of cadence?

   (a) half (b) imperfect authentic (c) perfect authentic (d) deceptive

5. Diagram the structure of phrases 1–2 in the following space.

6. Which harmony precedes the dominant at the end of the second phrase?

   (a) ii (b) V^6_5/V (c) V7/V (d) IV

7. Use the workspace provided to capture the excerpt.

   (a) Notate the rhythm of the melody and bass in compound duple meter on the single-line staves. Write a meter signature, and include bar lines. Beam notes to show beat grouping.

   (b) Below each rhythm staff, and under each note, write the solfège syllables or scale-degree numbers for the melody and bass. Begin the melody on *sol* ($\hat{5}$) and the bass on *do* ($\hat{1}$).

   (c) Combine your answers to complete the notation of the pitches and rhythm of the melody and bass. Begin on G4 and C4 respectively. Write the appropriate clefs, key signature, and meter signature.

NAME ______________________________

Workspace

Rhythm:

Melody:

Solfège syllables:

Scale-degree numbers:

Solfège syllables:

Scale-degree numbers:

Notation:

Rhythm:

Bass:

Solfège syllables:

Scale-degree numbers:

Solfège syllables:

Scale-degree numbers:

NAME ______________________

Contextual Listening 20.6

In this CL exercise you will:

- Identify cadences in an art song
- Identify melodic sequences
- Notate the pitches of a melody and bass that outline secondary harmonies
- Identify the harmonic intervals of the left-hand accompaniment

In this excerpt from an art song, a young man tries to persuade a young woman to let him court her. Study the text, and then listen to the excerpt and complete the following exercises.

Guten Abend, mein Schatz,	Good evening, my sweetheart,
guten Abend, mein Kind!	good evening, my dear!
Ich komm' aus Lieb' zu dir,	I come out of love for you,
Ach, mach' mir auf die Tür,	Oh, open your door,
mach' mir auf die Tür!	open your door for me!

1. Which is the meter signature of this excerpt?

   (a) $\frac{2}{4}$ (b) $\frac{3}{4}$ (c) $\frac{6}{8}$ (d) $\frac{9}{8}$

Questions 2-7 refer only to phrases 1-2, which conclude with the second statement of "Guten Abend, mein Kind!"

2. During phrase 1, the piano accompaniment is best described by which statement?
   (a) The piano introduction anticipates the motive in the voice.
   (b) The piano doubles the vocal melody in octaves.
   (c) The piano concludes the phrase with a chord progression based on ascending fifths.
   (d) All of the above.
   (e) None of the above.

3. The melodic sequence in phrase 1, which occurs after the piano introduction, is best described by which of the following?
   (a) Each measure descends by step. (b) Each measure descends by thirds.
   (c) Each measure ascends by step. (d) Each measure ascends by thirds.

4. Phrase 1 concludes with which type of cadence?
   (a) half (b) imperfect authentic (c) perfect authentic (d) deceptive

5. During phrase 2, which statement about the piano accompaniment is true?
   (a) The lower part arpeggiates the chords.
   (b) The highest part doubles the vocal melody.
   (c) The accompaniment includes block chords.
   (d) The highest part concludes with descending parallel thirds.
   (e) All of the above.

NAME ______________________________

6. Phrase 2 concludes with which harmonic progression?

   (a) V^6_5-I (b) ii^6-V (c) $vii^{ø7}$/V-V (d) V^4_3/V-V

7. Use the workspace provided to capture the first vocal phrase.

   (a) Notate the rhythm of the vocal melody of phrase 1 in simple triple meter on the single-line staff. Choose a meter signature, and include bar lines. Beam notes to show beat grouping.

   (b) Below each rhythm staff, and under each note, write the solfège syllables or scale-degree numbers of phrase 1's vocal melody.

   (c) Combine your answers to complete the notation of the pitches and rhythm of vocal phrase 1 beginning on A4. Write the appropriate clefs, key signature, and meter signature.

Workspace

Rhythm:

Melody:

Solfège syllables:

Scale-degree numbers:

Notation:

Questions 8-16 refer to the music that begins with phrase 3 ("Ich komm' aus . . .").

8. In the vocal part in phrase 3, the first three melodic pitches outline a triad of which quality and inversion?

   (a) m^6_3 (b) m^6_4 (c) M^6_3 (d) M^6_4

9. The second chord outlined by the voice is of which quality and inversion?

   (a) MM^6_5 (b) Mm7 (c) mm^4_3 (d) dm^4_2

10. Use the workspace provided to capture phrase 3.

    (a) Notate the rhythm of the vocal melody and bass line of phrase 3 on the single-line staves. Choose a meter signature, and include bar lines. Beam notes to show beat grouping.

    (b) Below each rhythm staff, and under each note, write the solfège syllables or scale-degree numbers of vocal melody and bass line.

    (c) Combine your answers to complete the notation of the pitches and rhythm of the vocal melody and bass line of phrase 3. Begin on E4 and A1 respectively. Write the appropriate clefs, key signature, and meter signature.

    (d) Beneath the bass staves, write one Roman numeral per measure under the first six measures of phrase 3 (i.e., under pitches 1-9).

Workspace

Rhythm:

Melody:

Solfège syllables:
Scale-degree numbers:

Solfège syllables:
Scale-degree numbers:

Notation:

Rhythm:

Bass:

Solfège syllables:
Scale-degree numbers:

Solfège syllables:
Scale-degree numbers:

11. How are bass pitches 1-3 and 7-9 in phrase 3 related to the piano melody in the introduction?

    (a) transposed down a fifth (b) melodic inversion

    (c) rhythmic augmentation (d) same pitches played backward (retrograde)

NAME ________________________________

12. Near the end of the bass line (beginning with the last seven bass pitches), how do the chromatic pitches embellish *sol* ($\hat{5}$)?

(a) double neighbor tones (b) passing tones

(c) consonant skips (d) suspensions

13. The excerpt concludes with which chord progression? (Focus on the chord quality of the last four bass pitches.)

(a) I-vi-ii^6-V (b) ii^6-V^7/V-V-I (c) vii^{ø7}/V-V$^{8-7}_{\substack{6-5\\4-3}}$-I (d) V^7/V-V$^{4-3}$-I

14. Listen to the entire excerpt once again. Which is its phrase structure?

(a) introduction **a^1 a^2-a^3-b** (b) introduction **a^1-a^2-b-c**

(c) introduction **a-b-a-c** (d) introduction **a-b-c-d**

CHAPTER 21

Tonicizing Scale Degrees Other Than V

In this chapter you'll learn to:

- Aurally identify secondary dominants and leading-tone chords to scale degrees other than V in excerpts from piano works
- Learn methods for understanding tonicization in a general way
- Recognize these harmonies quickly by listening for the chromatic solfège syllable leading upward and downward to tonicized chords
- Notate melodies and bass lines that outline these harmonies and develop the ability to interpret their function in different keys

Preparatory Listening

Complete the *Try It* dictations to review the following concepts and skills:

- Determining the solfège syllables or scale-degree numbers for the soprano and bass in model SATB phrases
- Associating solfège syllables or scale-degree numbers with secondary dominant and leading-tone IV (iv), vi (VI), ii, and III
- Converting solfège syllables and scale-degree numbers to pitches and notating them on the staff
- Applying Roman numerals to show tonicizations

Try It

Listen to model SATB phrases that are played once each. The key signature, meter signature, and first bass pitch are given.

- Focus on the bass line first, and notate its pitches.
- Beneath the bass pitches, write Roman numerals that represent the harmony; if more than one chord seems possible, write all the possibilities and choose the correct one after additional hearings.
- Show the tonicization with a slash (e.g., V^6/V) or as indicated by your teacher.
- Focus last on the soprano, determining the starting pitch by comparing it to the first bass pitch, then notate the entire soprano line.
- Add bar lines including the double bar at the end.
- If you are working by yourself, sing each part aloud with solfège syllables, scale-degree numbers, and/or letter names.

NAME ______________________________

1.

2.

3.

4.

5.

6.

7.

8.

NAME ______________________________

Contextual Listening

These listening methods can help you understand tonicization aurally. Sing each melody in two ways.

(1) Sing only the top line, which gives solfège syllables and scale-degree numbers in the original key (F). *Di-re* ($\sharp\hat{1}$-2) suggests a dominant-to-tonic progression (D-T) of ii (e.g., V/ii-ii). Likewise, *fi-sol* ($\sharp\hat{4}$-$\hat{5}$) implies a D-T progression of V (e.g., V/V-V).

(2) Sing the top line of syllables or numbers in measure 1, the second line in measure 2, and the third line in measure 3. Because *di* ($\sharp\hat{1}$) leads to *re* ($\hat{2}$), ii is being tonicized, and because *fi* ($\sharp\hat{4}$) leads to *sol* ($\hat{5}$), V is being tonicized. This method reflects these tonicizations, and makes it easy to hear how the motive in measure 1 is transposed to nontonic scale degrees.

With the second method it is also easy to infer harmonies from these tonicizations. If the *do-ti-do* ($\hat{1}$-$\hat{7}$-$\hat{1}$) melody in measure 1 can be harmonized with I-V-I, then the *do-ti-do* ($\hat{1}$-$\hat{7}$-$\hat{1}$) melody in measure 2 would support the same progression in the key of ii (ii: i-V-i).

Movable *do*

Method 1: Bracket notation

1. Is the chromatic pitch in phrase 2 a melodic embellishment or part of a chord that tonicizes a nontonic scale degree?

2. Because the chromatic pitch is part of a secondary-dominant-function chord, write a bracket to indicate you hear a secondary relationship.

3. Write the solfège syllable or scale-degree number of the chromatic pitch.

4. To which scale degree does this chromatic pitch lead?

5. Write the Roman numeral of that scale degree under the bracket, to indicate which chord is being tonicized.

6. Thinking now *in the key of your answer to* question 5, write the dominant-tonic (D-T) progression above the bracket. Begin with the chord that contains the chromatic

pitch and follow the same listening strategies you have used since learning to take harmonic dictation.

Hear a *sol-do* ($\hat{5}$-$\hat{1}$) bass line?

Hear a seventh, *fa* ($\hat{4}$), over the dominant chord?

Solution:

Method 2: Slash notation

1. Is the chromatic pitch a melodic embellishment or part of a chord that tonicizes a nontonic scale degree?

2. Because the chromatic pitch is part of a secondary-dominant-function chord, write a "slash" to indicate that you hear a secondary relationship.
3. Write the solfège syllable or scale-degree number of the chromatic pitch.
4. To which scale degree does this chromatic pitch lead?
5. Write the Roman numeral of that scale degree *after the slash*, to indicate which chord is being tonicized. Write the Roman numeral again, since this is the tonicized chord.
6. Thinking now in the key of your answer to question 5, identify the dominant chord and its inversion, and write this Roman numeral *before the slash*.

   Bass pitch sounds like *sol* ($\hat{5}$)?

   Hear a seventh, *fa* ($\hat{4}$), over the dominant chord?

   Solution:

Method 3: Colon notation

1. Is the chromatic pitch a melodic embellishment or part of a chord that tonicizes a nontonic scale degree?

2. Because the chromatic pitch is part of a secondary-dominant-function chord, write a colon to indicate that you hear a secondary relationship.
3. Write the solfège syllable or scale-degree number of the chromatic pitch.
4. To which scale degree does this chromatic pitch lead?
5. Write the Roman numeral of that scale degree *before the colon*, to indicate which chord is being tonicized.
6. Thinking now in the key of your answer to question 5, write the dominant-tonic (D-T) progression *after the colon*. Begin with the chord that contains the chromatic pitch.

   Hear a *sol-do* ($\hat{5}$-$\hat{1}$) bass line?

   Hear a seventh, *fa* ($\hat{4}$), over the dominant chord?

   Solution:

NAME ______________________

Contextual Listening 21.1

In this CL exercise you will:

- Listen for a chromatic pitch that does not appear in the melody and bass line of a work for piano
- Determine the scale degree that this pitch tonicizes
- Notate the melody and bass line of the second phrase
- Determine the harmonic progression of secondary chords

Listen to an excerpt from a work for piano you studied previously, and complete the following exercises.

This exercise focuses on phrase 2 only (mm. 5-8) which begins with a quarter-note anacrusis.

1. Use the workspace provided to capture the excerpt.
   (a) Notate the rhythm of the melody and bass parts of the second phrase (mm. 5-8) on the single-line staves. Begin with a quarter-note anacrusis in each part. Choose a meter signature, and include bar lines (including one to show the anacrusis). Beam notes to show beat grouping.
   (b) Below each rhythm staff, and under each note, write the solfège syllables or scale-degree numbers for the melody and bass parts of the second phrase (mm. 5-8). Begin both parts on *sol* ($\hat{5}$). Write your entire answer in the tonic key. Then, beneath this answer, use colon notation to more clearly reveal the tonicization of a different scale degree.
   (c) Combine your answers to complete the notation of the pitches and rhythm of the melody and bass parts of the second phrase (mm. 5-8). Begin on E♭5 and E♭3 respectively. Include the appropriate clefs, key signature, and meter signature.

NAME ______________________________

Workspace

Rhythm:

Melody:

Solfège syllables:

Scale-degree numbers:

Notation:

Rhythm:

Bass:

Solfège syllables:

Scale-degree numbers:

NAME ______________________________

Contextual Listening 21.4

In this CL exercise you will:

- Listen for chromatic pitches that tonicize various scale degrees in a work for keyboard
- Determine the scale degree that is being tonicized
- Notate the melody and bass line
- Use Roman numerals to show the tonicization in three ways

Listen to a two-phrase excerpt from a keyboard work, and complete the following exercises. This composition is based on a five-pitch motive. The motive is transposed, tonicizing different scale degrees.

1. Which is the meter signature of this excerpt?

   (a) $\frac{2}{2}$ (b) $\frac{3}{2}$ (c) $\frac{4}{2}$ (d) $\frac{6}{2}$

2. Phrase 1 concludes with which type of cadence?

   (a) Phrygian (b) imperfect authentic

   (c) perfect authentic (d) deceptive

Exercises 1-3 refer to phrase 1 only.

3. Use the workspace provided to capture the excerpt.

   (a) Notate the rhythm of the melody and bass line of phrase 1 on the single-line staves. Write the meter signature, and include bar lines.

   (b) Below each rhythm staff, and under each note, write the solfège syllables or scale-degree numbers for the melody and bass line of phrase 1. Write your entire answer in the tonic key. Then, beneath this answer, use colon notation to more clearly reveal the tonicization of a different scale degree. Vertically align the syllables or numbers.

   (c) Combine your answers to complete the notation of the pitches and rhythm of the melody and bass line of phrase 1. Begin on F4 and D3 respectively. Write the appropriate clefs, key signature, and meter signature.

   (d) Write Roman numerals beneath the bass pitches. Follow the strategies you practiced in CL exercises 21.1 and 21.2, and notate your answer with each of the three methods: bracket, slash, and colon.

   (e) Write P or N above each embellishing tone in the melody.

NAME ______________________

Workspace

Rhythm:

Melody:

Solfège syllables:

Scale-degree numbers:

Solfège syllables:

Scale-degree numbers:

Notation:

Rhythm:

Bass:

Solfège syllables:

Scale-degree numbers:

Solfège syllables:

Scale-degree numbers:

Exercise 4 refers to phrase 2 only.

4. Use the workspace provided to capture the excerpt.

   (a) Notate the rhythm of the melody and bass line of phrase 2 on the single-line staves. Write the meter signature, and include bar lines.

   (b) Below each rhythm staff, and under each note, write the solfège syllables or scale-degree numbers for the melody and bass line of phrase 2. Write your entire answer in the tonic key. Then, beneath this answer, use colon notation to more clearly reveal the tonicization of a different scale degree. Vertically align the syllables or numbers.

   (c) Combine your answers to complete the notation of the pitches and rhythm of the melody and bass line of phrase 2. Begin on F4 and D3 respectively. Write the appropriate clefs, key signature, and meter signature.

   (d) Write Roman numerals beneath the bass pitches. Follow the strategies you practiced in CL exercises 21.1 and 21.2, and notate your answer with each of the three methods: bracket, slash, and colon.

NAME ______________________________

Workspace

Rhythm:

Melody:

Solfège syllables:

Scale-degree numbers:

Solfège syllables:

Scale-degree numbers:

Notation:

Rhythm:

Bass:

Solfège syllables:
Scale-degree numbers:

Solfège syllables:
Scale-degree numbers:

The remaining exercises refer to the entire excerpt.

5. How long is each of the subphrases of the excerpt?

   (a) one measure (b) two measures (c) three measures (d) four measures

6. Conduct the hypermeter as you listen. Which describes the phrase rhythm of the excerpt?

   (a) regular (b) irregular

7. The excerpt concludes with which type of cadence?

   (a) Phrygian (b) imperfect authentic

   (c) perfect authentic (d) deceptive

8. Draw a diagram of the phrase structure of the excerpt in the following space.

Chromatic Harmony and Form

CHAPTER 22

Modulation to Closely Related Keys

In this chapter you'll learn to:

- Aurally identify modulations to closely related keys
- Locate and identify diatonic pivot chords that connect two different keys
- Notate melodies and bass lines of vocal and instrumental excerpts that begin in one key and modulate to another

---

Preparatory Listening

Complete the *Try It* dictations to familiarize yourself with the following concepts and skills:

- Determining the solfège syllables or scale-degree numbers for the soprano and bass of model SATB phrases
- Converting solfège syllables and scale-degree numbers to pitches and notating them on the staff
- Applying Roman numerals to show tonicizations
- Identifying diatonic pivot chords between two closely related keys

Try It

Listen to model modulating SATB progressions that are played once each. The key signature, meter signature, and first bass pitch are given.

- Focus on the bass line first, and notate its pitches.
- Beneath the bass pitches, write Roman numerals to identify each harmony; if more than one chord seems possible, write all the possibilities and choose the correct one after additional hearings.
- Use the last bass note and chord quality as a guide to help you determine the key to which the progression has modulated, and then work backward to determine solfège syllables and Roman numerals.
- The pivot chord will appear before the chord that functions primarily or exclusively in the new key, often immediately preceding the cadence.
- Indicate the pivot chord in the original key and the new key; this chord will have two different Roman numerals of the same quality and inversion.
- Focus last on the soprano, and utilize it to refine your chord choices.

NAME ______________________________

- Add bar lines including the double bar at the end.
- If you are working by yourself, sing each part aloud with solfège syllables, scale-degree numbers, and/or letter names.

1.

2.

3.

4.

5.

6.

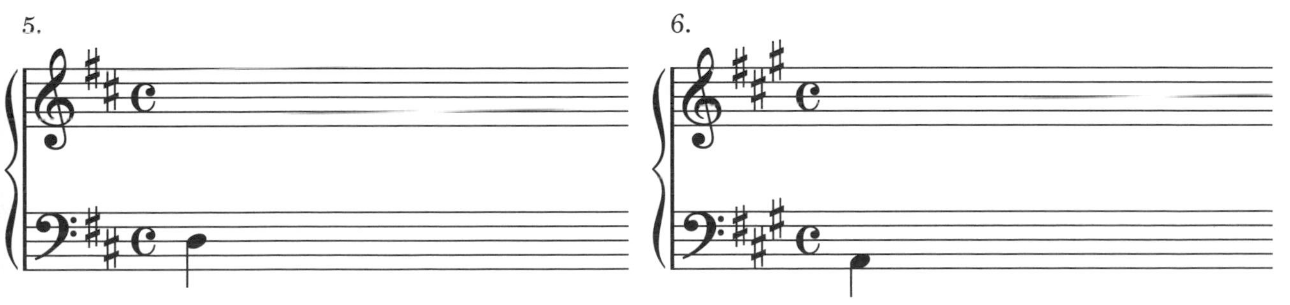

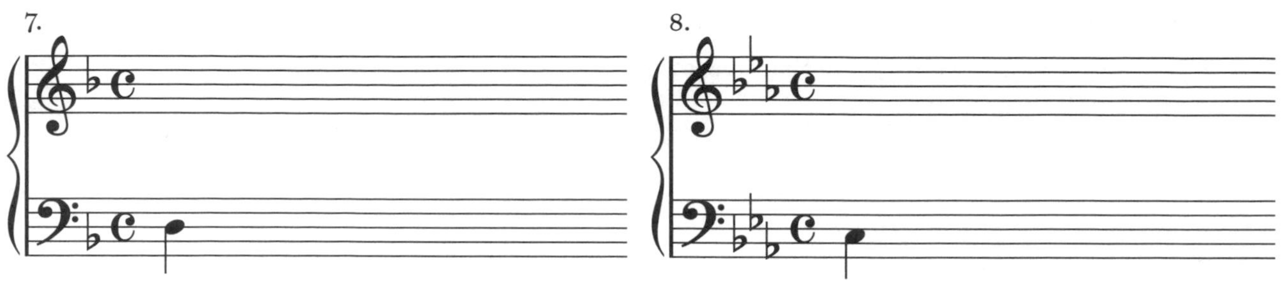

7.
8.

9.

NAME ______________________________

Contextual Listening 22.1

In this CL exercise you will:

- Determine the key change and indicate it using a Roman numeral in a work for piano
- Map the bass line to solfège syllables, scale-degree numbers, or letter names, then notate the bass line
- Locate the diatonic pivot and identify it in two keys
- Identify harmonies using Roman numerals
- Indicate phrase relationships in a two-phrase period

Listen to an excerpt from a piano sonata, which is two phrases long, and complete the following exercises.

1. Sing the bass pitches on a neutral syllable. By the end of the excerpt, which scale degree do they tonicize? ______

Strategy: Sustain this tonicized pitch, and listen to the beginning again. After you hear the original tonic pitch, sing up or down the scale until you reach the newly tonicized pitch.

2. Write the Roman numeral of the tonicized scale degree. ______ This Roman numeral is the key to which the excerpt modulates.
3. Listen again, and pay close attention to phrase 2. Since the excerpt is in major, listen for a chromatic pitch—typically *fi* ($\sharp\hat{4}$). The pivot chord precedes the chord that contains this chromatic pitch.
4. Now sing the entire bass line with solfège syllables or scale-degree numbers. Begin in the tonic key. At the pivot chord, switch your solfège syllables or scale-degree numbers to the new key.
5. Which best describes the period formed by these two phrases?
   (a) parallel (b) contrasting
   (c) modulatory parallel (d) modulatory contrasting
6. Use the workspace provided to capture the excerpt.
   (a) Notate the rhythm of the bass line on the single-line staves in $\frac{3}{4}$ meter. Write the meter signature, and include bar lines. Beam notes to show beat grouping.
   (b) Below the rhythm staves, and under each note, write the solfège syllables or scale-degree numbers for the bass line. Begin in the tonic key. At the pivot chord, write the Roman numeral of the new key (your answer to question 3) underneath. From that point on, write syllables *in the new key*.
   (c) Combine your answers to complete the notation of the pitches and rhythm of the bass line. Begin on D3. Write the appropriate clefs, key signature (and any accidentals), and meter signature.
   (d) Beneath each bass pitch, write the Roman numeral of the chord that harmonizes it. Begin in the tonic and switch to the new key at the pivot chord. Refer to your answers to previous questions for help.

Workspace

Rhythm:

Bass:

Solfège syllables:
Scale-degree numbers:

Solfège syllables:
Scale-degree numbers:

Notation:

NAME ______________________

Contextual Listening 22.2

In this CL exercise you will:

- Determine the key change and indicate it using a Roman numeral in a work for piano
- Map the bass line to solfège syllables, scale-degree numbers, or letter names, then notate the bass line
- Locate the diatonic pivot and identify it in two keys
- Identify harmonics using Roman numerals
- Indicate phrase relationships in a two-phrase period

Listen to a two-phrase excerpt from a piano sonata, and complete the following exercises.

1. Sing the bass pitches on a neutral syllable. By the end, which scale degree do they tonicize? ______

Strategy: Sustain this tonicized pitch and listen to the beginning again. After you hear the original tonic pitch, sing up or down the scale until you reach the newly tonicized pitch.

2. Write the Roman numeral of the tonicized scale degree. ______ This Roman numeral is the key to which the excerpt modulates.

3. Briefly describe the method of modulation in this excerpt.

4. Sing the bass line with solfège syllables or scale-degree numbers, beginning in the tonic key. At the new key, switch your solfège syllables or scale-degree numbers.

5. Which best describes the period formed by these two phrases?

   (a) parallel (b) contrasting

   (c) modulatory parallel (d) modulatory contrasting

6. (a) Listen again and conduct the hypermeter. Is the phrase rhythm (1) regular or (2) irregular?

   (b) If your answer is *irregular* (2), briefly describe the nature of the phrase expansion(s).

7. Use the workspace provided to capture the excerpt.

   (a) Notate the rhythm of the bass line on the single-line staves in simple triple meter. Begin with an anacrusis of two eighth notes. Write the meter signature, and include bar lines. Beam notes to show beat grouping.

   (b) Below the rhythm staves, and under each note, write the solfège syllables or scale-degree numbers for the bass line. Begin in the tonic key. At the location of the key change, write the Roman numeral of the new key (your answer to question 2) underneath. From that point on, write syllables *in the new key*.

(c) Combine your answers to complete the notation of the pitches and rhythm of the bass line. Begin on A3 with an anacrusis of two eighth notes. Write the appropriate clefs, key signature (and any accidentals), and meter signature.

(d) Beneath each bass pitch, write the Roman numeral of the chord that harmonizes it. Begin in the tonic and switch to the new key at the pivot chord. Refer to your answers to previous questions for help.

Workspace

Rhythm:

Bass:

Solfège syllables:

Scale-degree numbers:

Solfège syllables:

Scale-degree numbers:

Notation:

NAME ______________________________

Contextual Listening 22.3

In this CL exercise you will:

- Determine the key change and indicate it using a Roman numeral in an art song
- Identify cadences
- Locate and identify the diatonic pivot chord in two keys

Listen to two phrases from an art song, and complete the following exercises. Sometimes composers write progressions or cadences in a secondary key, but never reach the secondary tonic. You can, however, still infer the secondary tonic.

1. Sing the bass pitches on a neutral syllable. By the end of phrase 1, which scale degree do they tonicize? ______

Strategies: Sustain this tonicized pitch and listen to the beginning again. After you hear the original tonic pitch, sing up or down the scale until you reach the newly tonicized pitch. To find the cadence of phrase 1, listen for the end of a phrase of text.

2. Write the Roman numeral of the tonicized scale degree. ______ This is the key to which phrase 1 moves.
3. Write phrase 1's cadence type and the key in which it occurs (your answer to question 2).
4. Using a neutral syllable, sing the bass pitches again. By the end of phrase 2, which scale degree do the bass pitches tonicize? (Phrase 2 features a dominant pedal. Sing this pitch, then sing up a P4 to find the implied tonic pitch.) ______
5. Write the Roman numeral of the tonicized scale degree. ______ This is the key to which phrase 2 moves.
6. Write phrase 2's cadence type and the key in which it occurs (your answer to question 5).

NAME ______________________________

Contextual Listening 22.4

In this CL exercise you will:

- Identify the meter of chamber work
- Indicate the key change with a Roman numeral
- Map the bass and melody to solfège syllables, scale-degree numbers, or letter names, then notate the melody and bass line
- Locate the diatonic pivot and identify it in two keys
- Identify harmonies using Roman numerals
- Indicate phrase relationships in a two-phrase period

Listen to an excerpt from a trio sonata, and complete the following exercises.

1. Which of these represents the meter of this excerpt?
   (a) simple duple (b) simple triple
   (c) simple quadruple (d) compound triple
2. Using a neutral syllable, sing the bass pitches. By the end of the excerpt, which scale degree do the pitches tonicize? ______
3. Write the Roman numeral of the tonicized scale degree. ______ This is the key to which the excerpt modulates.
4. Since the excerpt begins in minor, listen for the subtonic pitch. The pivot chord usually precedes the chord that contains the subtonic pitch.
5. Now sing the entire bass line with solfège syllables and scale-degree numbers. Begin in the tonic key. At the pivot chord, switch your solfège syllables and scale-degree numbers to the new key.
6. Bass pitch 4 features which type of cadence?
   (a) Phrygian cadence in the original key (b) PAC in the original key
   (c) Phrygian cadence in the new key (d) PAC in the new key
7. The excerpt concludes with which type of cadence?
   (a) Phrygian cadence in the original key (b) PAC in the original key
   (c) Phrygian cadence in the new key (d) PAC in the new key
8. Which is the phrase structure of this excerpt?
   (a) modulatory parallel period (b) parallel double period
   (c) modulatory contrasting period (d) contrasting double period

9. Use the workspace provided to capture the excerpt.

(a) Notate the rhythm of the melody and bass parts on the single-line staves in simple triple meter. Choose a meter signature, and include bar lines. Beam notes to show beat grouping.

(b) Below the bass rhythm staff, and under each note, write the solfège syllables or scale-degree numbers for the bass part. Begin in the tonic key. At the pivot chord, write the Roman numeral of the new key, and then switch your solfège syllables or scale-degree numbers to the new key.

(c) Below the melody rhythm staff, and under each note, write the solfège syllables or scale-degree numbers for the melody. Begin in the tonic key. At the pivot chord, write the Roman numeral of the new key, and then switch your solfège syllables or scale-degree numbers to the new key.

(d) Combine your answers to complete the notation of the pitches and rhythm of the melody and bass parts. Begin on E5 and A3 respectively. Write the appropriate clefs, key signature (and any accidentals), and meter signature.

(e) Beneath each bass pitch, write the Roman numeral of the chord that harmonizes it. Begin in the tonic and switch to the new key at the pivot chord. Refer to your answers to previous questions for help.

Workspace

Rhythm:

Melody:

Solfège syllables:
Scale-degree numbers:

Solfège syllables:
Scale-degree numbers:

Notation:

Rhythm:

Bass:

Solfège syllables:
Scale-degree numbers:

Solfège syllables:
Scale-degree numbers:

Binary and Ternary Forms

NAME

In this chapter you'll learn to:

- Show relationships between sections within a composition using letter names
- Determine whether a section of a composition is continuous or sectional
- Make distinctions between ternary forms and rounded binary forms
- Use Roman numerals to demonstrate the key of a composition's internal sections

Preparatory Listening

Complete the *Try It* dictations to review the following concepts and skills:

- Determining the solfège syllables or scale-degree numbers for the soprano and bass in model SATB phrases
- Applying Roman numerals to bass lines
- Determining cadence types: authentic, deceptive, half, plagal

Try It

Listen to model SATB phrases that are played once each. The key signature, meter signature, and first bass pitch are given.

- Focus on the bass line first, and notate its pitches.
- Beneath the bass pitches, write Roman numerals to identify each harmony; if more than one chord seems possible, write all the possibilities and choose the correct one after additional hearings.
- Focus last on the soprano, and utilize it to refine your chord choices.
- Identify the cadence of each progression using the abbreviations PAC, IAC, HC, DC, and PC
- Add bar lines including the double bar at the end.
- If you are working by yourself, sing each part aloud with solfège syllables, scale-degree numbers, and/or letter names.

1.
2.
3.
4.
5.
6.

NAME ______________________________

Contextual Listening 23.1

In this CL exercise you will:

- Describe with letter names the design of a traditional melody
- Identify with Roman numerals the key of its second section
- Identify the form of the excerpt
- Determine balance between sections
- Determine if sections are continuous (open) or sectional (closed)

Listen to an excerpt from a ballet, and complete the following exercises.

1. Which is the section design of the excerpt?

   (a) **A A** (b) **A A′** (c) **‖: A :‖: B :‖** (d) **A A′ B A′**

2. Section 2 concludes in which key?

   (a) I (b) IV (c) V (d) vi

3. Which is the form of the excerpt?

   (a) simple binary (b) rounded binary
   (c) simple ternary (d) composite ternary

Before proceeding . . .

- If your answer to question 3 was (a) or (b), complete question 4 and question 5. (Don't complete question 6.)
- If your answer to question 3 was (c), you have finished this example. (Don't complete question 4 through question 6.)
- If your answer to question 3 was (d), skip to question 6. (Don't complete question 4 and question 5.)

4. Is the binary (a) sectional or (b) continuous?

5. (a) Which is the form of section 1?

   (1) parallel period (2) contrasting period
   (3) simple binary (4) rounded binary

   If your answer was (3) or (4), complete parts (b) and (c).

   (b) Is the binary (1) sectional or (2) continuous?

   (c) Are the sections balanced?

6. (a) Which is the form of section 2?

   (1) parallel period (2) contrasting period
   (3) simple binary (4) rounded binary

   If your answer was (3) or (4), complete parts (b) and (c).

   (b) Is the binary (1) sectional or (2) continuous?

   (c) Are the sections balanced?

NAME ______________________________

Contextual Listening 23.2

In this CL exercise you will:

- Draw a formal diagram of a work for keyboard
- Describe the design of the work with letter names
- Identify with Roman numeral the key of its second section
- Identify the form of the excerpt
- Determine balance between sections
- Determine if sections are continuous (open) or sectional (closed)

As you listen to this keyboard piece, draw a formal diagram.

What is the design of each section?

1. Does section 2 begin with melodic material that is (a) the same (**A**), (b) similar (**A′**), or (c) different (**B**)?
2. Write the design letters for the beginning of each section. ______ and ______

Is the binary form simple or rounded?

3. (a) Are the sections roughly equal, or (b) is the second section significantly longer than the first?
4. Does section 2 feature a return of music from the beginning? If so, what is the third design letter? ______
5. Is the form (a) simple or (b) rounded binary?

Is the form sectional or continuous?

6. At the end of section 1, is there an authentic cadence in the tonic?
7. Is the form (a) sectional or (b) continuous?

Are the sections balanced?

8. Does the end of section 2 sound similar to the end of section 1?
9. Are the sections balanced?

Invention, Fugue, and Other Contrapuntal Genres

NAME ____________________

In this chapter you'll learn to:

- Identify contrapuntal relationships and techniques found in inventions, fugues, and other contrapuntal keyboard generes
- Notate eighteenth-century two-part contrapuntal excerpts
- Define the components of a fugual exposition

Preparatory Listening

Complete the *Try It* dictations to review the following concepts and skills:

- Recognizing different types of melodic and rhythmic embellishments in two-part, note-to-note counterpoint
- Notating both parts in embellished note-to-note counterpoint

Try It

Listen to contrapuntal excerpts that are played twice with a pause in between. Each example is preceded by two "count-off" measures to set the tempo; a two-part excerpt beginning on the given pitches follows.

- Notate the pitches using whole notes, half notes, quarter notes, and eighth notes.
- Divide each dictation into two halves separated by a bar line; always end with a double bar.
- Below the staff write the interval between the upper and lower parts.
- If you are working by yourself, sing each part aloud with solfège syllables, scale-degree numbers, and/or letter names.

1.

2.

3.
4.
5.
6.
7.
8.
9.
10.

NAME ______________________________

Contextual Listening 24.1

In this CL exercise you will:

- Determine the meter of a contrapuntal work for keyboard
- Identify cadences
- Notate melody and bass parts
- Assign Roman numerals to identify harmonic functions
- Assess the regularity of phrase rhythm

Listen to an excerpt from a keyboard work, and complete the following exercises. To help you remember what you hear, draw a phrase diagram.

1. Which is the meter signature of this excerpt?

   (a) $\frac{2}{4}$ (b) $\frac{3}{4}$ (c) $\frac{4}{4}$ (d) $\frac{9}{8}$

2. Phrase 1 concludes with which type of cadence?

   (a) authentic (b) plagal (c) deceptive (d) Phrygian

3. Use the workspace provided to capture the excerpt.

   (a) Notate the rhythm of the melody and bass on the single-line staves in $\frac{3}{4}$ meter. Save time by writing ⁓ for mordents (the first embellishment you hear in the melody) and *tr* for the trills. Write the meter signature, and include bar lines. Beam notes to show beat grouping.

   (b) Below each rhythm staff, and under each note, write the solfège syllables or scale-degree numbers for the melody and bass beginning on *sol* ($\hat{5}$) and *do* ($\hat{1}$) respectively.

   (c) Combine your answers to complete the notation of the pitches and rhythm of the melody and bass parts. Begin on A4 and D3 respectively. Write the appropriate clefs, key signature (and any accidentals), and meter signature.

   (d) Beneath each bass pitch, write the Roman numeral of the chord that harmonizes it.

   (e) Above each dissonant embellishing tone in the melody, write P, IN, or ANT (for anticipation).

4. Conduct as you listen, focusing on the phrase rhythm. Is the phrase rhythm (a) regular or (b) irregular?

5. Briefly explain your answer to question 4.

Workspace

Rhythm:

Melody:

Solfège syllables:
Scale-degree numbers:

Solfège syllables:
Scale-degree numbers:

Notation:

Rhythm:

Bass:

Solfège syllables:
Scale-degree numbers:

Solfège syllables:
Scale-degree numbers:

NAME ______________________________

Contextual Listening 24.2

In this CL exercise you will:

- Identify and notate the subject, answer, and link (codetta) of a three-part fugal exposition
- Identify the techniques used to treat statements of the subject
- Notate the counterpoint that accompanies the subject

Listen to a three-voice fugue for keyboard, and complete the following exercises. For our purposes, the three voices are called voice 1 (highest part), voice 2 (middle part), and voice 3 (lowest part). In all exercises, write the *original* key signature (and any accidentals) and meter signature. Beam notes to show beat grouping.

Exercises 1–6 refer to the exposition.

1. Write the twelve notes of the *subject* presented by voice 1 with solfège syllables or scale-degree numbers. Ignore the trill on pitch 11.

2. Notate the subject in simple triple meter. Begin with an eighth rest, then D4.

3. Voice 2 enters with the *answer*. In the key of the minor dominant, write the answer with solfège syllables or scale degrees.

4. (a) Notate the answer in the bass clef and circle the last note. Begin with an eighth rest.

(b) Is this a real or tonal answer? Explain your deduction.

(c) After the answer, there is a short *link* that concludes when voice 3 enters. Notate this link on the staff in question 4(a).

5. After the link, voice 3 enters and restates the subject an octave lower than originally stated by voice 1. Notate the subject from question 2. Begin on D3 (preceded by an eighth rest).

6. Combine your answers from questions 2, 4, and 5, and notate the subject-answer-link-subject of the exposition in the correct order. Align the three voices vertically and notate all necessary rests prior to the entrance of each voice.

Exercises 7-11 refer to subsequent statements of the theme.

7. Listen again to CL 24.2a through 24.2c. The theme (subject or answer) is developed in a variety of ways.

   Passage A (CL 24.2a): Which contrapuntal device occurs in this passage?

   (1) augmentation (2) stretto (3) retrograde (4) inversion

   Passage B (CL 24.2b): Which contrapuntal device occurs in this passage?

   (1) augmentation (2) stretto (3) retrograde (4) inversion

   Passage C (CL 24.2c): Which *two* contrapuntal devices are presented in this passage?

   (1) augmentation (2) stretto (3) retrograde (4) inversion

8. Listen again to CL 24.2a. Notate voices 3 and then 2, beginning on A2 (preceded by an eighth rest). Align the two voices vertically, and include the rest prior to the entrance of voice 2.

9. Listen again to CL 24.2b, and notate the melody of voice 3. Begin on on A2 (preceded by an eighth rest).

NAME ______________________________

10. Listen again to CL 24.2c. Notate the melodies for voice 1 and voice 3, beginning on E5 and A2, respectively.

11. Listen to passage D (CL 24.2d). Notate the melodies for voices 1 and 2. Begin voice 1 on A5 (preceded by an eighth rest).

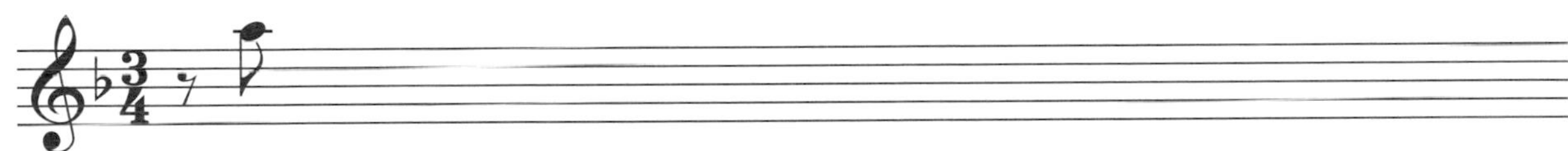

Exercises 12 and 13 refer to the motivic development and episodes.

12. Listen to passage E (CL 24.2e), the beginning of the fugue. Starting with the last pitch of the subject, A4, notate only the remainder of voice 1; this music is the counterpoint to the answer you wrote for question 4(a).

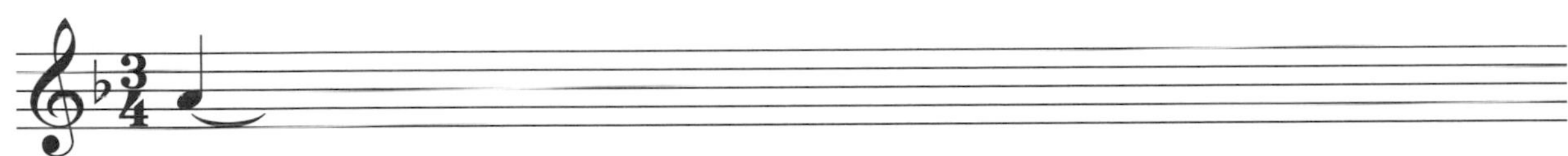

13. Following the initial exposition of a fugue, a passage called an episode leads to the second key area where the subject is again presented. The motive you notated in question 12 is developed in passage F (CL 24.2f). Begin on A3 in the bass clef and C♯4 and E4 in the treble clef, and notate all three voices. Align the voices, and notate a rest prior to the entrance of voice 1.

Exercises 14 and 15 refer to the codetta and subdominant extension.

14. Passage G (CL 24.2g) is a short *codetta* that includes a subdominant extension and changes the texture to include six voices. Notate this codetta, beginning on D5 and D3 (voice 1 and voice 3) respectively.

15. Listen to the fugue in its entirety (CL 24.2), and comment on the features that you find most interesting.

NAME ______________________________

Contextual Listening 24.3

In this CL exercise you will:

- Notate the motive of a two-part contrapuntal work for keyboard
- Identify the techniques used to treat statements of the motive
- Apply Roman numerals to indicate harmonic function
- Identify sequences by type
- Identify cadences and sections
- Notate segments of both the melody and the bass part

Listen to a work for keyboard and complete the following exercises. To help guide your listening, the piece is divided into parts 1-5, each of which may be subdivided into segments as described next. Listen first to the entire work (CL 24.3). Then listen to each part separately as necessary.

Part 1 consists of six segments, each one ten pitches long, that occur in the upper voice. Segment 1 is called the motive (or subject or theme).

segment number:	1 (motive)	2	3	4	5	6
pitches:	1-10	11-20	21-30	31-40	41-50	51-60

Exercises 1-15 focus on part 1 (CL 24.3a).

1. Write the pitches of the motive with solfège syllables or scale-degree numbers.

2. Notate the pitches and rhythm of the motive in simple quadruple meter on the staff provided. Begin on B♭4. Write the appropriate clef, key signature (and any accidentals), and meter signature. Beam notes to show beat grouping. The shortest rhythmic value is the thirty-second note.

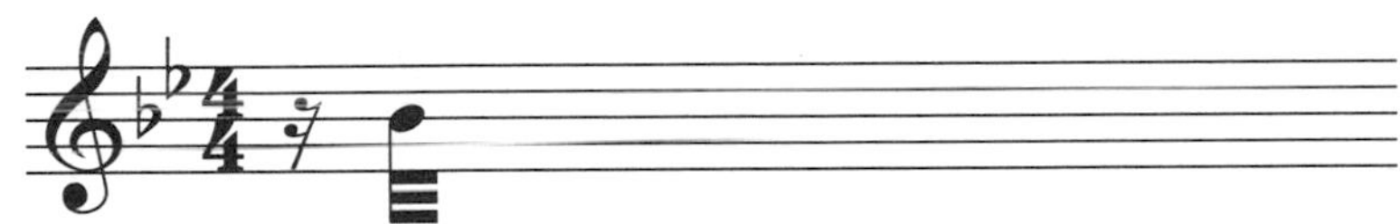

3. Write the pitches of segment 2 with solfège syllables or scale-degree numbers.

4. Notate the pitches and rhythm of segment 2.

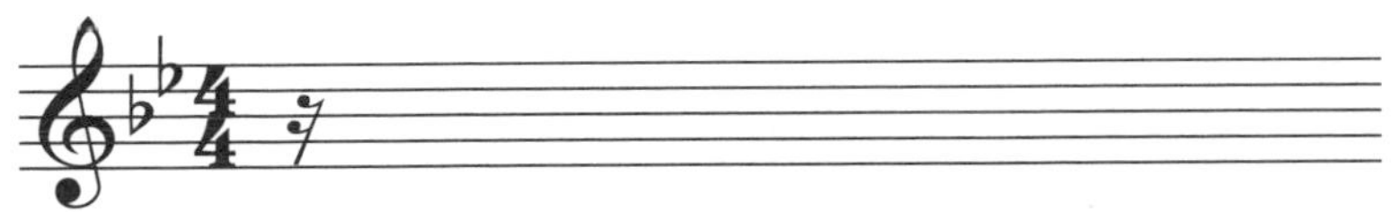

5. Segment 2 relates to the motive in which of the following ways?
   (a) melodic inversion (b) transposition
   (c) rhythmic diminution (d) retrograde

6. Segment 2 implies which secondary dominant chord?
   (a) V/ii (b) V/IV (c) V/V (d) V/vi

7. Write the pitches of segment 3 with solfège syllables or scale-degree numbers.

8. Notate the pitches and rhythm of segment 3.

9. Segment 3 relates to the motive in which of the following ways?
   (a) melodic inversion (b) transposition
   (c) rhythmic diminution (d) retrograde

10. Notate the pitches and rhythm of segment 4.

11. Segment 4 relates to the motive in which of the following ways?
    (a) melodic inversion (b) transposition
    (c) rhythmic diminution (d) retrograde

12. Notate the pitches and rhythm of segments 5 and 6.

13. Segments 5-6 relate to the motive in which of the following ways?
    (a) melodic inversion (b) transposition
    (c) rhythmic diminution (d) retrograde

14. Segments 1, 3, and 5 outline which harmonic progression?
    (a) tonic-dominant-tonic (b) tonic-predominant-dominant
    (c) tonic-predominant-tonic (d) dominant-tonic-predominant

15. Which procedural term best describes all of part 1?
    (a) exposition (b) episode (bridge)
    (c) secondary (counter-) exposition (d) coda

NAME ______________________________

Exercises 16-22 focus on part 2 (CL 24.3b), which begins immediately after segment 6 ends. Here, the lower and upper voices alternate initially. Part 2 features a total of seven segments (7-13), each one six pitches long.

16. Notate the pitches and rhythm of both voices on the following staves. Begin on B♭3 in the bass. Write the appropriate clefs, key signature (and any accidentals), and meter signature. Beam notes to show beat grouping.

17. Segment 7 relates to the motive in which of the following ways?
    - (a) fragmentation of the motive's beginning
    - (b) transposition down one octave
    - (c) interval change on pitch 6
    - (d) all of these

18. Compared with segment 7, segment 8 is changed in which way?
    - (a) transposition
    - (b) melodic inversion
    - (c) rhythmic augmentation
    - (d) retrograde

19. Segments 7-13 outline which sequence?
    - (a) descending fifths
    - (b) descending thirds
    - (c) descending parallel $\frac{6}{3}$ chords
    - (d) ascending 5-6

20. Part 2 concludes with which type of cadence?
    - (a) perfect authentic
    - (b) imperfect authentic
    - (c) half
    - (d) deceptive

21. Segment 13 features which type of phrase expansion?
    - (a) introduction
    - (b) internal expansion
    - (c) cadential extension
    - (d) none

22. Which procedural term best describes all of part 2?
    - (a) exposition
    - (b) episode (bridge)
    - (c) secondary (counter-) exposition
    - (d) coda

Immediately after segment 13, the lower voice descends with a three-pitch arpeggio. Part 3 begins on the following downbeat and includes twelve segments (14–25), each one ten pitches long. Exercises 23–30 focus on part 3 (CL 24.3c).

23. Part 3 begins in which related key?

    (a) ii (b) IV (c) V (d) vi

24. Compare the texture at the beginning of the piece with that of the beginning of part 3 (segments 14–19). The texture of part 3 is best described by which of the following?

    (a) Texture is unchanged.

    (b) Texture changes to chordal homophony.

    (c) Texture changes to imitative polyphony.

    (d) Texture is inverted (invertible counterpoint).

25. Which procedural term best describes the beginning of part 3 (segments 14–19)?

    (a) exposition (b) episode (bridge)

    (c) secondary (counter-) exposition (d) coda

26. Segment 21 includes which secondary-dominant-function chord?

    (a) V^7/ii (b) V^7/IV (c) V^7/V (d) V^7/vi

27. Segment 23 includes which secondary-dominant-function chord?

    (a) V^7/ii (b) V^7/IV (c) V^7/V (d) V^7/vi

28. Segment 25 includes which secondary-dominant-function chord?

    (a) V^7/ii (b) V^7/IV (c) V^7/V (d) V^7/vi

29. Compare the answers to questions 26–28. Taken together, they outline which sequence?

    (a) descending fifths (b) descending thirds

    (c) descending parallel $^6_3$ chords (d) ascending 5–6

30. Part 3 concludes with which type of cadence and in which key?

    (a) PAC (ii) (b) IAC (ii) (c) HC (ii) (d) Phrygian (ii)

Part 4 begins on a very low pitch with the first of seven variations of the motive (segments 26–32), each one eight pitches long (CL 24.3d).

31. The relationship between the voices may be described by which term?

    (a) stretto (overlap) (b) canon at two octaves

    (c) imitative polyphony (d) all of these

NAME ______________________________

32. Beginning with C2, notate *only* the first pitch of segments 26-32. Four of these pitches will appear in the bass staff and three in the treble.

33. Examine *only* the bass pitches in question 32. Despite their direction, which sequence is implied by these pitches?

(a) descending fifths (b) descending thirds

(c) descending parallel $^6_3$ chords (d) ascending 5-6

At end of part 4, both voices perform rhythmically identical six-pitch segments that lead to an IAC in the tonic key (segments 33-43).

34. Which of the following describes the relationship of these six-pitch segments to the motive?

(a) fragmentation of the motive's beginning

(b) interval change on pitch 6

(c) alternation between original and inverted forms of the motive

(d) all of the above

Part 5 begins immediately after the IAC in the tonic key and continues until the end (segments 44-end, CL 24.3e).

35. At the beginning of part 5, which describes the relationship between the voices?

(a) stretto (overlap) (b) canon at the octave

(c) imitative polyphony (d) all of these

36. The last three bass pitches imply which harmonic progression?

(a) ii^6-V-I (b) IV-V^7-I (c) V^{6-5}_{4-3}-I (d) V^{8-7}-I

Variation

In this chapter you'll learn to:

- Aurally understand the organization of continuous and sectional variations
- Anticipate typical practices in variation forms
- Specify what has been varied in a musical idea
- Define phrase structures and design within sectional variations

Preparatory Listening

Complete the *Try It* dictations to review the following concepts and skills:

- Determining the solfège syllables or scale-degree numbers for the soprano and bass of model SATB phrases
- Converting solfège syllables and scale-degree numbers to pitches and notating them on the staff
- Applying Roman numerals to show tonicizations
- Identifying diatonic pivot chords between two closely related keys

Try It

Listen to model modulating SATB phrases that are played once each. The key signature, meter signature, and first bass pitch are given.

- Focus on the bass line first, and notate its pitches.
- Beneath the bass pitches, write Roman numerals to identify each harmony; if more than one chord seems possible, write all the possibilities and choose the correct one after additional hearings.
- Use the last bass note as a guide to help you determine the key to which the progression modulates, and then work backward to determine solfège syllables and Roman numerals.
- The pivot chord will appear before the chord that functions primarily (or exclusively) in the new key, often immediately preceding the cadence.
- Indicate the pivot chord in the original key and the new key; this chord will have two different Roman numerals of the same quality and inversion.
- Focus last on the soprano, and utilize it to refine your chord choices.

NAME ______________________

- Add bar lines including the double bar at the end.
- If you are working by yourself, sing each part aloud with solfège syllables, scale-degree numbers, and/or letter names.

Continuous variations

Continuous variations are usually based on a short, phrase-length theme, in contrast to the binary or ternary small forms of sectional variations. This "theme" is either a recurring bass line (a **ground bass** or **passacaglia**) or a recurring harmonic progression (**chaconne**). The variations often feature phrase overlaps and other musical features that give them their continuous effect, in contrast to the "full stop" PACs typical of sectional variations.

NAME ____________________

Contextual Listening 25.1

In this CL exercise you will:

- Map the bass line of a vocal duet with basso continuo to solfège syllables, scale-degree numbers, or letter names, then notate the bass line
- Describe how the vocal parts relate to each other
- Explain the continuous nature of the variations

The following exercises are based on an excerpt from a vocal duet with basso continuo. Focus your listening on the repeating bass line. Then listen to how the vocal parts create lovely contrapuntal lines against the bass.

1. Use the workspace provided to capture the excerpt.
   (a) Notate the rhythm of the repeating portion of the bass line on the single-line staff in simple triple meter. Choose a meter signature, and include bar lines.
   (b) Below the single-line staff, and under each note, write the solfège syllables or scale-degree numbers of the repeating portion of the bass line.
   (c) Combine your answers to complete the notation of the pitches and rhythm of the repeating portion of the bass line beginning on G2. Write the appropriate clef, key signature, and meter signature.

Workspace

Notation:

Rhythm:

Bass:

Solfège syllables:

Scale-degree numbers:

2. Briefly describe how the two vocal parts relate to each other.

3. What characterizes these variations as continuous?

NAME ______________________

Sectional variations

Many movements or pieces are based on modified repetitions of an entire songlike small form (such as an **a a b a** phrase structure, a parallel period, or a rounded binary form). These are called **sectional variations**. The phrase structure and harmonic outline of the original small form—the theme—usually remain consistent in the variations, but composers might change just about anything else, including:

- mode (major to minor, for example)
- melodic figuration (in a **figural variation**, the same melodic figure appears throughout)
- timbre (or orchestration)
- texture, including textural inversions (e.g., the melody moves from the highest to the lowest voice)
- articulation
- dynamics
- rhythmic beat division
- tempo
- character
- register

Sectional variations usually appear back-to-back, but sometimes there are interludes, transitions, or retransitions between them. (Transitions move the music to a new tonal area, whereas retransitions modulate back to the original key and theme.) Classical and Romantic composers almost always use the entire structure in each variation. In more-recent works, composers might truncate the structure of some variations, including only the first or second half of the theme, for example.

NAME ____________________

Contextual Listening 25.2

In this CL exercise you will:

- Identify the phrase structure in a set of continuous variations
- Determine the sectional divisions and associate letter names with them
- Specify what has been varied in each variation

The following exercises are based on a theme and five variations for piano. First listen to the theme (CL 25.2), then each variation in turn (CL exercises 25.2a-25.2e).

Exercises 1–4 refer only *to the theme, which may be divided into two large sections. Draw a phrase diagram to help you as you listen. Section 1 consists of four phrases.*

1. Which is the phrase design of section 1?

   (a) **a a b a** (b) **a b a b** (c) **a b a c** (d) **a b c d**

2. Which is the overall phrase structure of section 1?

   (a) two parallel periods (b) two contrasting periods
   (c) one parallel double period (d) one contrasting double period

3. Now listen to the design of the entire theme. Which is the design of the theme's sections?

   (a) **A A′** (b) **A B** (c) **A A′ B A′** (d) **A B A C A**

4. Once again, consider the entire theme. Is its form (a) sectional or (b) continuous?

5. Now compare each variation with the theme, and list answers to the two questions posed. For ideas of what to listen for, refer to the bulleted list on page 269. Once you've finished, listen again to the theme and each variation.

	What remains the same?	*What is changed?*
Variation 1 (CL 25.2a)		
Variation 2 (CL 25.2b)		
Variation 3 (CL 25.2c)		
Variation 4 (CL 25.2d)		
Variation 5 (CL 25.2e)		

NAME ______________________________

Contextual Listening 25.3

In this CL exercise you will:

- Identify the phrase structure in a set of continuous variations
- Determine the sectional divisions and associate letter names with them
- Identify the form of the theme
- Map the melody and bass line to solfège syllables, scale-degree numbers, or letter names, then notate the melody and bass line
- Specify what has been varied in each variation

The following exercises are based on an excerpt from a ballet you studied previously. Listen to the entire theme followed by five variations.

Exercises 1-7 refer only to the theme.

1. In the first half of the theme, which describes the accompaniment to the clarinet melody?
   (a) Violins sustain pitches *sol* ($\hat{5}$) and *do* ($\hat{1}$).
   (b) Violins sustain the pitches of the V chord.
   (c) Violins play the melody in augmentation.
   (d) Violins play the melody in canon.

2. Use the workspace provided to capture the excerpt.
   (a) Notate the rhythm of the melody in phrases 3 and 4 on the single-line staff in common time. Write the meter signature, and include bar lines. Beam notes to show beat grouping.
   (b) Below the single-line staff, and under each note, write the solfège syllables or scale-degree numbers for the melody of phrases 3 and 4.
   (c) Combine your answers to complete the notation of the pitches and rhythm of the melody of phrases 3 and 4 beginning on D♭5. Write the appropriate clef, key signature, and meter signature.

Workspace

Rhythm:

Melody:

Solfège syllables:
Scale-degree numbers:

Solfège syllables:
Scale-degree numbers:

Notation:

3. At the beginning of phrase 3, which instruments double the clarinet melody?
   (a) violin and flute (b) oboe and violin
   (c) flute and piano (d) cello and oboe
4. Which is the phrase design of the theme?
   (a) **a a′ b a″** (b) **a a′ b c** (c) **a b a′ c** (d) **a b c d**
5. Which is the phrase structure of the theme?
   (a) two parallel periods (b) parallel double period
   (c) parallel period followed by a contrasting period (d) contrasting double period
6. Which is the form of the theme?
   (a) simple binary (b) rounded binary (c) ternary (d) rondo

After the initial statement of the theme, there is a brief modulatory interlude. Variation 1 begins after this interlude, with the clarinet in its high register. Exercises 7-9 refer to Variation 1.

7. Compared with the key of the theme, how is the key transposed in Variation 1.
   (a) up a step (b) up a third (c) down a step (d) down a third
8. At the beginning of Variation 1, the clarinet melody is doubled by which instrument?
   (a) violin (b) bassoon (c) flute (d) piano
9. How much of the theme is featured in this variation?
   (a) phrases 1 and 2 only (b) phrases 2, 3, and 4
   (c) phrases 3 and 4 only (d) all phrases

NAME ______________________

Exercises 10-12 refer to Variation 2, which consists of only three phrases.

10. At the beginning of Variation 2, which of the following occurs?
    (a) chromatic variations of the theme
    (b) figural variations of the theme
    (c) theme in inversion
    (d) piano ostinato in the accompaniment

11. At the beginning of phrase 2, how is the theme developed?
    (a) melodic inversion (b) canon at the octave
    (c) rhythmic diminution (d) fragments used in a sequence

12. The composer does not use all the theme's phrases in Variation 2. Which describes the portions of the theme he does include?
    (a) phrase 1 with one note change; varied repetition of phrase 1; phrase 2
    (b) phrase 1 with one note change; phrase 3; phrase 4
    (c) phrase 2; phrase 3; varied repetition of phrase 3
    (d) phrase 2; phrase 3; phrase 4

After Variation 2, there is a short modulatory transition. Exercises 13-15 refer to Variation 3, which begins after the transition in a faster tempo.

13. Compared with Variation 2, how is Variation 3 transposed?
    (a) up a third (b) up a fourth (c) a tritone (d) down a fourth

14. Which describes the texture of Variation 3?
    (a) nonimitative polyphony (b) chordal homophony
    (c) heterophony (d) monophony

15. In Variation 3, how much of the theme is featured?
    (a) phrases 1 and 2 only (b) phrases 2, 3, and 4
    (c) phrases 3 and 4 only (d) all phrases

Exercises 16-19 refer to Variation 4, which begins slower suddenly.

16. At the very beginning of this variation, listen carefully to the flute and bassoon. Which describes how the composer develops the theme?
    (a) The flute plays the **a** phrase while the bassoon plays the **b** phrase.
    (b) The flute plays the **b** phrase while the bassoon plays the **a** phrase.
    (c) The flute and bassoon play the **a** phrase, doubled in octaves.
    (d) The flute and bassoon play the **b** phrase, doubled in octaves.

17. Which of the following is the role of the strings?
    (a) They accompany the winds with sustained chords.
    (b) They accompany the winds with pizzicato chords.
    (c) They play the bass line.
    (d) They rest.

18. How many phrases comprise Variation 4?

(a) one phrase (b) two phrases (c) three phrases (d) all of the theme

19. Which is the last harmonic interval?

(a) unison/octave (b) third (c) fourth (d) fifth

The remaining exercises refer to Variation 5, which is louder and in a slow, majestic tempo.

20. Use the workspace provided to capture the excerpt.

(a) Notate the rhythm of the bass line of Variation 5 on the single-line staff. Choose meter signature(s), and include bar lines. Beam notes to show beat grouping. There are meter changes at the end so that the last note falls on a downbeat.

(b) Below the single-line staff, and under each note, write the solfège syllables or scale-degree numbers for the bass line of Variation 5.

(c) Combine your answers to complete the notation of the pitches and rhythm of the bass line of phrases 3 and 4 beginning on C in any octave you wish. Write the appropriate clef, key signature, and meter signature(s).

Workspace

Notation:

Rhythm:

Bass:

Solfège syllables:

Scale-degree numbers:

21. Variation 5 consists of which part of the theme?

(a) the first half (b) the middle (phrases 2 and 3)

(c) the second half (d) all of it

Modal Mixture

NAME ______________________

In this chapter you'll learn to:

- Aurally identify modally altered harmonies
- Apply borrowed Roman numerals to indicate modal mixture
- Identify cadences by type
- Identify types of six-four chords

Preparatory Listening

Complete the *Try It* dictations to familiarize yourself with the following concepts and skills:

- Determining the solfège syllables or scale-degree numbers for the soprano and bass of model SATB phrases: T-D-T, T-PD-D-T, plagal extensions, and descending bass lines
- Converting solfège syllables and scale-degree numbers to pitches and notating them on the staff
- Identifying harmonies with Roman numerals

Try It

Listen to model SATB phrases that are played once each. The key signature, meter signature, and first bass pitch are given.

- Focus on the bass line first, and notate its pitches.
- Listen for and indicate any chords that seem peculiar given your expectations of chord quality.
- Beneath the bass pitches, write Roman numerals to identify each harmony; if more than one chord seems possible, write all the possibilities and choose the correct one after additional hearings.
- Focus last on the soprano, and utilize it to refine your chord choices.
- Add bar lines including the double bar at the end.
- If you are working by yourself, sing each part aloud with solfège syllables, scale-degree numbers, and/or letter names.

1.
2.
3.
4.
5.
6.

NAME ______________________________

Contextual Listening 26.1

In this CL exercise you will:

- Identify the meter of a work for piano
- Determine the solfège syllables or scale-degree numbers of the melody and bass, and convert this to notation on the staff
- Associate harmonies with Roman numerals and identify the type of six-four chord that appears
- Identify cadences and embellishing tones by type
- Identify instances of modal mixture

Listen to an excerpt from a piano trio, and complete the following exercises.

1. Which is the meter signature of this excerpt?

   (a) $\frac{3}{4}$ (b) $\frac{4}{4}$ (c) $\frac{6}{8}$ (d) $\frac{9}{8}$

2. Use the workspace provided to capture the excerpt.

   (a) Notate the rhythm of the melody and bass on the single-line staves in the meter you chose for question 1. Write the meter signature, and include bar lines. Beam notes to show beat grouping.

   (b) Below each rhythm staff, and under each note, write the solfège syllables or scale-degree numbers for the melody and bass. Begin in the tonic key. At each pivot chord, write the Roman numeral of the new key, and then switch your solfège syllables or scale-degree numbers to the new key.

   (c) Combine your answers to complete the notation of the pitches and rhythm of the melody and bass. Begin on B♭3 and G1 respectively. Write the appropriate clefs, key signature (and any accidentals), and meter signature.

   (d) Beneath each bass pitch, write the Roman numeral of the chord that harmonizes it. Begin in the tonic and switch to the new key at each pivot chord. Refer to your answers to previous questions for help.

   (e) Circle the Roman numeral for each chord that is an example of modal mixture.

   (f) Identify each dissonant embellishing tone in the melody with P or IN.

Workspace

Rhythm:

Melody:

Solfège syllables:
Scale-degree numbers:

Solfège syllables:
Scale-degree numbers:

Notation:

Rhythm:

Bass:

Solfège syllables:
Scale-degree numbers:

Solfège syllables:
Scale-degree numbers:

3. Briefly discuss the internal structure of this phrase.

4. The excerpt employs which type of $^6_4$ chord?

   (a) passing (b) neighboring (c) cadential (d) arpeggiating

5. The cadential extension includes which type of resolution?

   (a) deceptive (b) plagal (c) Phrygian (d) Lydian

NAME ______________________________

Contextual Listening 26.2

In this CL exercise you will:

- Identify the meter of a work for piano and the type of accompanimental pattern in the left hand
- Determine the solfège syllables or scale-degree numbers of the melody and bass, and convert this to notation on the staff
- Associate harmonies with Roman numerals
- Identify cadences, phrase structures, and embellishing tones
- Identify instances of modal mixture

Listen to an excerpt from a piano sonata, and complete the following exercises.

1. Which of these represents the meter of this excerpt?
   (a) simple triple (b) simple quadruple
   (c) compound triple (d) compound quadruple
2. Which best describes the bass line of this excerpt?
   (a) basso continuo (b) pedal point
   (c) Alberti bass (d) walking bass
3. The highest melodic pitch is which type of embellishing tone?
   (a) anticipation (b) suspension
   (c) passing tone (d) incomplete neighbor
4. The scale that descends from the highest melodic pitch is which type?
   (a) major (b) natural (descending melodic) minor
   (c) harmonic minor (d) ascending melodic minor
5. Just after the highest melodic pitch, which of the following resolutions occurs?
   (a) deceptive (b) Phrygian (c) plagal (d) Picardy
6. Compared with the first chord, on which chord does the excerpt end?
   (a) I (b) ♭III (c) V (d) ♭VI
7. Which is the phrase structure of this excerpt?
   (a) parallel period (b) modulatory parallel period
   (c) contrasting period (d) modulatory contrasting period
8. Use the workspace provided to capture the excerpt.
   (a) Notate the rhythm of the melody and bass parts on the single-line staves in the meter you chose for question 1. Begin with a quarter note in the melody. Write the meter signature, and include bar lines. Beam notes to show beat grouping.
   (b) Below the bass rhythm staff under the initial note of each beat, write the solfège syllables or scale-degree numbers for the bass part using quarter notes to indicate full beats. Begin in the tonic key. At the pivot chord, write the Roman numeral of the new key, and then switch your solfège syllables or scale-degree numbers to the new key.

(c) Below the melody rhythm staff, and under each note, write the solfège syllables or scale-degree numbers for melody. Begin in the tonic key. At the pivot chord, write the Roman numeral of the new key, and then switch your solfège syllables or scale-degree numbers to the new key.

(d) Combine your answers to complete the notation of the pitches and rhythm of the melody and bass. Begin on B♭4 and B♭3 respectively. Write the appropriate clefs, key signature (and any accidentals), and meter signature.

(e) Indicate the harmonic progression by writing Roman numerals beneath the bass staff. Begin in the tonic and switch to the new key at the pivot chord. Refer to your answers to previous questions for help.

(f) Circle the Roman numeral of each chord that is an example of modal mixture.

Workspace

Rhythm:

Melody:

Solfège syllables:
Scale-degree numbers:

Solfège syllables:
Scale-degree numbers:

Solfège syllables:
Scale-degree numbers:

Solfège syllables:
Scale-degree numbers:

Notation:

NAME ______________________________

Rhythm:

Bass: 𝄆 ______________________________

Solfège syllables:

Scale-degree numbers:

𝄆 ______________________________

Solfège syllables:

Scale-degree numbers:

𝄆 ______________________________

Solfège syllables:

Scale-degree numbers:

𝄆 ______________________________

Solfège syllables:

Scale-degree numbers:

NAME ________________________

Contextual Listening 26.3

In this CL exercise you will:

- Identify the meter of a work for piano and voice
- Determine the solfège syllables or scale-degree numbers of the melody and bass, and convert this to notation on the staff
- Associate harmonies with Roman numerals
- Identify cadences and phrase structures
- Associate the introductory harmonies with Roman numerals and identify the type of six-four chord that appears
- Identify instances of modal mixture

This example is a folk song arranged for chorus. The setting is deeply rooted in traditional music, but, as you will hear, many of the sounds stretch the boundaries of functional tonality. Listen first to the entire excerpt, then as directed in the following exercises.

1. Which is the meter signature of this excerpt?

   (a) $\frac{2}{4}$ (b) $\frac{3}{4}$ (c) $\frac{9}{8}$ (d) $\frac{12}{8}$

2. Listen from the beginning until the voices enter. The chord that accompanies the first vocal pitch is the tonic. Is the tonic (a) major or (b) minor?

3. Use the workspace provided to capture the excerpt.

   (a) Notate the rhythm of only the five introductory chords in dotted-half notes on the bass rhythm staff using the meter you chose for question 1. Write the meter signature, and include bar lines.

   (b) For the five introductory chords, write the solfège syllables or scale-degree numbers for the bass line.

   (c) Combine your answers to complete the notation of the introductory bass pitches and rhythm.

   (d) Above each bass pitch, write the quality of the triad associated with it. Then write Roman numerals below the bass note. Use the quality of each triad to help you decide whether that Roman numeral should be uppercase or lowercase.

   (e) Circle the Roman numeral of each chord in the introduction that is an example of modal mixture.

   (f) Notate the rhythm of the melody on the upper single-line staff in the meter you chose for question 1. Align your notes to begin after the introductory bass pitches. Write the meter signature, and include bar lines.

   (g) Below the melody rhythm staff, and under each note, write the solfège syllables or scale-degree numbers for the melody. Begin on *do* ($\hat{1}$).

   (h) Combine your answers to complete the notation pitches and rhythm of the melody beginning on B♭4. Notate the melody as the composer did, using accidentals without a key signature. Write the appropriate clef and meter signature.

NAME ______________________________

Workspace

Rhythm:

Bass: 𝄃 ______________________________

Solfège syllables:

Scale-degree numbers:

Notation:

Rhythm:

Introduction (8 measures)

Introduction: 𝄃 ______________________________

Solfège syllables:

Scale-degree numbers:

Melody: 𝄃 ______________________________

Solfège syllables:

Scale-degree numbers:

𝄃 ______________________________

Solfège syllables:

Scale-degree numbers:

4. Briefly describe the internal structure of each vocal phrase.

5. At the beginning of vocal phrase 2, which are the qualities of the first two triads in the piano accompaniment?

   (a) M-M (b) M-m (c) m-M (d) m-m

6. Which are the qualities of the last two chords in the piano accompaniment?

   (a) Mm7-M$^5_3$ (b) mm7-M$^5_3$ (c) dm7-m$^5_3$ (d) dd7-m$^5_3$

CHAPTER 27

The Neapolitan Sixth and Augmented-Sixth Chords

In this chapter you'll learn to:

- Aurally identify the neapolitan sixth and augmented-sixth chords
- Apply borrowed Roman numerals to these chromatic harmonies
- Identify cadences by type
- Identify nonchord tones by type

Preparatory Listening

Complete the *Try It* dictations to familiarize yourself with the following concepts and skills:

- Determining the solfège syllables or scale-degree numbers for the soprano and bass of model SATB phrases that present the Neapolitan sixth and augmented-sixth chords
- Converting solfège syllables and scale-degree numbers to pitches and notating them on the staff
- Applying Roman numerals to show harmonic progressions

Try It

Listen to model SATB phrases that are played once each. The key signature, meter signature, and first bass pitch are given.

- Focus on the bass line first, and notate its pitches.
- Beneath the bass pitches, write Roman numerals to identify each harmony; if more than one chord seems possible, write all the possibilities and choose the correct one after additional hearings.
- Focus last on the soprano, and utilize it to refine your chord choices.
- Add bar lines including the double bar at the end.
- If you are working by yourself, sing each part aloud with solfège syllables, scale-degree numbers, and/or letter names.

NAME ______________________________

NAME ____________________

Contextual Listening 27.1

In this CL exercise you will:

- Identify the meter of a symphonic excerpt
- Determine the solfège syllables or scale-degree numbers of the melody and bass, and convert this to notation on the staff
- Associate harmonies with Roman numerals
- Identify the cadence

Listen to an excerpt from a symphony, and complete the following exercises.

1. Which of these represents the meter of this excerpt?
   (a) simple duple   (b) simple triple
   (c) compound duple   (d) compound triple
2. Which instrument doubles the violins' melody?
   (a) clarinet   (b) bassoon   (c) horn   (d) trombone
3. Use the workspace provided to capture the excerpt.
   (a) Notate the rhythm of the melody and bass parts on the single-line staves in the meter you chose for question 1, beginning with a quarter note. Write the meter signature, and include bar lines. Beam notes to show beat grouping.
   (b) Below the single-line staves, and under each note, write the solfège syllables or scale-degree numbers for the melody and bass parts.
   (c) Combine your answers to complete the notation of the pitches and rhythm of the melody and bass parts beginning on G♯4 and E3 respectively (but be aware that the bass line is doubled an octave lower). Write the appropriate clefs, key signature (and any accidentals), and meter signature.
   (d) Beneath the bass pitches, write the Roman numerals.
   (e) Write the harmonic interval numbers between the treble and bass staves.

NAME ______________________________

Workspace

Rhythm:

Melody: 𝄆

Solfège syllables:
Scale-degree numbers:

Notation:

Rhythm:

Bass: 𝄆

Solfège syllables:
Scale-degree numbers:

4. Between bass pitches 3-4, which melodic interval occurs?
   (a) P4 (b) A4 (c) d5 (d) P5
5. The excerpt concludes with which type of cadence?
   (a) half (b) imperfect authentic (c) perfect authentic (d) plagal
6. In the second half of the melody, the chromaticism is due to which of the following?
   (a) modulation to the relative minor (b) modulation to the mediant
   (c) Neapolitan sixth (d) modal mixture

NAME ______________________

Contextual Listening 27.2

In this CL exercise you will:

- Identify the meter of a work for piano
- Determine the solfège syllables or scale-degree numbers of the melody and bass, and convert this to notation on the staff
- Aurally identify the harmonic progression that concludes each phrase

Listen to an excerpt from a work for piano, and complete the following exercises.

1. Which is the meter of this excerpt?

   (a) $\frac{2}{4}$ (b) $\frac{3}{4}$ (c) $\frac{6}{8}$ (d) $\frac{9}{8}$

2. Which is the melody's first melodic interval?

   (a) M2 (b) m3 (c) M3 (d) P4

3. How does the rhythm of phrase 2 compare with that of phrase 1?

   (a) the same throughout

   (b) the same at the beginning, but different at the end

   (c) different at the beginning, but the same at the end

   (d) different throughout

4. Use the workspace provided to capture the excerpt.

   (a) Notate the rhythm of the melody on the single-line staves in the meter you chose for question 1. Begin with a dotted-eighth and sixteenth note anacrusis. Write the meter signature, and include bar lines (including one to show the anacrusis). Beam notes to show beat grouping.

   (b) Below the single-line staves, and under each note, write the solfège syllables or scale-degree numbers for the melody beginning on *mi* ($\hat{3}$).

   (c) Combine your answers to complete the notation of the pitches and rhythm of the melody beginning on G♯4. Write the appropriate clef, key signature (and any accidentals), and meter signature.

NAME ___________________________

Workspace

Rhythm:

Melody: 𝄥

Solfège syllables:

Scale-degree numbers:

𝄥

Solfège syllables:

Scale-degree numbers:

Notation:

5. Phrase 1 concludes with which harmonic progression?

   (a) IV-Fr^6-V (b) ii^6-vii^{ø6}/V-V (c) IV^6-V^6-I (d) V$^{6-5}_{4-3}$-I

6. Phrase 2 concludes *in the key of vi* with which harmonic progression?

   (a) V^7-i (b) vii^{o7}-I (c) iv^6-It^6-V (d) iv-N6-V

7. Which are the last two harmonic intervals between the melody and bass line?

   (a) 4-6 (b) 5-8 (c) 10-8 (d) 10-10

NAME ______________________

Contextual Listening 27.3

In this CL exercise you will:

- Identify the meter of an art song
- Determine the solfège syllables or scale-degree numbers of the melody and bass, and convert this to notation on the staff
- Associate harmonies with Roman numerals
- Identify nonchord tones

Listen to an excerpt from an art song, and complete the following exercises.

1. Which of these represents the meter of this excerpt?
   (a) simple duple (b) simple triple
   (c) compound triple (d) compound quadruple
2. The beginning features all of the following *except* a(n)
   (a) tonic pedal point. (b) slow harmonic rhythm.
   (c) rhythmic ostinato in the accompaniment. (d) Alberti bass.
3. Melodic pitch 3 is which type of dissonant embellishing tone?
   (a) passing tone (b) neighbor tone
   (c) appoggiatura (d) anticipation
4. The first melodic skip is which interval?
   (a) M3 (b) P4 (c) P5 (d) m6
5. The highest melodic pitch is which of the following?
   (a) *do* ($\hat{1}$) (b) *fa* ($\hat{4}$) (c) *le* ($\flat\hat{6}$) (d) *ti* ($\hat{7}$)
6. Compared with the beginning of the excerpt, the end is
   (a) transposed to the relative key. (b) an almost literal repetition.
   (c) rhythmically diminished. (d) in a different meter.
7. Use the workspace provided to capture the excerpt.
   (a) Notate the rhythm of the melody and bass line on the single-line staves in the meter you chose for question 1, with the eighth note as the beat unit. Begin at the point where the voice enters. Write the meter signature, and include bar lines. Beam notes to show beat grouping.
   (b) Below the bass rhythm staff, and under each note, write the solfège syllables or scale-degree numbers for the melody and bass line.
   (c) Combine your answers to complete the notation of the pitches and rhythm of the melody and bass line. Begin on D5 and G2 respectively. Write the appropriate clefs, key signature (and any accidentals), and meter signature.
   (d) Beneath the bass pitches, write the Roman numerals and figures.
   (e) *Musical challenge!* Transcribe the inner voices of the accompaniment. Refer to your answers to previous questions for help.

NAME ______________________________

Workspace

Rhythm:

Melody:

Solfège syllables:

Scale-degree numbers:

Solfège syllables:

Scale-degree numbers:

Solfège syllables:

Scale-degree numbers:

Solfège syllables:

Scale-degree numbers:

Notation:

Rhythm:

Bass:

Solfège syllables:

Scale-degree numbers:

Solfège syllables:

Scale-degree numbers:

Solfège syllables:

Scale-degree numbers:

Solfège syllables:

Scale-degree numbers:

NAME ______________________________

Contextual Listening 27.4

In this CL exercise you will:

- Identify the meter of a work for piano
- Determine the solfège syllables or scale-degree numbers of the melody and bass, and convert this to notation on the staff
- Associate harmonies with Roman numerals
- Identify the cadence
- Describe the organization of the phrase

Listen to an excerpt from a work for piano, and complete the following exercises.

1. Which is the meter signature of this excerpt?

   (a) $\frac{2}{4}$ (b) $\frac{3}{4}$ (c) $\frac{6}{8}$ (d) $\frac{9}{8}$

2. Use the workspace provided to capture the excerpt.

   (a) Notate the rhythm of the melody and bass on the single-line staves in the meter you chose for question 1, beginning with an eighth note. Write the meter signature, and include bar lines. Beam notes to show beat grouping.

   (b) Below the single-line staves, and under each note, write the solfège syllables or scale-degree numbers for the melody and bass.

   (c) Combine your answers to complete the notation of the pitches and rhythm of the melody and bass. Begin on E4 and E2 respectively. Write the appropriate clefs, meter, key signatures, bar lines, and accidentals. Beam notes to show beat grouping.

   (d) Beneath the bass pitches, write the Roman numerals and figures.

3. The fourth melodic pitch is which type of embellishing tone?

   (a) neighbor (b) passing (c) suspension (d) anticipation

Workspace

Rhythm:

Melody:

Solfège syllables:
Scale-degree numbers:

Solfège syllables:
Scale-degree numbers:

Notation:

Rhythm:

Bass:

Solfège syllables:
Scale-degree numbers:

Solfège syllables:
Scale-degree numbers:

4. During the last four pitches, the inner voice outlines which tetrachord?
   (a) major (b) minor (c) harmonic (d) Phrygian (natural minor)
5. The excerpt concludes with which type of cadence?
   (a) half (b) imperfect authentic (c) perfect authentic (d) deceptive
6. Briefly describe the internal organization of the phrase.

Vocal Forms

NAME ______________________

In this chapter you'll learn to:

- Analyze English and German texts
- Explain how a composer conveys the meaning of a text
- Notate vocal melodies and bass lines

Preparatory Listening

Complete the *Try It* dictations to review the following concepts and skills:

- Determining the solfège syllables or scale-degree numbers for the soprano and bass of model SATB phrases that present modal mixture, the Neapolitan sixth chord, and the augmented-sixth chord
- Converting syllables and numbers to pitches and notating them on the grand staff
- Applying Roman numerals to show harmonic progressions

Try It

Listen to model SATB phrases that are played once each. The key signature, meter signature, and first bass pitch are given.

- Focus on the bass line first, and notate its pitches.
- Beneath the bass pitches, write Roman numerals to identify each harmony; if more than one chord seems possible, write all the possibilities and choose the correct one after additional hearings.
- Focus last on the soprano, and utilize it to refine your chord choices.
- Add bar lines including the double bar at the end.
- If you are working by yourself, sing each part aloud with solfège syllables, scale-degree numbers, and/or letter names.

1.
2.
3.
4.
5.
6.
7.

NAME ______________________________

Contextual Listening 28.1

In this CL exercise you will:

- Identify the meter an art song
- Determine the solfège syllables or scale-degree numbers of the melody and bass, and convert this to notation on the staff
- Identify ways that the composer conveys the meaning or emotion of the text

Listen to a phrase from an art song, and complete the following exercises.

Wind o' the Westland blow, blow,
Bring me the dreams of long ago,
Long, long ago.

1. Which is the meter signature of this excerpt?

   (a) $\frac{3}{4}$ (b) $\frac{4}{4}$ (c) $\frac{6}{8}$ (d) $\frac{9}{8}$

2. Which technique is featured in the bass line?

   (a) pedal point (b) Alberti bass (c) basso continuo (d) walking bass

3. Use the workspace provided to capture the excerpt.

   (a) Notate the rhythm of the melody on the single-line staves in the meter you chose for question 1. Write the meter signature, and include bar lines. Beam notes to show beat grouping.

   (b) Below the single-line staves, and under each note, write the solfège syllables or scale-degree numbers for the melody.

   (c) Combine your answers to complete the notation of the pitches and rhythm of the melody beginning on B♭4. Write the appropriate clef, key signature (and any accidentals), and meter signature.

Workspace

Rhythm:

Melody:

Solfège syllables:

Scale-degree numbers:

Solfège syllables:

Scale-degree numbers:

Notation:

4. List several ways the music conveys the meaning or emotion of the text.

NAME ______________________________

Contextual Listening 28.2

In this CL exercise you will:

- Identify the accompaniment pattern of an art song
- Determine the solfège syllables or scale-degree numbers of the melody and bass, and convert this to notation on the staff
- Explain how the composer expands a phrase
- Explain how the composer conveys the meaning of specific words in the text

Study the text to an excerpt from an art song before listening for the first time. Then complete the following exercises.

Ach Veilchen, armes Veilchen, wie blühst du aus dem Schnee?
(O violet, poor violet, how do you bloom in the snow?)
Im kurzen Sonnenweilchen, dann langem Winterweh, dann langem Winterweh.
(In the sun for a brief moment, then in long winter's pain, then in long winter's pain.)

1. Which is the rhythm of the accompaniment throughout much of the excerpt?

2. Use the workspace provided to capture the excerpt.
   (a) Notate the rhythm of the melody and bass on the single-line staves in the meter you chose for question 1. Write the meter signature, and include bar lines. Beam notes to show beat grouping.
   (b) Below the single-line staves, and under each note, write the solfège syllables or scale-degree numbers for the melody and bass.
   (c) Combine your answers to complete the notation of the pitches and rhythm of the melody and bass. Begin on B♭4 and E♭3 respectively. There is no need to double the bass one octave lower. Write the appropriate clefs, key signature (and any accidentals), and meter signature.
   (d) At each change of harmony, write the Roman numerals below the bass pitch.

Workspace

Rhythm:

Melody:

Solfège syllables:
Scale-degree numbers:

Solfège syllables:
Scale-degree numbers:

Notation:

Rhythm:

Bass:

Solfège syllables:
Scale-degree numbers:

Solfège syllables:
Scale-degree numbers:

NAME ______________________

3. The excerpt consists of a single phrase. Briefly describe the techniques the composer employs to expand this phrase.

4. How does the composer evoke the meaning of "dann langem Winterweh" ("then in long winter's pain") at the end of the excerpt?

5. List two ways that the composer signifies the meaning of "weh" ("pain").

NAME ______________________

Contextual Listening 28.3

In this CL exercise you will:

- Identify phrase structure, design, and form in an aria from a cantata
- Determine the solfège syllables or scale-degree numbers of the melody and bass, and convert this to notation on the staff
- Identify harmonic progressions and cadences
- Discuss the dual meaning of the text and the ways in which the composer conveys this

This aria, "Schafe können sicher weiden," is from J. S. Bach's Cantata No. 208 (*The Hunt*). It is likely that Bach's patron, Duke Wilhelm Ernst, commissioned the cantata as a birthday present for a prominent duke called Christian. The aria is sung by the character Pales, Roman goddess of flocks and shepherds. Study the poetic translation, then listen to the aria and complete the following exercises.

Schafe können sicher weiden,	Sheep can safely graze,
wo ein guter Hirte wacht,	where a good shepherd watches over them.
Wo Regenten wohl regieren,	Where rulers govern well,
kann man Ruh und Frieden spüren	one can feel rest and peace
und was Länder glücklich macht.	and that which makes countries content.

Exercises 1-4 refer to the entire song. To help you remember what you hear, sketch a diagram as you listen.

1. Which is the section design of the entire aria?

   (a) **A A** (b) **A A′** (c) **A B** (d) **A B A**

2. Section 2 concludes in which key?

   (a) I (b) IV (c) V (d) vi

3. Is the form of the entire song (a) sectional or (b) continuous?

4. Which is the form of the entire aria?

   (a) simple binary (b) rounded binary

   (c) simple ternary (d) composite ternary

Before proceeding . . .

- If your answer to question 4 was (a) or (b), complete question 5 and question 6 and skip to question 9. (Don't complete questions 7 or 8.)
- If your answer to question 4 was (c), skip to question 9. (Don't complete questions 5-8.)
- If your answer to question 4 was (d), skip to question 7. (Don't complete questions 5 or 6.)

5. Is the binary (a) sectional or (b) continuous?

6. Are the sections balanced?

7. (a) Which is the form of section 1?
   (1) parallel period (2) contrasting period
   (3) simple binary (4) rounded binary

   If your answer was (3) or (4), complete parts (b) and (c).

   (b) Is the binary (1) sectional or (2) continuous?

   (c) Are the sections balanced?

8. (a) Which is the form of section 2?
   (1) parallel period (2) contrasting period
   (3) simple binary (4) rounded binary

   If your answer was (3) or (4), complete parts (b) and (c).

   (b) Is the binary (1) sectional or (2) continuous?

   (c) Are the sections balanced?

Exercises 9-14 refer only to the music of section 1.

9. At the beginning, at which interval are the flutes doubled?
   (a) third (b) fifth (c) sixth (d) octave

10. At the end of the introduction, at which interval are the flutes doubled?
    (a) third (b) fifth (c) sixth (d) octave

11. Use the workspace provided to capture the excerpt.
    (a) Notate the rhythm of the vocal melody, which begins in measure 5, on the single-line staves in common time. Write *tr* for the trill. Write the meter signature, and include bar lines. Beam notes to show beat grouping.
    (b) Below the single-line staves, and under each note, write the solfège syllables or scale-degree numbers for the melody.
    (c) Combine your answers to complete the notation of the pitches and rhythm of the melody beginning on B♭4. Write the appropriate clef, key signature (and any accidentals), and meter signature.

Workspace

Rhythm:

Melody: ‖

Solfège syllables:

Scale-degree numbers:

‖

Solfège syllables:

Scale-degree numbers:

‖

Solfège syllables:

Scale-degree numbers:

‖

Solfège syllables:

Scale-degree numbers:

Notation:

12. The beginning of the vocal melody opens with which harmonic progression?

    (a) I-I-vii^{ø7}-I (b) I-ii^6-V-I (c) I-ii$^4_2$-V$^6_5$-I (d) I-IV-V$^4_2$-I^6

13. After the vocal part cadences, section 1 concludes with an instrumental postlude. Which best describes the final instrumental cadence of section 1?

    (a) IAC in I

    (b) PAC in V

    (c) deceptive resolution followed by a PAC in I

    (d) PAC in vi followed by a HC in IV

14. Which is the form of section 1?

    (a) introduction + parallel period + codetta

    (b) introduction + contrasting period + codetta

    (c) introduction + parallel double period

    (d) introduction + contrasting double period

15. From the beginning of section 2, what are the first two keys tonicized?

    (a) ii then IV (b) IV then V (c) V then I (d) vi then ii

16. This secular song's text can have a dual meaning, one that honors Duke Christian and another that refers to Bach's deeply held Christian beliefs. Discuss each meaning and how Bach paints this text in his music.

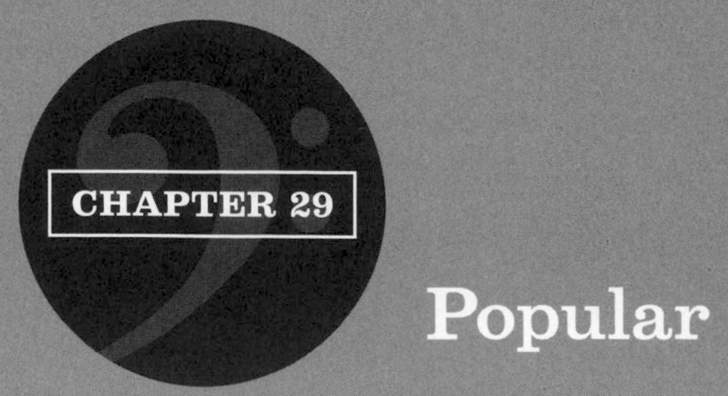

Popular Music

In this chapter you'll learn to:

- Notate swung melodies
- Hear and identify seventh chords that contain altered pitches
- Associate Roman numerals with popular-music chord symbols
- Transcribe excerpts from jazz, blues, and popular-song repertoires

Preparatory Listening

Complete the *Try It* dictations to familiarize yourself with the following concepts and skills:

- Identifying seventh chords that contain altered pitches
- Notating short jazz and blues riffs

Try It

Listen to isolated tonic-, and dominant-, and predominant-function harmonies related to the key of C, each of which is played once. Notate each harmony on the grand staff and supply the correct lead-sheet chord symbol. The exercises may include chords with extensions (added sixth and ninth chords); mixture chords and diminished sevenths; chords with suspensions (sus chords); and chords with altered fifths. The bass pitches are given.

- Focus on the bass note and silently arpeggiate through the chord; this might require that you arpeggiate up to the thirteenth of the chord!
- To determine altered pitches, compare the notes you hear with the diatonic pitches that would normally appear in the chord.
- Consider the quality of a root-position chord that would normally occur above each bass note
- If you are working by yourself, sing each part aloud with solfège syllables, scale-degree numbers, and/or letter names.

NAME ______________________________

1.

2.

3.

4.

5.

6.

7.

8.

Listen to short ii-V-I progressions related to the key of C major or C minor, each of which is played once. For each of the three chords, notate the bass and soprano lines, then determine chord quality and any extensions, alterations, or mixture. Note the upper voices in the treble clef. The first bass pitch is given.

- Focus on the bass line first, and notate its pitches.
- Above the top staff write letter names to indicate chord roots.
- Focus last on the soprano, and utilize it to refine your chord choices.

Listen to short "riffs" based on the blues scale, each of which is played once. Notate each riff in the indicated meter. The first note and key signature of each are given.

- Sing the notated first note and the blues scale associated with it.
- Notate the first and last notes first, then fill in the notes in between.

NAME ______________________________

Contextual Listening 29.1

In this CL exercise you will:

- Determine the meter of a jazz standard
- Notate the melody and bass
- Determine the harmonic sequence
- Associate Roman numerals with popular-music chord symbols

Listen to one phrase from a jazz standard, and complete the following exercises.

1. Which is the meter of this excerpt?

   (a) $\frac{3}{4}$ (b) $\frac{4}{4}$ (c) $\frac{6}{8}$ (d) $\frac{9}{8}$

2. On what sequence is the excerpt based?

   (a) ascending second (b) descending third

   (c) descending fourth (d) descending fifth

3. Use the workspace provided to capture the excerpt.

   (a) Notate the rhythm of the melody and bass parts on the single-line staves in the meter you chose for question 1. Write the meter signature, and include bar lines. Beam notes to show beat grouping.

   (b) Below the single-line staves, and under each note, write the solfège syllables or scale-degree numbers for the melody and bass beginning on *do* ($\hat{1}$) and *fa* ($\hat{4}$) respectively.

   (c) Combine your answers to complete the notation of the pitches and rhythm of the melody and bass. Begin on A4 and D3 respectively. Write the appropriate clefs, key signature, and meter signature.

   (d) Write the Roman numerals below the bass pitches.

   (e) Write the popular-music chord symbols above the melody.

Workspace

Rhythm:

Melody:

Solfège syllables:
Scale-degree numbers:

Solfège syllables:
Scale-degree numbers:

Notation:

Rhythm:

Bass:

Solfège syllables:
Scale-degree numbers:

Solfège syllables:
Scale-degree numbers:

4. Bass pitches 1-3, 4-6, and 7-9 form which linear intervallic pattern (LIP) with the sustained high notes in the melody?

   (a) 10-10 (b) 10-7 (c) 8-6 (d) 5-10

5. Bass pitches 1 and 3, 4 and 6, and 7 and 9 form which LIP with the highest part of the accompaniment?

   (a) 10-10 (b) 10-7 (c) 8-6 (d) 5-10

6. The final cadence is extended by which resolution?

   (a) Dorian (b) Phrygian (c) plagal (d) deceptive

NAME ________________________________

Contextual Listening 29.2

In this CL exercise you will:

- Determine the meter of a popular song
- Notate the melody and bass
- Identify the linear intervallic pattern (LIP) between the melody and bass

Listen to an excerpt from a popular song, and complete the following exercises.

1. Which is the meter signature of this excerpt?

   (a) $\frac{2}{4}$ (b) $\frac{3}{4}$ (c) $\frac{9}{8}$ (d) $\frac{12}{8}$

2. In chords 3-6, which is the linear intervallic pattern (LIP)?

   (a) 6-6 (b) 8-5 (c) 10-7 (d) 10-10

3. Use the workspace provided to capture the excerpt.

   (a) Notate the rhythm of the melody and bass on the single-line staves in the meter you chose for question 1. Begin with a quarter-note and eighth-note anacrusis. Write the meter signature, and include bar lines (including one to show the anacrusis). Beam notes to show beat grouping.

   (b) Below the single-line staves, and under each note, write the solfège syllables or scale-degree numbers for the melody and bass.

   (c) Combine your answers to complete the notation of the pitches and rhythm of the melody and bass. Begin on C4 and F2 respectively. Write the appropriate clefs, key signature (and any accidentals), and meter signature.

   (d) Write the Roman numerals below the bass pitches.

   (e) Write the popular-music chord symbols above the melody.

Workspace

Rhythm:

Melody:

Solfège syllables:
Scale-degree numbers:

Solfège syllables:
Scale-degree numbers:

Solfège syllables:
Scale-degree numbers:

Notation:

NAME ______________________________

Rhythm:

Bass:

Solfège syllables:

Scale-degree numbers:

Solfège syllables:

Scale-degree numbers:

Solfège syllables:

Scale-degree numbers:

NAME ______________________

Contextual Listening 29.3

In this CL exercise you will:

- Identify the trumpet rhythm from a blues excerpt
- Identify the scale from which the melody derives
- Notate the riffs played by the trumpet and piano at concert pitch
- Transpose the trumpet riff for a B♭ instrument
- Identify the bass pitches that accompany the trumpet

Much instrumental jazz is derived from song. Listen to an excerpt from one such composition, and complete the following exercises. All exercises refer to the music that occurs *after the introduction.*

1. After the introduction, which of the following best represents the jazz rhythm of the trumpet?

2. The pitches of the melody are chosen from which scale?

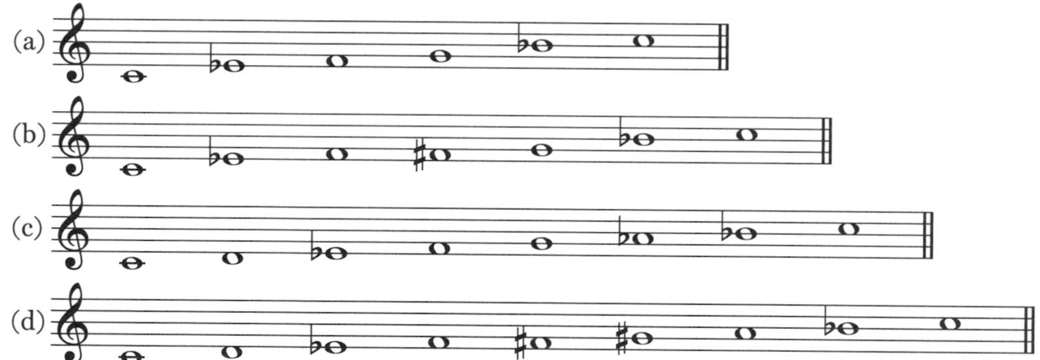

3. The initial melodic segment, or riff (four measures plus the pickup), is heard six times during the excerpt. Notate the concert pitches of this riff next, beginning with E♭4. Write an appropriate clef, the meter signature, and any accidentals.

4. Beginning with F4, notate the pitches of this riff for B♭ trumpet. Write an appropriate clef, the meter signature, and any accidentals. Remember that the trumpet's pitches are a M2 higher than they sound.

5. Midway through the excerpt, the piano echoes the trumpet's riff. Notate the pitches of the four-measure piano riff next, beginning with E♭4. Write an appropriate clef, the meter signature, and any accidentals.

6. Beginning with C5, notate the pitches of the piano riff for the E♭ alto saxophone. Write an appropriate clef, the meter signature, and any accidentals. The saxophone's pitches are written a M6 higher than they sound.

7. In the second half of the excerpt, which of the following best describes the texture?

   (a) chordal homophony (b) heterophony

   (c) fugal imitation (d) accompanied call and response

8. While the trumpet plays, tap the beat and listen to the bass pitches at the beginning of each measure. Write the chord roots that sound on beat 1 in each measure.

measure:	___	___	___	___	___	___	___	___
	1	2	3	5	7	9	10	11

CHAPTER 30

Chromatic Harmony and Voice-Leading

In this chapter you'll learn to:

- Hear and aurally identify chromatic harmony and voice-leading in works for piano and chamber ensemble
- Determine phrase structures and large-scale form
- Identify sequences and linear intervallic patterns (LIPs)
- Identify cadences by type
- Identify nonchord tones by type

Preparatory Listening

Complete the *Try It* dictations to review the following concepts and skills:

- Determining the solfège syllables or scale-degree numbers for the soprano and bass of model SATB phrases that present a variety of harmonic sequences
- Converting solfège syllables and scale-degree numbers to pitches and notating them on the staff
- Applying Roman numerals to show harmonic progressions
- Identifying sequences and linear intervallic patterns (LIPs) by type

Try It

Listen to model SATB phrases that are played once each. The key signature, meter signature, and first bass pitch are given.

- Focus on the bass line first, and notate its pitches.
- Beneath the bass pitches, write Roman numerals to identify each harmony; if more than one chord seems possible, write all the possibilities and choose the correct one after additional hearings.
- Focus last on the soprano, and utilize it to refine your chord choices.
- Above the top staff indicate the harmonic interval between the soprano and bass (e.g., 5-6).
- To the left of the grand staff identify the type of sequence (e.g., descending 5ths)
- Add bar lines including the double bar at the end.
- If you are working by yourself, sing each part aloud with solfège syllables, scale-degree numbers, and/or letter names.

NAME ___________________________

1.

2.

3.

4.

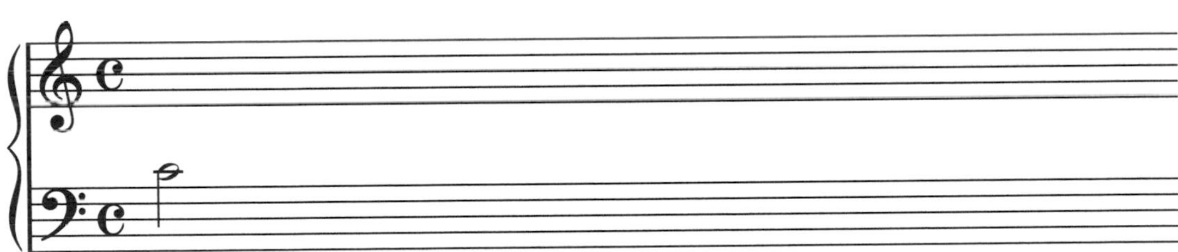

5.

6.

NAME ______________________________

Contextual Listening 30.1

In this CL exercise you will:

- Identify the meter of a work for piano
- Determine the solfège syllables or scale-degree numbers of the melody and bass, and convert this to notation on the staff
- Identify linear intervallic patterns (LIPs)
- Draw a diagram to show internal phrase structures
- Identify the design and form of the excerpt
- Apply Roman numerals and identify nonchord tones

This three-phrase excerpt is from a piano sonata. Listen first to the entire excerpt. Then listen in three stages, focusing on the first, second, then third phrase.

1. Which is the meter signature of this excerpt?

   (a) $\begin{smallmatrix}3\\4\end{smallmatrix}$ (b) $\begin{smallmatrix}4\\4\end{smallmatrix}$ (c) $\begin{smallmatrix}6\\8\end{smallmatrix}$ (d) $\begin{smallmatrix}9\\8\end{smallmatrix}$

The following questions refer only to phrase 1, the music up to the rolled chords.

2. How is the melody of the second subphrase related to that of the first?

   (a) melodic inversion (b) rhythmic augmentation

   (c) transposed up a step (d) unrelated

3. Phrase 1 cadences with which of the following harmonic progressions?

   (a) I: V$^{6-5}_{4-3}$ (b) I: IV–V–I (c) V: V$^{6-5}_{4-3}$–I (d) V: ii^6–V^7–I

4. Draw a diagram of the internal structure for phrase 1. Label each subphrase with a letter and, if present, any type(s) of phrase expansion.

Exercises 5-9 refer only to subphrases 1 and 2 of phrase 1.

5. Use the workspace provided to capture the first phrase.

   (a) Notate the rhythm of the melody and bass on the single-line staves in the meter you chose for question 1. Begin with a dotted-eighth-sixteenth-note anacrusis. Write the meter signature, and include bar lines. Beam notes to show beat grouping.

   (b) Below the single-line staves, and under each note, write the solfège syllables or scale-degree numbers for the melody and bass.

   (c) Combine your answers to complete the notation of the pitches and rhythm of the melody and bass. Begin on D5 and D4 respectively. Write the appropriate clefs, key signature, and meter signature.

   (d) Write the Roman numerals below the bass pitches.

   (e) Above each embellishing tone in the melody, write P, N, or IN.

Workspace

Rhythm:

Melody:

Solfège syllables:
Scale-degree numbers:

Notation:

Rhythm:

Bass:

Solfège syllables:
Scale-degree numbers:

Exercises 6-8 refer only to phrase 2, which begins with the rolled chords in the high register.

6. Listen to the intervals between the melody and bass at the beginning of phrase 2. The phrase begins with which of the following linear intervallic patterns?

   (a) 8-5 (b) 7-6 (c) 10-7 (d) 10-10

7. Use the workspace provided to capture the second phrase.

   (a) Notate the rhythm of the melody and bass line on the single-line staves. Write the meter signature, and include bar lines. Beam notes to show beat grouping.

   (b) Below the single-line staves, and under each note, write the solfège syllables or scale-degree numbers for the melody and bass beginning on *te* ($\flat\hat{7}$) and *sol* ($\hat{5}$) respectively.

   (c) Combine your answers to complete the notation of the pitches and rhythm of the melody and bass. Begin on A♭5 and F3 respectively and start with a quarter-note anacrusis. Refer to your answer to question 6 to see and hear the linear intervallic pattern. Write the appropriate clefs, key signature (and any accidentals), and meter signature.

   (d) Write the Roman numerals below the bass pitches.

NAME ______________________________

Workspace

Rhythm:

Melody: 𝄆 ______________________________

Solfège syllables:

Scale-degree numbers:

𝄆 ______________________________

Solfège syllables:

Scale-degree numbers:

Notation:

Rhythm:

Bass: 𝄆 ______________________________

Solfège syllables:

Scale-degree numbers:

𝄆 ______________________________

Solfège syllables:

Scale-degree numbers:

8. (a) As you listen to phrase 2, conduct the hypermeter. Is the phrase rhythm (1) regular or (2) irregular?

   (b) If your answer was *irregular,* briefly describe the nature of the phrase expansion.

Exercises 9-13 refer only to phrase 3.

9. How is the beginning of phrase 3 different from the beginning of phrase 1?
   (a) The music is transposed.
   (b) The higher and lower parts have switched places.
   (c) Phrase 3 is a melodic inversion.
   (d) Phrase 3 is rhythmically augmented.

10. Write the Roman numerals of the opening chord progression for phrase 3 (i.e., the music of subphrases 1 and 2).

11. Which of the following is the final chord progression of the excerpt?
   (a) iii-IV-vi-V^{6-5}_{4-3}-I (b) IV^6-I^6-ii^6-ii-V-I
   (c) vi-ii^6-ii-V^7-I (d) vi-IV-ii^6-V^{6-5}_{4-3}-I

12. Which is the phrase design of the entire excerpt?
   (a) **a b c** (b) **a b a′** (c) **a b a** (d) **a a′ a″**

13. Which is the form of the entire piece?
   (a) simple binary (b) rounded binary
   (c) simple ternary (d) composite ternary

NAME ______________________________

Contextual Listening 30.2

In this CL exercise you will:

- Identify the meter of a work for piano
- Determine the solfège syllables or scale-degree numbers of the melody and bass, and convert this to notation on the staff
- Identify sequences and linear intervallic patterns (LIPs)
- Identify phrase structures, design, and the form of the excerpt
- Apply Roman numerals and identify nonchord tones

Listen to an excerpt from a keyboard work, and complete the following exercises.

1. Which is the meter signature of this excerpt?

   (a) $\frac{2}{4}$ (b) $\frac{3}{4}$ (c) $\frac{9}{8}$ (d) $\frac{12}{8}$

2. Which is the section design of the entire movement?

   (a) **A A** (b) **A A′** (c) **A B** (d) **A B A′**

3. Which is the form of the entire movement?

   (a) simple binary (b) rounded binary

   (c) simple ternary (d) composite ternary

   - If your answer was (a) or (b), complete question 4 and question 5, then skip to question 8. (Don't complete questions 6–7.)
   - If your answer was (c), skip to question 8. (Don't complete questions 4–7.)
   - If your answer was (d), skip to question 6. (Don't complete questions 4–5.)

4. Is the binary (a) sectional or (b) continuous?

5. Are the sections balanced?

6. (a) Which is the form of section 1?

   (1) parallel period (2) contrasting period

   (3) simple binary (4) rounded binary

   If your answer was (3) or (4), complete parts (b) and (c).

   (b) Is the binary (1) sectional or (2) continuous?

   (c) Are the sections balanced?

7. (a) Which is the form of section 2?

   (1) parallel period (2) contrasting period

   (3) simple binary (4) rounded binary

   If your answer was (3) or (4), complete parts (b) and (c).

   (b) Is the binary (1) sectional or (2) continuous?

   (c) Are the sections balanced?

Exercises 8-12 refer only to section 2, phrase 1.

8. Using a neutral syllable, sing the bass pitches. By the end of the phrase, which scale degree do they tonicize? _____

Strategy: Sustain this tonicized pitch and listen to the beginning of the excerpt again. After you hear the original tonic pitch, sing up or down the scale until you reach the newly tonicized pitch.

9. Use the workspace provided to capture a sketch of section 2, phrase 1.
   (a) On the single-line staves, and in the meter you chose for question 1, notate solid, stemless noteheads for the melodic and bass pitches that *occur on the first six downbeats of section 2*. Write the meter signature, and include bar lines. Beam notes to show beat grouping.
   (b) Below the single-line staves, and under each note, write the solfège syllables or scale-degree numbers for the melody and bass line *occurring on the first six downbeats of section 2*.
   (c) Combine your answers to complete the notation of the pitches and rhythm of the melody and bass *occurring on the first six downbeats of section 2*. Begin on C5 (melody) and A3 (bass). Write the appropriate clefs, key signature (and any accidentals), and meter signature.
   (e) Write the harmonic intervals that occur between the soprano and bass.

NAME ______________________________

Workspace

Rhythm:

Melody:

Solfège syllables:

Scale-degree numbers:

Notation:

Rhythm:

Bass:

Solfège syllables:

Scale-degree numbers:

10. What linear intervallic pattern (LIP) occurs?

    (a) 5-8 (b) 6-6 (c) 8-10 (d) 10-10

11. Which sequence occurs in the phrase?

    (a) descending fifths (b) descending thirds

    (c) ascending 5-6 (d) ascending fifths

12. Use the workspace provided to capture all the notes in the first phrase of section 2.

    (a) Below the single-line staves, and under each note, write the solfège syllables or scale-degree numbers for *all of the melody and bass notes* in the first phrase of section 2. Refer to your work in question 9b for help.

    (b) Combine your answers to complete the notation of the pitches and rhythm for the entire first phrase of section 2. Refer to your work in question 9c for help. Begin on C5 (melody) and A3 (bass). Write the appropriate clefs, key signature (and any accidentals), and meter signature.

    (c) Write the Roman numerals below the bass pitches. Show any secondary relationships, and at the appropriate location, indicate the modulation.

    (d) Identify each dissonant embellishing tone in the melody as passing (P) or neighbor (N).

Workspace

Rhythm:

Melody:

Solfège syllables:
Scale-degree numbers:

Solfège syllables:
Scale-degree numbers:

Notation:

Rhythm:

Bass:

Solfège syllables:
Scale-degree numbers:

Solfège syllables:
Scale-degree numbers:

NAME ____________________

Contextual Listening 30.3

In this CL exercise you will:

- Identify the meter of a chamber work
- Determine the solfège syllables or scale-degree numbers of the melody and bass, and convert this to notation on the staff
- Identify sequences and linear intervallic patterns
- Identify phrase structures, design, and the form of the excerpt
- Apply Roman numerals and identify nonchord tones

Listen to a two-phrase excerpt from a chamber work (CL 30.3). You may also listen to a reduction in which the embellishments have been removed (CL 30.3a).

1. Which is the meter signature of this excerpt?

   (a) $\frac{2}{4}$ (b) $\frac{3}{4}$ (c) $\frac{4}{4}$ (d) $\frac{9}{8}$

Exercise 2 refers only to phrase 1.

2. Use the workspace provided to capture phrase 1.
   (a) Notate the rhythm of the melody and bass on the single-line staves in the meter you chose for question 1. Write the meter signature, and include bar lines. Beam notes to show beat grouping.
   (b) Below the single-line staves, and under the notes occurring on each downbeat, write the solfège syllables or scale-degree numbers for the melody and bass. Write ∾ for the turn.
   (c) Below the single-line staves, and under each note, write the remaining solfège syllables or scale-degree numbers for the melody and bass. Write ∾ for the turn.
   (d) Combine your answers to complete the notation of the pitches and rhythm of the melody and bass. Begin on B4 and G3 respectively. Write the appropriate clefs, key signature (and any accidentals), and meter signature.
   (e) Write the Roman numerals below the bass pitches.
   (f) Above each embellishing tone in the melody, write P or N.

Workspace

Rhythm:

Melody:

Solfège syllables:
Scale-degree numbers:

Solfège syllables:
Scale-degree numbers:

Notation:

Rhythm:

Bass:

Solfège syllables:
Scale-degree numbers:

Solfège syllables:
Scale-degree numbers:

The remaining excercises refer only to phrase 2, which begins when the opening motive returns.

3. Use the workspace provided to capture phrase 2.
   (a) Notate the rhythm of the bass part on the single-line staves in the meter you chose for question 1. Listen to the cello *pizzicati* at the beginning of the phrase. Write the meter signature, and include bar lines. Beam notes to show beat grouping.
   (b) Below the single-line staves, and under each note, write the solfège syllables or scale-degree numbers for the bass part.

(c) Combine your answers to complete the notation of the pitches and rhythm of the bass part. Begin on G2. Write the appropriate clefs, key signature (and any accidentals), and meter signature.

Workspace

Notation:

Rhythm:

Bass:

Solfège syllables:
Scale-degree numbers:

Solfège syllables:
Scale-degree numbers:

Solfège syllables:
Scale-degree numbers:

4. At the beginning of phrase 2, how is the melody developed?
   (a) The melody overlaps with another melodic statement.
   (b) The melody is doubled in sixths.
   (c) The melody is in a canon at the octave.
   (d) The melody sounds in the lowest part.
5. The first three harmonies of phrase 2 belong to which key?
   (a) relative minor (b) parallel minor
   (c) dominant (d) submediant
6. Which type of sequence occurs during phrase 2?
   (a) descending fifths (b) descending thirds
   (c) ascending 5-6 (d) ascending fifths

7. Which of the following is the linear intervallic pattern at the beginning of the sequence?

   (a) 6-6 (b) 7-10 (c) 10-6 (d) 10-10

8. Phrase 2 concludes with which cadence?

   (a) HC in I (b) PAC in I (c) HC in V (d) PAC in V

9. Briefly summarize the phrase expansion used in phrase 2. Refer to your answers to previous questions for ideas.

Chromatic Modulation

NAME ______________________

In this chapter you'll learn to:

- Hear and explain enharmonic reinterpretations of the Ger^{+6} chord, the V^7 chord, and the vii$^{\circ 7}$ chord in chromatic modulations
- Determine phrase structures and draw phrase diagrams
- Identify cadences by type
- Identify nonchord tones by type
- Hear the common-tone diminished seventh chord
- Describe relationships between phrases

Preparatory Listening

Complete the *Try It* dictations to familiarize yourself with the following concepts and skills:

- Determining the solfège syllables or scale-degree numbers for the soprano and bass of model SATB phrases that present the enharmonic reinterpretation of the Ger^{+6} chord, the V^7 chord, and the vii$^{\circ 7}$ chord in modulations
- Converting solfège syllables and scale-degree numbers to pitches and notating them on the staff
- Applying Roman numerals to show harmonic progressions

Try It

Listen to model SATB phrases that are played once each. The key signature, meter signature, and first bass pitch are given. The six dictations here are grouped into pairs. The first of each does not modulate; the second dictation modulates by means of enharmonic reinterpretation of the Ger^{+6} chord, the V^7 chord, or the vii$^{\circ 7}$ chord.

- Focus on the bass line first, and notate its pitches.
- Beneath the bass pitches, write Roman numerals to identify each harmony; if more than one chord seems possible, write all the possibilities and choose the correct one after additional hearings.
- Focus last on the soprano, and utilize it to refine your chord choices.
- For the second dictation of each pair, indicate the starting and ending keys, and show the enharmonic reinterpretation of the Ger^{+6} chord, the V^7 chord, or the vii$^{\circ 7}$ chord by providing a Roman numeral in both keys.

- Add bar lines including the double bar at the end.
- If you are working by yourself, sing each part aloud with solfège syllables, scale-degree numbers, and/or letter names.

NAME ________________________________

Contextual Listening 31.1

In this CL exercise you will:

- Determine the solfège syllables or scale-degree numbers of the melody and bass of an excerpt of a piano rag, and convert this to notation on the staff
- Identify cadences by types
- Identify phrase structures

Listen to a four-phrase excerpt from a piano rag, and complete the following exercises.

1. Use the workspace provided to capture the excerpt.
   (a) Notate the rhythm of the melody and bass line on the single-line staves in $\frac{2}{4}$ meter. Divide the excerpt into four-measure phrases. Write the meter signature, and include bar lines. Beam notes to show beat grouping.
   (b) Below the single-line staves, and under each note, write the solfège syllables or scale-degree numbers for the melody and bass. Divide the excerpt into four-measures phrases and show the key changes with Roman numerals.
   (c) Combine your answers to complete the notation of the pitches and rhythm of the melody and bass. Begin on E♭5 and E♭2 respectively. Write the appropriate clefs, key signature, and meter signature.
   (d) Write the Roman numerals below the bass pitches. Show tonicizations and modulations.
   (e) Circle each common-tone diminished-seventh chord symbol.

Workspace

Rhythm:

Melody:

Solfège syllables:

Scale-degree numbers:

Solfège syllables:

Scale-degree numbers:

Solfège syllables:

Scale-degree numbers:

Solfège syllables:

Scale-degree numbers:

Notation:

NAME ______________________________

Rhythm:

Bass:

Solfège syllables:

Scale-degree numbers:

Solfège syllables:

Scale-degree numbers:

Solfège syllables:

Scale-degree numbers:

Solfège syllables:

Scale-degree numbers:

2. Phrase 1 concludes with which cadence type?

(a) Phrygian (b) plagal (c) IAC (d) deceptive

3. Phrase 2 concludes with which cadence type?

(a) IAC in the tonic (b) PAC in the tonic

(c) HC in the tonic (d) PAC in the new key

4. Phrase 3 concludes with which cadence type?

(a) Phrygian (b) plagal (c) IAC (d) deceptive

5. Phrase 4 concludes with which cadence type?

(a) IAC in the tonic (b) PAC in the tonic

(c) IAC in the new key (d) PAC in the new key

6. Which of these represents the excerpt's phrase structure?

(a) parallel period (b) contrasting period

(c) parallel double period (d) contrasting double period

Contextual Listening 31.2

In this CL exercise you will:

- Identify the meter of a work for piano
- Determine the solfège syllables or scale-degree numbers of the melody and convert this to notation on the staff.
- Draw a phrase diagram
- Identify the hypermeter as regular or irregular
- Identify the type of modulation and indicate the keys involved using Roman numerals
- Aurally identify harmonic progressions

This excerpt from a piano work is in three parts. The first part is in a minor key, the second in a major key, and the third in a minor key. Listen to the entire excerpt, then focus on each part in turn.

1. Which is the meter signature of this excerpt?

   (a) $\frac{2}{4}$ (b) $\frac{3}{4}$ (c) $\frac{6}{8}$ (d) $\frac{9}{8}$

The following questions refer only to part 1.

2. Part 1 opens with which chord progression?

   (a) i-ii$^{\circ 6}$-i^6-V^6-i (b) i-iv-i^6-V^6-i (c) i-V$^4_2$-i-vii$^{\circ 7}$-i (d) i-vii$^{\circ 4}_{\ 3}$-i^6-V$^6_5$-i

3. Compared with the beginning of phrase 1, the beginning of phrase 2 is

   (a) a melodic inversion. (b) rhythmically augmented.

   (c) transposed up a third. (d) sequenced using the descending-fifth progression.

4. Part 1 concludes with a modulation to which key?

   (a) i (b) iv (c) V (d) VI

5. Use the workspace provided to capture the excerpt.

   (a) Notate the rhythm of the melody for part 1 on the single-line staves in the meter you chose for question 1. Write the meter signature, and include bar lines. Beam notes to show beat grouping.

   (b) Below the single-line staves, and under each note, write the solfège syllables or scale-degree numbers for the melody of part 1.

(c) Combine your answers to complete the notation of the pitches and rhythm for the melody of part 1 beginning on G4. Write the appropriate clefs, key signature (and any accidentals), and meter signature.

Workspace

Rhythm:

Melody:

Solfège syllables:

Scale-degree numbers:

Solfège syllables:

Scale-degree numbers:

Notation:

6. Using your answer to question 5c, sing the melodic pitches 2-5 slowly, then sing pitches 12-15. How is the contour of group 2 related to that of group 1?
   (a) identical
   (b) transposed down a third
   (c) transposed down a fourth
   (d) transposed down a fifth

7. (a) Conduct the hypermeter as you listen. Is the phrase rhythm (1) regular or (2) irregular?
   (b) If your answer was *irregular,* briefly describe the nature of the phrase expansion.

8. The modulation that connects the end of part 1 and the beginning of part 2 is which of the following?
   (a) diatonic common (pivot) chord
   (b) common tone
   (c) direct
   (d) sequential

The next questions refer to part 2 (the major-key section in the middle of the excerpt).

9. Compared with the phrases of part 1, phrase 1 of part 2 is of what length?
   (a) half as long
   (b) same length
   (c) one-and-a-half times the length
   (d) twice as long

10. Draw a diagram of the internal structure of phrase 1 of part 2. Label each subphrase with a letter and, if present, any type of phrase expansion.

11. (a) Conduct the hypermeter as you listen to part 2. Is the phrase rhythm (1) regular or (2) irregular?

    (b) If your answer was *irregular,* briefly describe why you think so.

The next questions refer to part 3 (the minor-key music at the end).

12. How is phrase 1 of part 3 related to phrase 1 of part 1?

    (a) identical

    (b) an exact transposition

    (c) the same contour with different pitches

    (d) the same rhythm with different pitches

13. The excerpt concludes on which chord?

    (a) i (b) iv (c) V (d) VI

14. (a) Conduct the hypermeter as you listen to the conclusion of part 3. Is the phrase rhythm (1) regular or (2) irregular?

    (b) If your answer was *irregular,* briefly describe the nature of the phrase expansion.

CHAPTER 32

Sonata, Sonatina, and Concerto

In this chapter you'll learn to:

- Aurally understand the organization of an entire sonata-form movement
- Anticipate typical tonal structures in sonata-form movements
- Associate themes with tonal areas
- Define phrase structures within large formal areas

Preparatory Listening

Complete the *Try It* dictations to review the following concepts and skills:

- Determining the solfège syllables or scale-degree numbers for the soprano and bass of model SATB phrases that present a variety of harmonic sequences
- Converting solfège syllables and scale-degree numbers to pitches and notating them on the staff
- Applying Roman numerals to show harmonic progressions
- Identifying sequences and linear intervallic patterns (LIPs) by type
- Determining the solfège syllables or scale-degree numbers for the soprano and bass of model SATB phrases that present the enharmonic reinterpretation of the Ger^{+6} chord, the V^{7} chord, and the vii^{o7} chord in modulations

Try It

Listen to model SATB phrases that are played once each. The key signature, meter signature, and first bass pitch are given.

- Focus on the bass line first, and notate its pitches.
- Beneath the bass pitches, write Roman numerals to identify each harmony; if more than one chord seems possible, write all the possibilities and choose the correct one after additional hearings.
- Focus last on the soprano, and utilize it to refine your chord choices.
- Above the top staff indicate the harmonic interval between the soprano and bass (e.g., 5-6).
- To the left of the grand staff identify the type of sequence (e.g., descending fifths)

NAME ______________________________

- Add bar lines including the double bar at the end.
- If you are working by yourself, sing each part aloud with solfège syllables, scale-degree numbers, and/or letter names.

1.

2.

3.

4.

Listen to model SATB phrases that are played once each. The key signature, meter signature, and first bass pitch are given.

- Focus on the bass line first, and notate its pitches.
- Beneath the bass pitches, write Roman numerals to identify each harmony; if more than one chord seems possible, write all the possibilities and choose the correct one after additional hearings.
- Focus last on the soprano, and utilize it to refine your chord choices.
- Indicate the starting and ending keys, and show the enharmonic reinterpretation of the Ger^{+6} chord, the V^{7} chord, or the vii^{o7} chord by providing a Roman numeral in both keys.
- Add bar lines, including the double bar at the end.
- If you are working by yourself, sing each part aloud with solfège syllables, scale-degree numbers, and/or letter names.

NAME ______________________________

Contextual Listening 32.1

In this CL exercise you will:

- Determine the broad formal elements of an entire movement from a piano sonata
- Identify cadences and phrase structures within sections
- Determine the solfège syllables or scale-degree numbers of the melody and bass, and convert this to notation on the staff
- Describe the relationships between phrases
- Identify sequences by type

Listen to a movement from a piano sonata, and complete the following exercises. Approximate timings are given to help you locate specific passages.

1. Which is the meter signature of this excerpt?

   (a) $\frac{2}{4}$ (b) $\frac{3}{4}$ (c) $\frac{6}{8}$ (d) $\frac{9}{8}$

Exercises 2-6 refer only to phrase 1 of the first theme group (FTG; 0"-14").

2. At the beginning of *the second half* of phrase 1 (5"), which describes the bass line?

   (a) rhythmic augmentation of melody (b) creates a pedal point

   (c) imitates the melody (d) Alberti bass

3. Which of the following is the cadential progression of phrase 1?

   (a) ii6-V7-I (b) IV-V-I (c) V^{6-5}_{4-3}-I (d) vi-V7-I

4. Use the workspace provided to capture phrase 1 of the first theme group.

   (a) Notate the rhythm of the melody for phrase 1 on the single-line staves in the meter you chose for question 1. Write the meter signature, and include bar lines. Beam notes to show beat grouping.

   (b) Below the single-line staves, and under each note, write the solfège syllables or scale-degree numbers for the melody of phrase 1.

   (c) Combine your answers to complete the notation of the pitches and rhythm of the melody for phrase 1. Begin on F4. Write the appropriate clefs, key signature, and meter signature.

   (d) Draw a bracket over melodic pitches 10-16 and label these pitches as motive x.

Workspace

Rhythm:

Melody:

Solfège syllables:
Scale-degree numbers:

Solfège syllables:
Scale-degree numbers:

Notation:

Phrases 2 and 3 of the first theme group feature dotted rhythms and a chordal texture. Exercises 5-9 refer only to these two phrases (15"-27").

5. Use the workspace provided to capture phrases 2 and 3 of the first theme group.
   (a) Notate the rhythm of the melody and bass for phrases 2 and 3 on the single-line staves in the meter your chose for question 1. Write the meter signature, and include bar lines. Beam notes to show beat grouping.
   (b) Below the single-line staves, and under each note, write the solfège syllables or scale-degree numbers for the melody and bass of phrases 2 and 3.
   (c) Combine your answers to complete the notation of the pitches and rhythm of the melody and bass for phrases 2 and 3. Begin on C6 and A4 respectively. Write the appropriate clefs, key signature, and meter signature.
   (d) Write the Roman numerals below the bass pitches.

NAME ______________________________

Workspace

Rhythm:

Melody:

Solfège syllables:

Scale-degree numbers:

Solfège syllables:

Scale-degree numbers:

Notation:

Rhythm:

Bass:

Solfège syllables:

Scale-degree numbers:

Solfège syllables:

Scale-degree numbers:

6. Phrase 2 concludes with which cadence type?

   (a) HC (b) IAC (c) PAC (d) deceptive

7. Phrase 3 concludes with which cadence type?

   (a) HC (b) IAC (c) PAC (d) deceptive

8. Which is the phrase structure of phrases 2 and 3?
   (a) parallel period (b) contrasting period
   (c) parallel double period (d) independent phrases
9. Compared with phrase 2, by which means is phrase 3 expanded?
   (a) introduction (b) internal repetition
   (c) internal sequence (d) cadential extension

Exercises 10-14 refer only to the transition (27"-49").

10. The beginning of the transition tonicizes which key?
    (a) ii (b) IV (c) V (d) vi
11. In the key of your answer to question 15, which is the opening chord progression? The implied harmony of the anacrusis is shown in parentheses.
    (a) (V^{6}_{5})-I-V^{6}_{4}-I^{6} (b) (V^{6}_{5})-I-$vii^{\varnothing 6}_{5}$-I^{6} (c) (V^{6}_{5})-I-$vii^{\circ 6}_{4}$-i^{6} (d) (V^{6}_{5})-i-V^{4}_{3}-i^{6}
12. The arrival on V in the new key of the second theme is preceded by which of the following chords?
    (a) V: $ii^{\varnothing 4}_{3}$ (b) V: iv^{6} (c) V: V^{7}/V (d) V: A^{6}
13. The arrival on V in the new key is prolonged by which means?
    (a) plagal extension (b) repeated ii-V progressions
    (c) sequence (d) suspensions
14. Is the transition (a) dependent (based on FTG) or (b) independent (not based on FTG)?

Exercises 15-22 refer only to the second theme group, which is made up of four phrases (49"-1'08").

15. Use the workspace provided to capture the first two phrases of the second theme group.
    (a) Notate the rhythm of the melody for the first two phrases of the second theme on the single-line staves. Write the meter signature, and include bar lines. Beam notes to show beat grouping. Omit the grace notes.
    (b) Below the single-line staves, and under each note, write the solfège syllables or scale-degree numbers for the first two phrases of the second theme.
    (c) Combine your answers to complete the notation of the pitches and rhythm of the second theme beginning on E5. Write the appropriate clefs, key signature (and any accidentals), and meter signature.
    (d) Draw a bracket over melodic pitches 10-16 and label these pitches as motive x.

NAME ______________________________

Workspace

Rhythm:

Melody: ‖ ______________________________

Solfège syllables:

Scale-degree numbers:

‖ ______________________________

Solfège syllables:

Scale-degree numbers:

Notation:

16. Phrase 1 of the second theme group concludes with which cadence type?

    (a) HC (b) IAC (c) PAC (d) plagal

17. Phrase 2 of the second theme group concludes with which cadence type?

    (a) HC (b) IAC (c) PAC (d) plagal

18. How does phrase 3 relate to phrase 1 of the second theme? Phrase 3 is

    (a) a variation that features neighbor tones and two-against-three rhythm.

    (b) a variation that features passing tones and different harmonies.

    (c) a contrast that features similar melodic material, but different harmonies.

    (d) a contrast that features different melodic material, rhythm, and harmonies.

19. Phrase 4 of the second theme group concludes with which cadence type?

    (a) HC (b) IAC (c) PAC (d) plagal

20. Phrases 1-4 of the second theme comprise which larger structure(s)?

    (a) two parallel periods (b) two contrasting periods

    (c) one parallel double period (d) one contrasting double period

Eliding with the cadence of phrase 4 of the second theme, a transition leads to the closing theme group (1'08"). We can call this transition t^2. Exercises 21-26 refer only to t^2.

21. Which is the opening chord progression in the key of V?

    (a) I-ii-V7-i (b) I-V7-i-V7 (c) I-vi-ii6-V (d) I-vii°7-i-vii°7

22. A sequence leads into this transition's cadence. On which progression is the sequence based?

(a) descending fifths (b) descending thirds

(c) ascending 5-6 (d) ascending fifths

23. The sequence features which linear intervallic pattern (LIP)? (The LIP begins on chord 2 of the sequence.)

(a) 7-6 (b) 10-5 (c) 10-7 (d) 10-10

24. The end of the sequence features which rhythmic device?

(a) syncopation (b) hemiola

(c) two-against-three beat divisions (d) rhythmic augmentation of S's theme

25. Briefly describe how this sequence relates to motive x.

26. The end of this transition remains in the key of V. Its cadence is extended by many repetitions of which two cadential chords?

(a) iv^6–V (b) N^6–V (c) V^6_5/V–V (d) $vii^{\circ 7}$/V–V

Exercises 27-29 refer only to the closing theme group: CT (1'25"-1'53").

27. Use the workspace provided to capture phrase 1 of the closing theme group, CT.

(a) Notate the rhythm of the melody and bass for phrase 1 of the CT on the single-line staves. Write the meter signature, and include bar lines. Beam notes to show beat grouping.

(b) Below the single-line staves, and under each note, write the solfège syllables or scale-degree numbers for the melody and bass of the CT.

(c) Combine your answers to complete the notation of the pitches and rhythm of the melody and bass for the CT. Begin on A4 and F3 respectively. Write the appropriate clefs, key signature, and meter signature.

(d) Write the Roman numerals below the bass pitches.

NAME ______________________

Workspace

Rhythm:

Melody:

Solfège syllables:

Scale-degree numbers:

Notation:

Rhythm:

Bass:

Solfège syllables:

Scale-degree numbers:

28. Phrase 1 concludes with which cadence type?

    (a) HC (b) IAC (c) PAC (d) plagal

29. List all the ways in which phrase 2 of the CT is expanded.

Exercises 30-32 refer only to the development (3'50").

30. Use the workspace provided to capture phrase 1 of the development.
    (a) Notate the rhythm of the melody and bass for phrase 1 of the development on the single-line staves. Write the meter signature, and include bar lines. Beam notes to show beat grouping.
    (b) Below the single-line staves, and under each note, write the solfège syllables or scale-degree numbers for the melody and bass of the development.
    (c) Combine your answers to complete the notation of the pitches and rhythm of the melody and bass for the development. Begin on G4 and E3 respectively. Write the appropriate clefs, key signature (and any accidentals), and meter signature.
    (d) Write the Roman numerals below the bass pitches.

Workspace

Rhythm:

Melody:

Solfège syllables:

Scale-degree numbers:

Solfège syllables:

Scale-degree numbers:

Notation:

Rhythm:

Bass:

Solfège syllables:

Scale-degree numbers:

Solfège syllables:

Scale-degree numbers:

31. Phrase 1 concludes with which cadence type?

    (a) HC (b) IAC (c) PAC (d) deceptive

32. How does phrase 2 relate to phrase 1?

    (a) identical melody and harmony

    (b) melodic variation with identical harmony

    (c) harmonic variation with identical melody

    (d) different melody and harmony

The beginning of the retransition elides with the cadence of phrase 2 of the development. Exercises 33-39 refer only to the music of the retransition (4'12").

33. On which portion of the music is the beginning of the retransition based?
    (a) phrase 1 of FTG (first theme group) (b) t (the transition)
    (c) phrase 1 of STG (second theme group) (d) t^2 (transition between STG and CT)

34. During the retransition, a four-chord harmonic progression occurs twice—first in the key of ii, then in the key of vi. Which of the following is that progression?
    (a) ii°–i^6–V^6–i (b) V^6_4–i^6–$vii^{\circ 7}$–i (c) $vii^{\circ 6}$–i^6–$vii^{\circ 7}$–i (d) $vii^{\circ 6}_5$–i^6–V^6_5–i

35. Which are the two chords at the cadence of the retransition?
    (a) vi: ii^6–V (b) vi: iv^6–V (c) vi: It^6–V (d) vi: N^6–V

The final exercises refer only to the recapitulation (4'44").

36. Compare the first theme group (FTG) of the recapitulation with FTG in the exposition. Which describes FTG in the recapitulation?
    (a) It is identical to FTG in the exposition.
    (b) It has same beginning, but the end is truncated.
    (c) The beginning is truncated, but the end is the same.
    (d) Each part of FTG is truncated.

37. Compare the transition (t) in the recapitulation with t in the exposition. Which describes t in the recapitulation?
    (a) It is identical to t in the exposition. (b) It is the same length, but cadences on V.
    (c) It is longer and cadences on V. (d) It contains a descending-fifth sequence.

38. Compare the second theme group (STG) in the recapitulation with STG in the exposition. Which describes STG in the recapitulation?
    (a) It is transposed to the tonic. (b) The second half is varied.
    (c) It is same length. (d) All of the above.

39. Beginning with t^2, the transition to the closing theme group, compare the entire end of the recapitulation with the end of the exposition. Which does *not* occur?
    (a) The transition to the CT (t^2) is longer.
    (b) The music of the CT is transposed to the tonic.
    (c) The CT includes the same melody and harmony.
    (d) The CT includes a codetta.

CHAPTER 33

Rondo, Sonata-Rondo, and Large Ternary

In this chapter you'll learn to:

- Aurally understand the organization of composite ternary and rondo forms
- Anticipate typical tonal structures in rondos and ternary forms
- Associate themes with tonal areas
- Define phrase structures within large formal areas

Preparatory Listening

Complete the *Try It* dictations to review the following concepts and skills:

- Identifying seventh chords that contain altered pitches
- Notating short jazz and blues riffs

Try It

Listen to isolated tonic-, dominant-, and predominant-function harmonies related to the key of C, each of which is played once. Notate each harmony on the grand staff and supply the correct lead-sheet chord symbol. The exercises may include chords with extensions (added sixth and ninth chords); mixture chords and diminished sevenths; chords with suspensions (sus chords); and chords with altered fifths. The bass pitches are given.

- Focus on the bass note and silently arpeggiate through the chord; this might require that you arpeggiate up to the thirteenth of the chord!
- To determine altered pitches, compare the notes you hear with the diatonic pitches that would normally appear in the chord.
- Consider the quality of a root-position chord that would normally occur above each bass note.
- If you are working by yourself, sing each part aloud with solfège syllables, scale-degree numbers, and/or letter names.

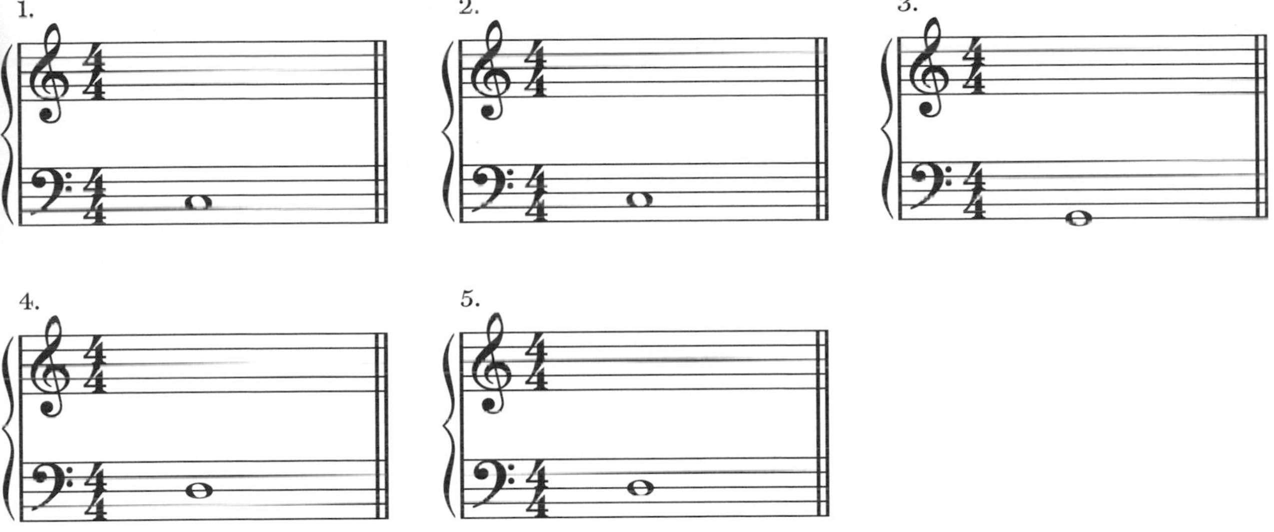

Listen to short ii-V-I progressions related to the key of C major or C minor, each of which is played once. For each of the three chords, notate the bass and soprano lines, then determine chord quality and any extensions, alterations, or mixture. Notate the upper voices in the treble clef. The first bass pitch is given.

- Focus on the bass line first, and notate its pitches.
- Above the top staff write letter names to indicate chord roots.
- Focus last on the soprano, and utilize it to refine your chord choices.

Listen to short "riffs" based on the blues scale, each of which is played once. Notate each riff in the indicated meter. The first note and key signature of each is given.

- Sing the notated first note and the blues scale associated with it.
- Notate the first and last notes first, then fill in the notes in between.

9.

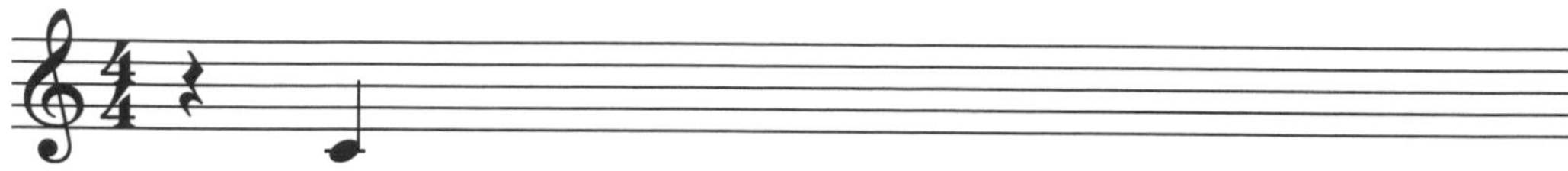

10.

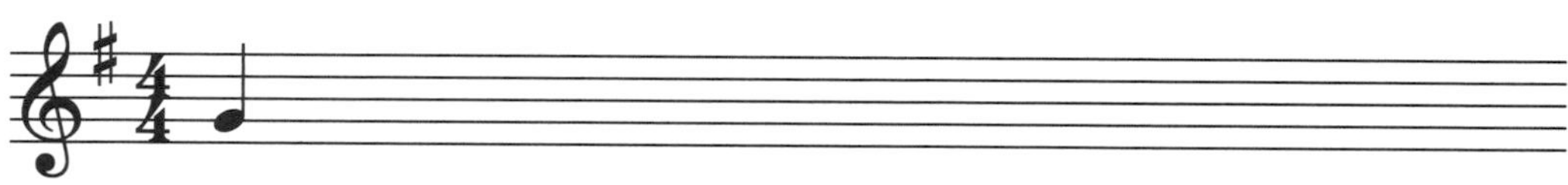

NAME ______________________________

Contextual Listening 33.1

In this CL exercise you will:

- Determine elements of a composite form as well as the internal design in a work for piano
- Explain your findings in prose

Listen to a work for piano and then write a brief paragraph that summarizes your answers to the following questions. Illustrate your paragraph with a diagram of the form; write design letters that represent all sections.

- Is the form ternary or rounded binary? List substantive musical reasons for your decision.
- Is the form a composite form? If so, what is the form of each individual section?
- Is the example sectional or continuous?
- If the form is binary, are its sections balanced?

Rondo

The plan of a rondo is simple: a refrain alternates with contrasting sections. Typical rondo designs are **A B A C A** and **A B A C A D** (or **B**) **A**.

	A	**B (C, D)**		**A**		
‖:	Refrain	Contrasting section	:‖	Refrain	Coda (optional)	‖
	(usually two or three repetitions)					

The character of rondos is often spirited and their tempos are often quick. Compared with the refrain, the contrasting sections are usually in a different key or mode (such as the parallel minor) and have different melodic ideas.

Rondos may be composite forms; for example, the refrain might be a binary form. Recurrences of the refrain may be abbreviated. Some rondos include retransitional passages that lead back to the tonic-key refrain. Rondos often conclude with a coda.

NAME ______________________________

Contextual Listening 33.2

In this CL exercise you will:

- Determine the sectional division of a rondo
- Associate letter names to sections
- Convey your musical conclusions in prose

Listen to a work for piano, and write a brief paragraph that summarizes your answers to the questions. Illustrate your paragraph with a diagram of the form; write design letters that represent all of the sections.

Strategies: If you hear an exact repetition of the section, that means that it is *one* section, not two. To hear the contrasting section(s) listen for both (1) a change of key, and (2) a change of the thematic idea.

1. The piece is divided into how many sections?

   (a) 3 (b) 4 (c) 5 (d) 7

2. Which is the piece's section design:

   (a) **A B A′** (b) **A B A′ B A″** (c) **A A′ B A″** (d) **A B A′ C A″ B A‴**

3. How do the sections differ in character from each other?

4. Is there a coda?

NAME ______________________________

Contextual Listening 33.3

In this CL exercise you will:

- Determine the meter of a rondo for piano
- Determine the sectional divisions and associate letter names with them
- Determine the solfège syllables or scale-degree numbers of the melody, and convert this to notation on the staff
- Identify cadences by type
- Identify nonchord tones by type

First listen to the entire movment of the piano sonata. As you listen, draw a diagram to help you remember the movement's structure.

1. Which is the meter signature of this excerpt?
   (a) $\frac{2}{4}$ (b) $\frac{3}{4}$ (c) $\frac{6}{8}$ (d) $\frac{9}{8}$

Exercises 2-8 refer only to the first segment, which is repeated (0"-15").

2. Segment 1 concludes with which type of cadence?
   (a) HC in the key of V (b) IAC in the key of I
   (c) PAC in the key of V (d) deceptive cadence in the key of I
3. Use the workspace provided to capture the excerpt.
   (a) Notate the rhythm of the melody on the single-line staves in the meter you chose for question 1. Write the meter signature, and include bar lines. Beam notes to show beat grouping.
   (b) Below the single-line staff, and under each note, write the solfège syllables or scale-degree numbers for the melody beginning on *sol* ($\hat{5}$). Begin in the tonic key. At the pivot chord, write the Roman numeral of the new key (your answer to question 2) underneath it. From that point on, write syllables *in the new key*.
   (c) Combine your answers to complete the notation of the pitches and rhythm of the melody beginning on A4. Write the appropriate clef, key signature (and any accidentals), and meter signature.

Workspace

Rhythm:

Melody:

Solfège syllables:
Scale-degree numbers:

Solfège syllables:
Scale-degree numbers:

Notation:

4. Melodic pitches 5 and 6 create which type of suspension? (Recall that suspensions are named according to the intervals above the bass pitch.)

   (a) 2-3 (b) 4-3 (c) 7-6 (d) 9-8

5. Melodic pitches 12 and 13 create which type of suspension?

   (a) 2-3 (b) 4-3 (c) 7-6 (d) 9-8

6. In the middle of the segment, the chromatic pitch is which type of embellishing tone?

   (a) passing (b) neighboring (c) suspension (d) anticipation

7. The end of the segment employs which type of $^6_4$ chord?

   (a) passing (b) neighboring (c) cadential (d) arpeggiated

Exercises 8-12 refer only to the section that immediately follows segment 1, which we will call an episode. The episode is repeated (15"-38").

8. Compare the beginning of the episode with the beginning of phrase 1. How is the initial motive of the episode related to the initial motive of phrase 1?

   (a) rhythmically augmented (b) transposed down one octave
   (c) inverted (d) wider melodic intervals

9. The first two chords of the episode create which harmonic progression?

   (a) V^6_5-I (b) vii$^{\circ 4}_{3}$-I^6 (c) V^4_3/ii-ii^6 (d) V^6_5/V-V

10. In the last phrase of the episode, the beginning of the melody is doubled in which of the following ways?

(a) thirds only (b) sixths only

(c) thirds, then sixths, then thirds (d) sixths, then thirds, then sixths

11. The last phrase of the episode employs which secondary dominant chord?

(a) V^4_3/iii (b) V^4_2/IV (c) V^6_5/V (d) V7/vi

12. The episode concludes with which of the following?

(a) a cadential $^6_4$ that leads to a PAC in the tonic

(b) a modulation to the relative minor key

(c) a descending-fifth sequence

(d) a textural inversion (the melody occurs in the lower part)

*Exercises 13-14 refer only to the **B** section, which immediately follows the episode and sounds in the parallel minor key (38"-1'20").*

13. Which is the opening chord progression of the **B** section?

(a) i-V7-VI (b) i-V^6_5-i (c) i-V^4_3-i6 (d) i-V^4_2-i6

14. The first half of the **B** section modulates to which key?

(a) III (b) IV (c) V (d) VI

Exercises 15-16 refer to the entire movement.

15. Which is the form of the movement's **A** section (0"-38")?

(a) simple binary (b) rounded binary

(c) simple ternary (d) composite ternary

16. Which is the form of the entire movement?

(a) rounded binary (b) ternary

(c) theme and variations (d) rondo

The Twentieth Century and Beyond

Modes, Scales, and Sets

In this chapter you'll learn to:

- Identify traditional tetrachords
- Combine tetrachords to create modes and scales
- Determine the scales and modes of twentieth-century songs and piano works
- Identify textures and compositional manipulations of themes and phrases
- Convert pitch-class integers and letter names to notation on the staff

Preparatory Listening

Complete the *Try It* dictations to review the following concepts and skills:

- Identifying tetrachord types (major, minor, Phrygian, harmonic, and whole-tone)
- Identifying scales and modes as combinations of tetrachord types

Try It

Traditional Tetrachords

Listen to traditional tetrachords presented in one-measure excerpts in common time. The first pitch is given. Notate the excerpt, and then identify the type of tetrachord (major, minor, Phrygian, harmonic, or whole-tone).

- For review, consider the number of half steps between each note of the tetrachord from lowest to highest:
  major: 2-2-1
  minor: 2-1-2
  Phrygian: 1-2-2
  harmonic: 1-3-1
  whole-tone: 2-2-2
- Sketch the rhythm above the staff.
- Focus aurally on the intervals between each successive note that you hear, and then sketch the pitches on the staff using sharps and flats where appropriate.
- Combine rhythm and pitches to complete the notation of the example.

NAME ______________________________

1.

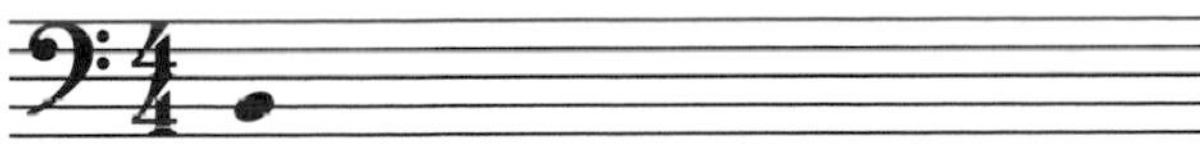

2.

3.

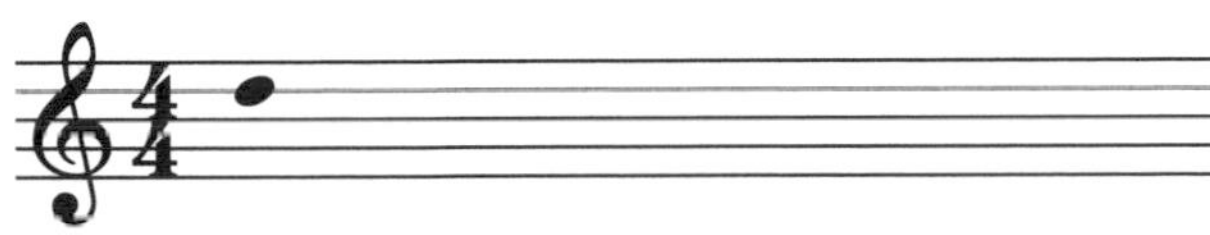

4.

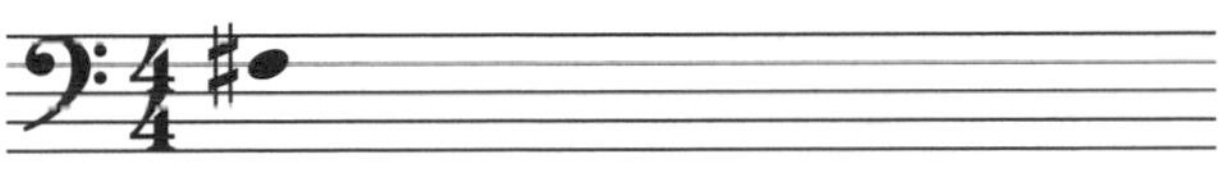

5.

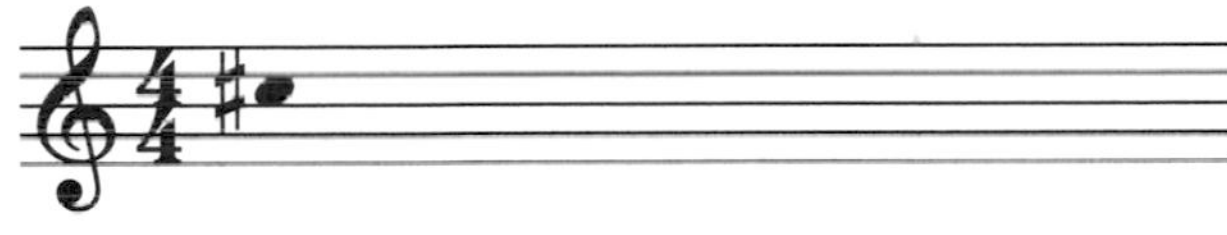

Modes and Scales

Listen to a traditional mode or scale presented in one-measure excerpts in common time. The first pitch is given. Notate the excerpt, then identify the two tetrachords from which the scale or mode is constructed: major, minor, Phrygian, harmonic, or whole-tone. Example: D4 is given, then E F G A B C D are played; Dorian mode = minor (tetrachord) + minor (tetrachord)

- Because the rhythm in each example is simple, notate pitches and rhythm at the same time in an ascending eighth-note scale.
- Notate any necessary sharps and flats to create the patterns that you have identified.
- Listen to the example again to internalize the collective sound and character of each scale or mode.

6.

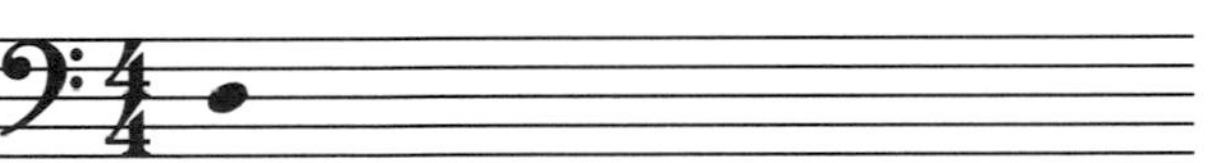

7.

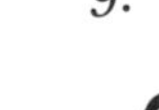

8.

9.

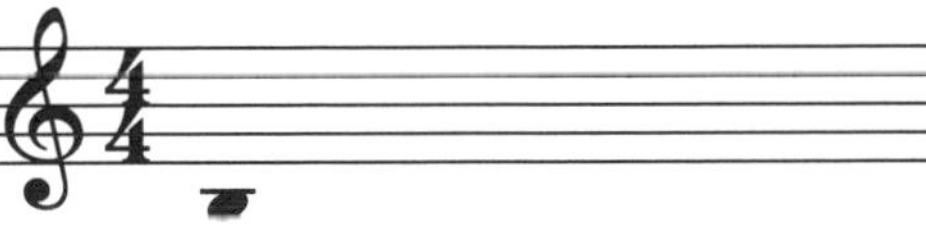

10.

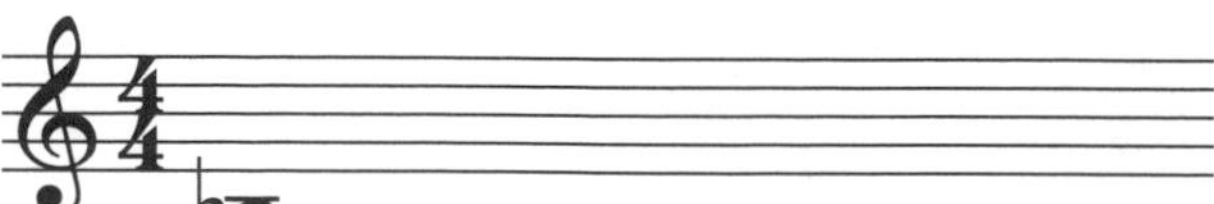

11.

12.

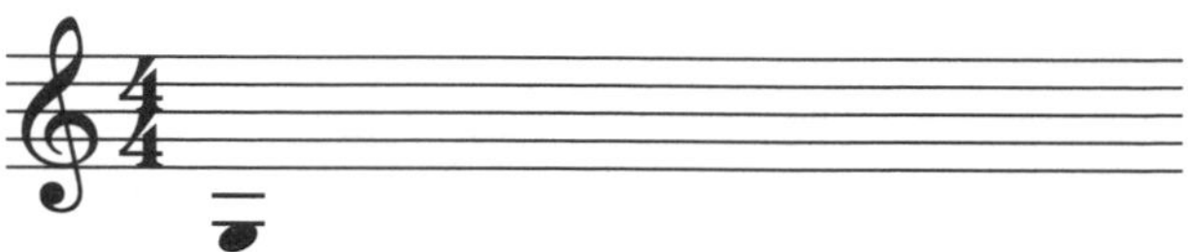

NAME ____________________

Contextual Listening 34.1

In this CL exercise you will:

- Identify the meter of a work for piano
- Identify the texture of the two parts
- Identify the scale on which the excerpt is based
- Convert pitch-class integers and letter names to notation on the staff

Listen to fourteen complete measures from a piano work, and complete the following exercises.

1. Which term represents the texture of the excerpt?

   (a) monophony (b) chordal homophony

   (c) nonimitative polyphony (d) imitative polyphony

2. Which is the meter signature of this excerpt?

   (a) $\frac{2}{8}$ (b) $\frac{3}{8}$ (c) $\frac{4}{8}$ (d) $\frac{5}{8}$

3. The excerpt begins with an introduction followed by two phrases. Compared with phrase 1, phrase 2:

   (a) begins and ends the same. (b) begins the same but ends differently.

   (c) begins differently but ends the same. (d) begins and ends differently.

4. On which collection is the excerpt based? To answer this question, first sing each of the possibilities below, and then compare these to the bass line of the excerpt.

   (a) Mixolydian mode (b) pentatonic

   (c) whole-tone (d) octatonic

5. Use the workspace provided to capture the excerpt.

   (a) Notate the rhythm of the melody and bass line on the single-line staves in the meter you chose for question 2. Write the meter signature, and include bar lines. Beam notes to show beat grouping.

   (b) Below the single-line staff, and under each note, write the pitch-class integers of the melody and bass using *t* for B♭ and *e* for B♮. For the melody, begin with 9 (A3) preceded by a grace note 2 (D4); begin the bass with 2 (D3).

   (c) Combine your answers to complete the notation of the pitches and rhythm of the melody and bass. Include the appropriate clef, meter signature, and accidentals. Beam your notes to show phrase beginnings and endings even if this conflicts with the meter.

Workspace

Rhythm:

Melody:

Pitch-class integers:

Pitch-class integers:

Notation:

Rhythm:

Bass:

Pitch-class integers:

Pitch-class integers:

NAME ______________________________

Contextual Listening 34.2

In this CL exercise you will:

- Identify the meter of a twentieth-century art song
- Identify the scale on which the excerpt is based
- Identify arpeggiated triad types
- Identify pitch intervals and contour between melodic pitches
- Notate the melody

Listen to a brief excerpt from an art song, and complete the following exercises.

1. On which scale is this excerpt based?

   (a) pentatonic (b) octatonic (c) whole-tone (d) Lydian

2. Which of these represents the meter of this excerpt?

   (a) simple triple (b) simple quadruple

   (c) compound duple (d) compound triple

3. In the vocal line, which is the quality of the arpeggiated triads?

   (a) major (b) minor (c) augmented (d) diminished

4. Use the workspace provided to capture the excerpt.

   (a) Notate the rhythm of the melody on the single-line staves in the meter you chose for question 2. Write the meter signature, and include bar lines. Beam notes to show beat grouping.

   (b) Below the single line staff, write the pitch-class integers of the vocal line using *t* for B♭ and *e* for B♮.

   (c) Combine your answers to complete the notation of the pitches and rhythm of the vocal melody beginning on E5. Include the appropriate clef, meter signature, and accidentals.

Workspace

Rhythm:

Melody: 

Pitch-class integers:

Notation:

5. At the beginning, which is a correct notation of the piano's pitches?

(a) 

(b) 

(c) 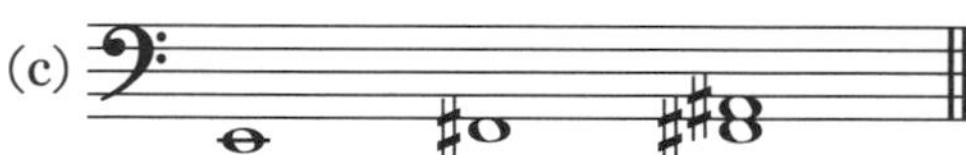

(d) 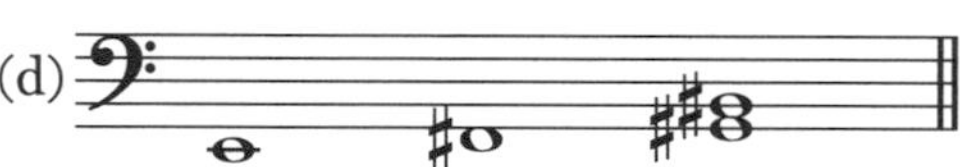

6. Briefly discuss the text painting of this excerpt.

NAME ______________________

Contextual Listening 34.3

In this CL exercise you will:

- Identify the scale on which a work for piano is based
- Name the type of repeated bass pattern
- Identify the texture of the excerpt
- Notate a melodic statement
- Describe the compositional treatment of a theme
- Identify the form of the excerpt

Listen several times to this composition for piano before completing the following exercises.

1. The beginning of the piece is based on which scale or mode?

   (a) Lydian mode (b) pentatonic (c) whole-tone (d) octatonic

2. The opening theme is doubled at which interval?

   (a) m3 (b) M3 (c) TT (d) m6

3. When the bass first enters, which of the following best represents the rhythm?

   (a) 

   (b) 

   (c) 

   (d) 

4. Which term describes the nature of the bass's repetition?

   (a) basso continuo (b) ostinato (c) sequence (d) passacaglia

5. Use the workspace provided to capture the excerpt.

   (a) Immediately after the first entrance of the bass, a second theme enters in the middle register (22″-52″). Notate the rhythm of the initial statement of this melody on the single-line staves in the meter shown in question 3.

   (b) Below the single-line staff, and under each note, write the pitch-class integers of the melody from 5(a) using *t* for B♭ and *e* for B♮. The first pitch is given on the following five-line staff. Ignore any octave doubling.

   (c) Combine your answers to complete the notation of the pitches and rhythm of the melody. The clef and first pitch are given.

Workspace

Rhythm:

Melody:

Pitch-class integers:

Pitch-class integers:

Notation:

4

6. The opening theme is heard six times at the beginning of the piece. Which best describes the texture during occurences 3-6?

   (a) chordal homophony (b) nonimitative polyphony

   (c) imitative polyphony (d) melody and accompaniment

7. After the initial statement of the second theme (which you notated in question 5), the *beginning* of this second theme is repeated and combined with the first theme (52″). Which of the following best describes the repetition at the beginning of theme 2?

   (a) exact (b) transposed

   (c) doubled using parallel chords (d) inverted fragment

8. After the repetition of theme 2 and just before the entrance of a third theme, the bass line consists of repeated pitches with long durations (1′16″). Listen several times to the beginning of the bass line (recall question 3; 16″), and compare these two places. How is the latter bass line related to the original statement of the bass line?

   (a) rhythmic augmentation (b) rhythmic diminution

   (c) transposition (d) inversion

9. At 2′23″, there is a change of character and tempo. On which scale is this new section based?

   (a) major (b) natural (descending melodic) minor

   (c) Phrygian mode (d) pentatonic

10. Which of the following is the role of the bass line throughout the composition?

(a) It has no consistent role.

(b) It serves as a pedal point.

(c) It defines the tonal centers of each section.

(d) It moves in contrary motion to the highest part.

11. Which is the form of the composition? Refer to your answers to previous questions to help you decide.

(a) simple binary (b) ternary (c) sonata (d) rondo

CHAPTER 35

Rhythm, Meter, and Form After 1900

In this chapter you'll learn to:

- Determine nontraditional meter signatures in early-twentieth-century works
- Identify combined meters
- Notate pitch-class collections in asymmetric meters
- Determine the scales and modes of instrumental and vocal works
- Identify the instruments in a work for wind instruments

Preparatory Listening

Complete the *Try It* dictations to review the following concepts and skills:

- Aurally identifying composite asymmetric meters
- Notating sets, scales, and modes in asymmetric meters

Try It

Asymmetric Meters

The following exercises present unordered pitch-class collections realized in two full measures in asymmetric meters. The shortest value is an eighth note. Each answer key represents one solution; others may be possible. The primary purpose of these exercises is to reinforce rhythmic and metric concepts, but, in doing so, you will also review pitch-class sets, scales, and modes. Although additional information is provided in the answer keys, just focus on the rhythm and pitches for now.

- Listen to the example several times to determine a repeated grouping of strong and weak notes.
- Write a composite eighth-note meter signature, for example $\frac{3+2+2}{8}$.
- Sketch the rhythm above the staff, using beams to show the groupings that you hear, and indicate the bar line between the two measures.
- Sketch the pitches on the staff as you listen for repeated notes and patterns.
- Combine rhythm and pitches to complete the notation of the example.

NAME ______________________________

1.

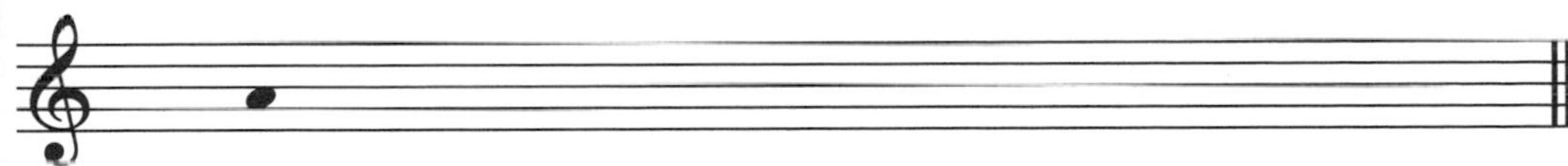

2.

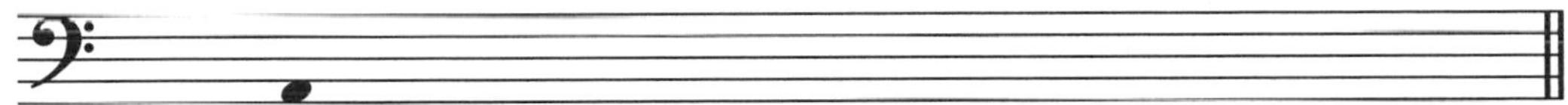

3.

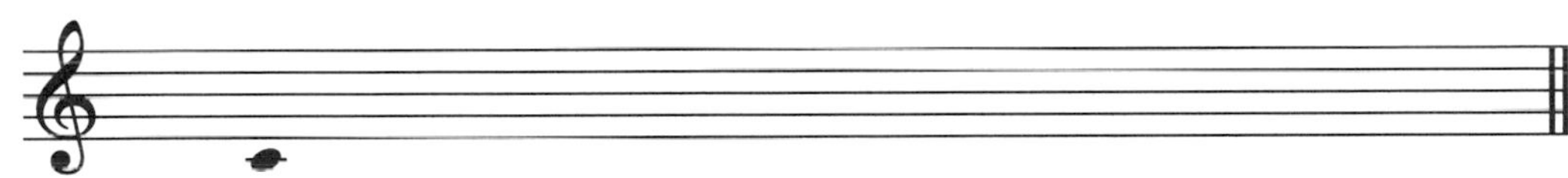

4.

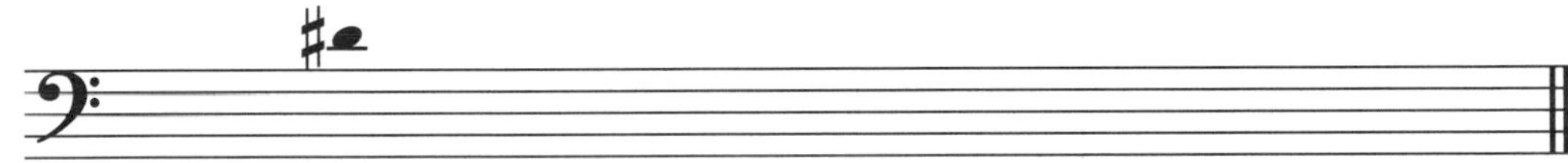

5.

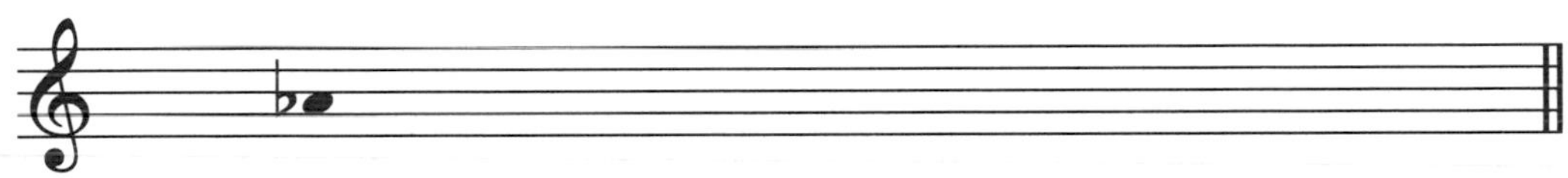

Changing Meters

Beginning with the given pitch, notate the rhythm and pitches of the example using changing meters. The shortest value is an eighth note.

- Listen to the example several times to determine two distinct meters and write appropriate meter signatures at the beginning of each measure.
- Sketch the rhythm above the staff, using beams to show the groupings that you hear.
- Sketch the pitches on the staff as you listen for repeated notes and patterns.
- Combine rhythm and pitches to complete the notation of the example.

6.

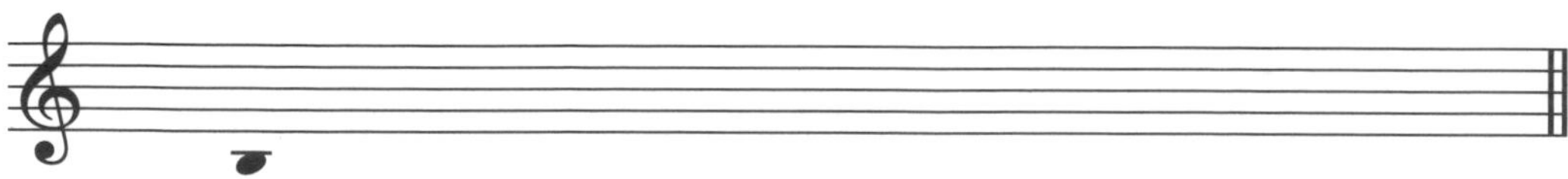

7.

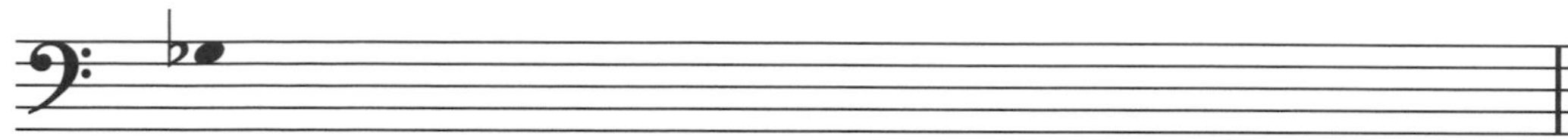

8.

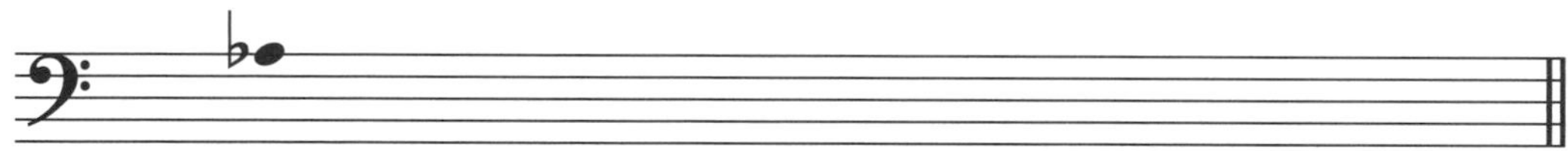

9.

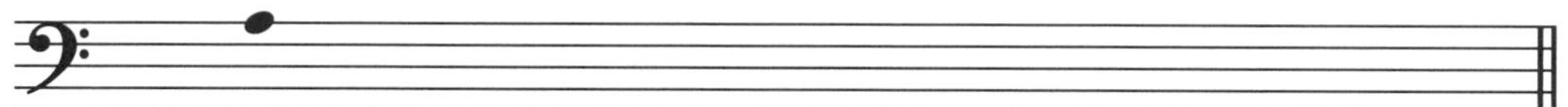

10.

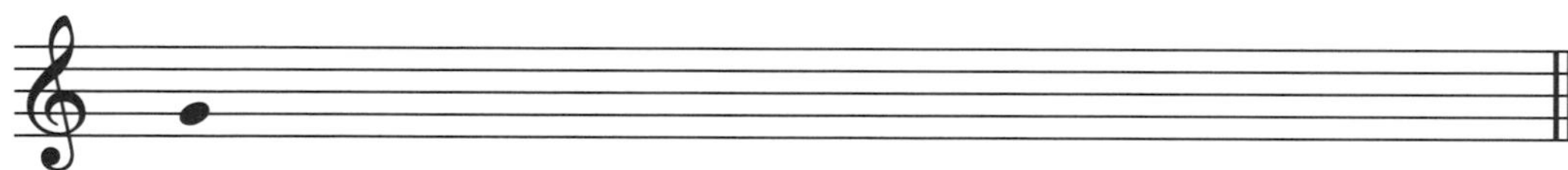

NAME ______________________

Contextual Listening 35.1

In this CL exercise you will:

- Identify the meter of a folk song and notate its rhythm
- Identify the scale or mode on which the excerpt is based
- Determine the solfège syllables or scale-degree numbers of the melody, and convert this to notation on the staff

Listen to an excerpt from a folk song, and complete the following exercises.

1. Use the workspace provided to capture the excerpt.
   (a) Notate the rhythm of the melody on the single-line staff. Each segment fits within one measure of a single meter signature. Choose a meter signature, and include bar lines. Beam notes to show beat grouping.
   (b) Below the single-line staff, and under each note, write the solfège syllables or scale-degree numbers beginning on *sol* ($\hat{5}$).
   (c) Combine your answers to complete the notation of the pitches and rhythm of the melody beginning on D5. Write the appropriate clef, key signature, and meter signature.

Workspace

Rhythm:

Melody:

Solfège syllables:
Scale-degree numbers:

Solfège syllables:
Scale-degree numbers:

Notation:

2. The melodic pitches might belong to all of the following scales or modes *except*
   (a) natural minor. (b) Dorian. (c) Phrygian. (d) Aeolian.

NAME ______________________________

Contextual Listening 35.2

In this CL exercise you will:

- Group phrase segments of a choral work into asymmetric measures
- Identify cadences and suspensions
- Determine the solfège syllables or scale-degree numbers of the melody, and convert this to notation on the staff
- Describe the phrase design

Listen to an excerpt from a carol, and complete the following exercises.

1. Use the workspace provided to capture the excerpt.
   (a) Segments 1-2 end with the word "sprung." Notate the rhythm of these two segments on the single-line staff. Each segment fits within one measure of a single meter signature. Choose a meter signature, and include bar lines. Beam notes to show beat grouping.
   (b) Below the single-line staff, and under each note, write the solfège syllables or scale-degree numbers of segments 1-2 beginning on *sol* ($\hat{5}$).
   (c) Combine your answers to complete the notation of the pitches and rhythm of segments 1-2 beginning on C5. Write the appropriate clef, key signature, and meter signature.

Workspace

Rhythm:

Melody:

Solfège syllables:
Scale-degree numbers:

Notation:

2. Segment 1 concludes with which type of cadence?
   (a) perfect authentic (b) imperfect authentic (c) half (d) deceptive
3. The dissonant suspensions near the end of segment 2 are of which type?
   (a) 2-3 (b) 4-3 (c) 7-6 (d) 9-8
4. Segment 2 concludes with which type of cadence?
   (a) perfect authentic (b) imperfect authentic (c) half (d) deceptive
5. Which is the best phrase design for the entire excerpt?
   (a) **‖: a :‖ b ‖: a′ :‖** (b) **‖: a b :‖ c ‖: a′ b :‖**
   (c) **a b a c a b a** (d) **a b a c a d a**

NAME ______________________________

Contextual Listening 35.3

In this CL exercise you will:

- Identify the instruments of a work for wind instruments
- Identify changing meter signatures by grouping notes into strong and weak beats
- Describe how statements of the theme relate to each other
- Identify cadences
- Determine the solfège syllables or scale-degree numbers of the initial theme, and convert this to notation on the staff
- Place the work in historical context

Listen to an excerpt from a work for wind instruments, and complete the following exercises.

1. The excerpt begins with which two melodic pitch intervals?

   (a) m3, M7 (b) m3, m7 (c) M3, M7 (d) M3, m7

2. Which instruments are in the ensemble?

   (a) oboe, flute, saxophone, bass clarinet, horn, trumpet, and trombones

   (b) oboes, flutes, clarinet, bassoon, trumpet, and trombone

   (c) flute, clarinet, bassoons, trumpets, and trombones

   (d) flute, clarinets, bass clarinet, trumpets, trombone, and tuba

The excerpt begins with a trumpet theme, which returns several times during the excerpt.

3. Use the workspace provided to capture the excerpt.

   (a) Notate the rhythm of the theme's first statement. Start without a meter, writing note heads only, and then write "↓" and "↑" above pitches to show the accented and unaccented beats in the melody. Place bar lines before each "↓" mark. The quarter note is the initial beat unit. Count the number of eighth notes between bar lines to determine the meter signature of each measure.

   (b) Below the single-line staff, and under each note, write the solfège syllables or scale-degree numbers beginning on *do* ($\hat{1}$).

   (c) Combine your answers to complete the notation of the pitches and rhythm of the melody beginning on E♭5. Write the appropriate clef, key signature, and meter signatures.

Workspace

Rhythm:

Melody:

Solfège syllables:
Scale-degree numbers:

Solfège syllables:
Scale-degree numbers:

Notation:

4. How does the third statement of the theme relate to the second? The third statement
   (a) follows it in canon. (b) is a melodic inversion.
   (c) is a rhythmic augmentation. (d) is a rhythmic diminution.
5. Beginning with its fourth statement, the theme is developed in all of the following ways *except* which of the following?
   (a) The opening pitch intervals are larger.
   (b) Only the initial portion is performed.
   (c) It is sequenced down by step.
   (d) It is now in compound meter.
6. The final cadence of the excerpt features which of the following?
   (a) a IV-I progression (b) mode mixture (minor tonic)
   (c) an augmented-sixth chord (d) a Phrygian resolution
7. Which articulation is heard throughout the excerpt?
   (a) legato (b) slurs (c) staccato (d) pizzicato
8. This excerpt is a parody of the music of which earlier period?
   (a) Renaissance (b) Baroque (c) Classical (d) Romantic

Music Analysis with Sets

NAME ______________________________

In this chapter you'll learn to:

- Determine the scales and modes of twentieth-century instrumental and choral works
- Identify textures and compositional manipulations of themes and phrases
- Transpose melodies for instruments notated in different clefs
- Determine pitch classes and letter names, and convert this to notation on the staff
- Determine the normal order and interval-class vector of a set

Preparatory Listening

Complete the *Try It* dictations to review the following concepts and skills:

- Aurally identifying trichords and notating them on the staff
- Determining the normal order and interval vectors of trichords

Try It

The trichord's first pitch is given. Notate all three pitches; enharmonic equivalents are equally correct. What is the set's normal order? Although additional information is provided in the answer keys, just focus on the normal order for now.

- Listen to the example and sketch its contour above the staff.
- Because the rhythm in each is example is simple, notate pitches and rhythm at the same time with beamed eighth notes.
- Determine the normal order using a separate sheet of manuscript paper.
- To the right of each example, write the normal order using this format: {___ ___ ___}
- To the right of each example, write its ic vector using this format: [______________] (no spaces between interval classes)

1.

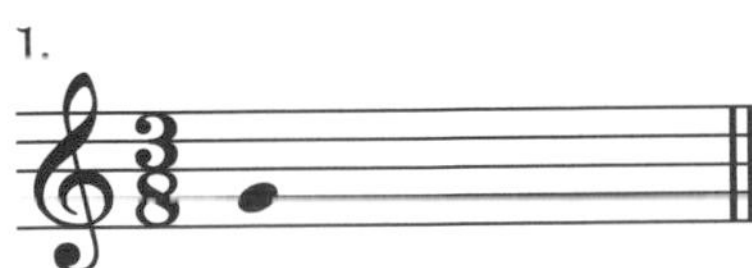

2.

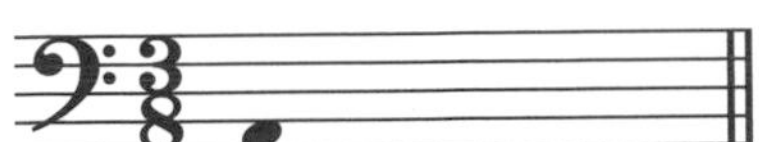

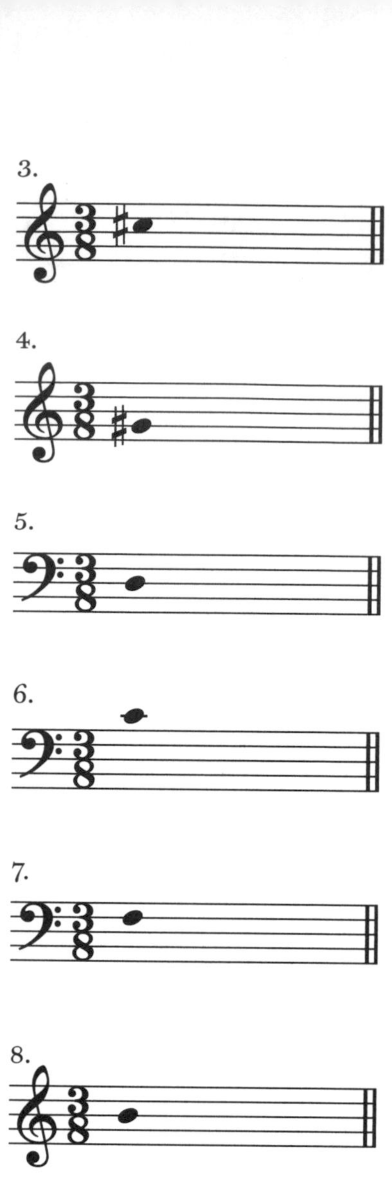

8.

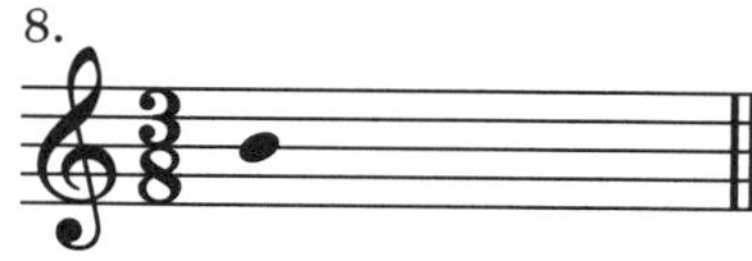

9.

10.

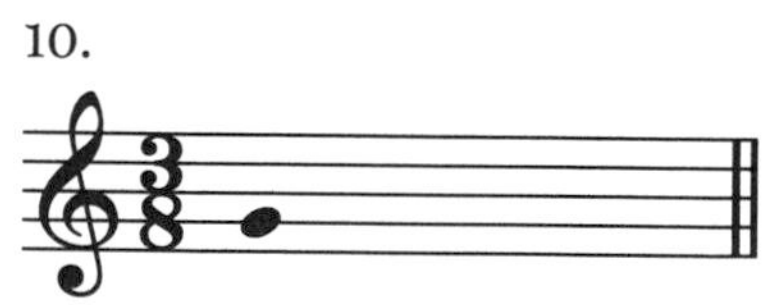

11.

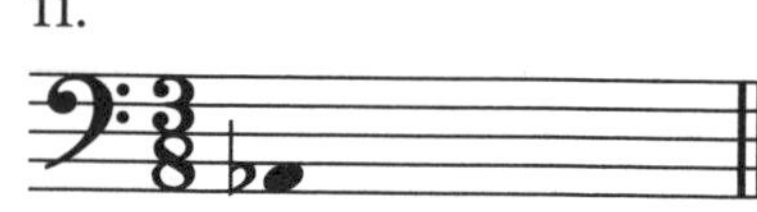

12.

NAME ______________________________

Contextual Listening 36.1

In this CL exercise you will:

- Identify the meter of a work for piano
- Identify the texture
- Identify tetrachords of the scale on which the excerpt is based
- Identify the final cadence by type
- Determine pitch classes and letter names, and convert this to notation on the staff

Listen to a piano work that is based on a folk melody, and complete the following exercises.

1. Which is the meter signature for this excerpt?

   (a) $\frac{2}{4}$ (b) $\frac{3}{4}$ (c) $\frac{6}{8}$ (d) $\frac{9}{8}$

2. Which is the texture of the excerpt?

   (a) imitative counterpoint (b) nonimitative counterpoint

   (c) melody and accompaniment (d) chordal homophony

3. Use the workspace provided to capture the excerpt.

   (a) Notate the rhythm of the melody on the single-line staves in the meter you chose for question 1. Write the meter signature, and include bar lines. Beam notes to show beat grouping.

   (b) Below the single-line staff, and under each note, write the pitch classes or letter names of the melody beginning on 9 (A).

   (c) The melody is doubled at the octave. Combine your answers to complete the notation of the pitches and rhythm of the upper voice beginning on A4. Write the appropriate clef, meter signature, and accidentals.

Workspace

Rhythm:

Melody:

Pitch classes:

Letter names:

Pitch classes:

Letter names:

Pitch classes:

Letter names:

Notation:

4. The end of the excerpt most resembles which traditional cadence? (Hint: Listen to the bass line.)

   (a) authentic (b) deceptive (c) plagal (d) Phrygian

5. Listen to the first half again, up to and including the punctuating chord. Notate each distinct pitch class you hear (in both the melody and bass). Rearrange these pitches and construct a scale that begins on B.

6. With which tetrachord does the scale begin?

   (a) major (b) minor (c) harmonic (d) Phrygian (natural minor)

7. With which tetrachord does the scale end?

   (a) major (b) minor (c) harmonic (d) Phrygian (natural minor)

NAME ______________________________

Contextual Listening 36.2

In this CL exercise you will:

- Identify the meter of a work for viola and piano
- Identify the scale on which the excerpt is based
- Determine pitch classes and letter names, and convert this to notation on the staff
- Transpose the work for alto saxophone

Listen to an excerpt from a chamber work, and complete the following exercises.

1. Which is the meter signature of this excerpt?

   (a) $\begin{smallmatrix}2\\4\end{smallmatrix}$ (b) $\begin{smallmatrix}3\\4\end{smallmatrix}$ (c) $\begin{smallmatrix}6\\8\end{smallmatrix}$ (d) $\begin{smallmatrix}9\\8\end{smallmatrix}$

2. On which type of scale is this excerpt based?

   (a) pentatonic (b) octatonic (c) whole-tone (d) Phrygian

3. At the end of each half of the excerpt, the viola sustains a long pitch. What is the quality of the chord that accompanies these sustained pitches?

   (a) major triad (b) augmented triad
   (c) major seventh chord (d) minor seventh chord

4. Use the workspace provided to capture the excerpt.

   (a) Notate the rhythm of the viola melody for the first half of the excerpt (to the first long sustained note) in the meter you chose for question 1. Write the meter signature, and include bar lines. Beam notes to show beat grouping.

   (b) Below the single-line staff, and under each note, write the pitch classes or letter names of the melody beginning on 9 (A).

   (c) Combine your answers to complete the notation of the pitches and rhythm of the viola melody beginning on A4 in treble clef (below middle C, switch to alto clef). Indicate all accidentals.

Workspace

Rhythm:

Melody:

Pitch classes:

Letter names:

Pitch classes:

Letter names:

Notation:

5. Transcribe the melody from question 4 for alto saxophone (up a M6). Begin on F♯5. Write the appropriate clef and accidentals.

6. After the first long sustained viola note, the melody you notated repeats, transposed to a higher pitch. Compared with the beginning, by what interval has the composer transposed the repetition?

   (a) M3 (b) P4 (c) TT (d) P5

NAME ______________________________

Contextual Listening 36.3

In this CL exercise you will:

- Identify functional relationships between chords in a work for piano
- Notate melodic pitches and reorder them into a familiar collection
- Determine pitch classes and letter names, and convert this to notation on the staff
- Identify scales and chord types

The following exercises are based on a work for piano. Listen to CL 36.3a, then complete exercises 1-6.

1. Which is a correct notation of chord 1?

(a) (b) (c) (d)

2. How is chord 2 related to chord 1?
   (a) subdominant chord
   (b) transposition of chord 1
   (c) chord members are from the same whole-tone scale
   (d) supplies the remaining pitches of the chromatic collection

3. Notate the pitches and rhythm of the melody. The first note is given.

4. Reorder the first five distinct pitch classes of the melody from question 3 into a pentachord that begins on B, and notate your answer.

5. What is the traditional name for the pentachord in question 4?
   (a) major (b) minor (c) harmonic (d) Phrygian (natural minor)

6. Which represents the pitch classes of this pentachord?
   (a) {e 0 3 4 6} (b) {e o 2 4 6} (c) {e 1 3 4 6} (d) {e 1 2 4 6}

Exercises 7-11 are based on another excerpt from the same work. CL 36.3b is the entire passage. CL 36.3c is the same passage without the parallel triads.

7. Notate the pitches and rhythm of the melody of this excerpt. (The melody is in the middle register.) The first note is given.

8. The melody's first four distinct pitch classes are from which tetrachord?

   (a) major (b) minor (c) harmonic (d) Phrygian (natural minor)

9. In the highest register, the parallel triads are of which quality?

   (a) major (b) minor (c) augmented (d) diminished

10. When considered together, the pitch classes of all four parallel triads belong to which scale?

    (a) whole-tone (b) pentatonic

    (c) octatonic (d) harmonic minor

11. The final chord is of which quality?

    (a) major triad (b) minor triad

    (c) major seventh (MM7) (d) minor seventh (mm7)

Sets and Set Classes

NAME ______________________

In this chapter you'll learn to:

- Identify the pitch classes of motives and themes
- Consider motivic pitches as unordered pitch-class sets
- Identify the normal order of motives and themes
- Analyze the interval content of motives and themes using an interval-class vector

Preparatory Listening

Complete the *Try It* dictations to review the following concepts and skills:

- Aurally identifying trichords and notating them on the staff
- Determining the normal order, prime form, set type, and interval vector of trichords

Try It

The trichords presented next also appeared in the previous chapter; the first pitch is given. Notate all three pitches; enharmonic equivalents are equally correct. To the right of each, complete the following.

- What is the set's normal order? { ___ ___ ___ }.
- What is its prime form? [___ ___ ___].
- What is its Forte number? (Consult the "Set-Class Table" appendix of the text.); for example, Forte SC 3-___
- What is its ic vector? [______________] (no spaces between interval classes)

1.

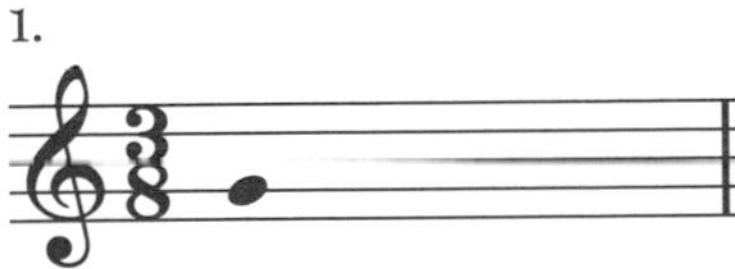

2.

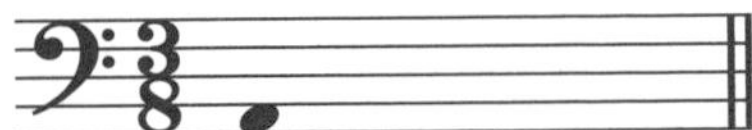

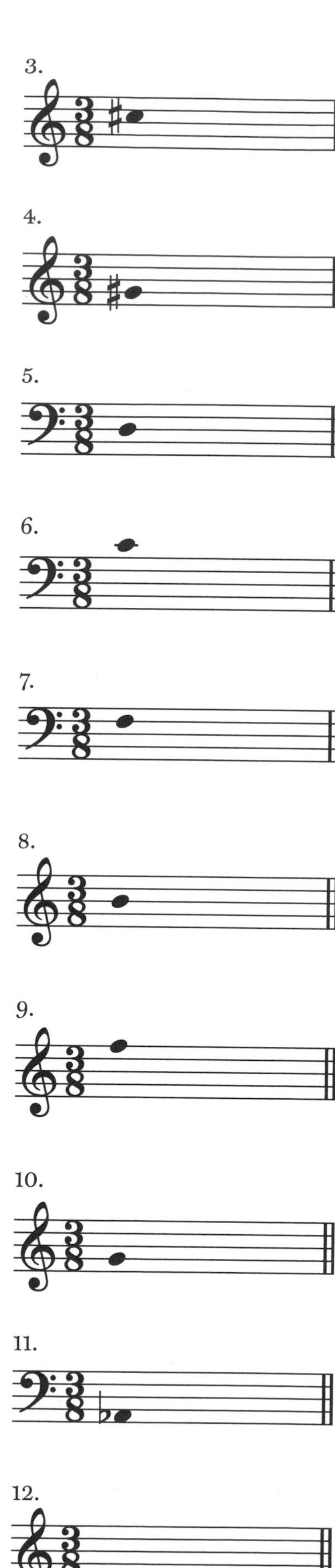
3.
4.
5.
6.
7.
8.
9.
10.
11.
12.

NAME ______________________________

Contextual Listening 37.1

In this CL exercise you will:

- Notate the melodic pitches of the theme from a twentieth-century chamber work
- Consider its pitches as an unordered set and place the pitch classes in normal order
- Analyze the interval content using an interval-class vector

Listen again to an excerpt of a chamber work heard in CL 36.2, and analyze the principal motive of the work.

1. Consider the viola's pitches 1-4 to be unordered pcset A. On the following staff, notate pcset A in ascending order. Beneath each pitch, write its pc integer.

2. Play and notate the four rotations of set A next. What is the normal order for set A? { ___ ___ ___ ___ }

3. Find the intervals between each pc in set A, and arrange them as an ic vector. The ic vector of set A is [___ ___ ___ ___ ___ ___].

4. What is interesting about this tetrachord's interval content?

NAME ______________________________

Contextual Listening 37.2

In this CL exercise you will:

- Notate the melodic pitches of the theme from an Impressionistic piano work
- Consider its pitches as an unordered set and place the pitch classes in normal order
- Analyze the interval content using an interval-class vector

Listen to a work you first studied in CL 34.3, and complete the following exercises.

1. Notate melodic pitches 1-7 on the staff. Begin on G♯5/A♭5. Enharmonic equivalents are acceptable.

2. Consider the distinct pcs of question 1 to be unordered pcset A. Notate these pitches on the following staff. Find the normal order and interval-class vector of set A.

   normal order { ___ ___ ___ ___ ___ ___ } ic vector [___ ___ ___ ___ ___ ___]

3. What is interesting about the interval content of this hexachord?

4. In the middle of the composition, the character changes and becomes more animated (2′23″). The composer has written a pentatonic scale that is played on the black keys of the piano. Notate the pitches of the "black-key" pentatonic scale on the following staff. Consider this pentatonic scale to be unordered pcset B. Find the normal order and interval-class vector of set B.

   normal order { ___ ___ ___ ___ ___ } ic vector [___ ___ ___ ___ ___ ___]

NAME ______________________________

Contextual Listening 37.3

In this CL exercise you will:

- Notate the melodic pitches of the theme from a twentieth-century piano work
- Consider its pitches as an unordered set and place the pitch classes in normal order
- Analyze the interval content using an interval-class vector

Listen to a work you first studied in CL 36.1 and complete the following exercises.

1. Begin on A4, and notate melodic pitches 1-13 on the following staff. Ignore the octave doubling. Enharmonic equivalents are acceptable.

2. Consider the distinct pcs in question 1 to be unordered pcset A. Notate these pitches on the following staff. Find the normal order and interval-class vector of set A.

   normal order { ___ ___ ___ ___ ___ ___ } ic vector [___ ___ ___ ___ ___ ___]

3. Consider melodic pitches 10-13 to be a subset of set A called set B. Notate these pitches on the following staff. Find the normal order and interval-class vector of set B.

   normal order { ___ ___ ___ ___ } ic vector [___ ___ ___ ___ ___ ___]

NAME ______________________________

Contextual Listening 37.4

In this CL exercise you will:

- Notate the pitches of chords from an Impressionistic piano work
- Consider its pitches as an unordered set and place the pitch classes in normal order
- Analyze the interval content of chords using interval-class vectors and identify their relationship to each other

The following exercises are based on a work for piano that you first studied in CL 36.3. Listen to CL 37.4a then complete exercises 1-4.

1. Chords 1 and 2 are shown next and are called sets A and B, respectively. Notate the distinct pitches of each set on the following staff. Find the normal order and ic vector for each set.

A normal order { __ __ __ __ __ } ic vector [__ __ __ __ __ __]

B normal order { __ __ __ __ __ } ic vector [__ __ __ __ __ __]

2. What is the relationship between sets A and B? Show how you determine their relationship.

3. Begin on F♯5, and notate melodic pitches 1-7. Ignore octave doubling. Enharmonic equivalents are acceptable.

4. Consider the distinct pcs of question 3 to be unordered pcset C. Notate these pitches on the staff below. Find the normal order and interval-class vector of set C.

C normal order { ___ ___ ___ ___ ___ } ic vector [___ ___ ___ ___ ___ ___]

Listen to another excerpt from the same work. CL 37.4b is the entire passage; CL 37.4c the same passage without the parallel triads.

5. Begin on G4, and notate melodic pitches 1-9 of this excerpt.

6. Consider the distinct pcs of question 5 to be unordered pcset D. Notate these pitches on the following staff. Find the normal order and interval-class vector of set D.

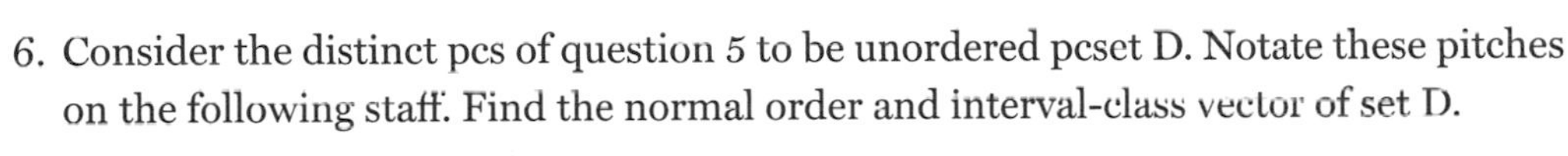

D normal order { ___ ___ ___ ___ } ic vector [___ ___ ___ ___ ___ ___]

7. Including melodic pitch 1, which is a correct notation of the first chord?

8. Consider the answer to question 7 to be unordered pcset E. Calculate the normal order and interval-class vector of set E.

E normal order { ___ ___ ___ ___ ___ } ic vector [___ ___ ___ ___ ___ ___]

9. What is the relationship between sets E and A? Show how you determine their relationship.

Ordered Sets and Serialism

In this chapter you'll learn to:

- Determine ordered segments in twentieth-century serial works
- Determine the serial relationships between segments
- Describe the compositional treatment of themes
- Identify scale and mode types
- Notate works by knowing the serial practices involved

Preparatory Listening

Complete the *Try It* dictations to review the following concepts and skills:

- Hearing relationships in pitch segments that have been manipulated through serial processes
- Notating pitch segments on the staff
- Determining the ordered pitch intervals and pitch-class intervals between adjacent notes of pitch segments

Try It

The following exercises present the identification and analysis of ordered segment P, followed by the identification of four segments related to P.

- Listen to the first example (a). This is ordered segment P, which begins with the given pitch.
- Notate all the pitches of P. Beneath each pitch, write its pc integer number.
- Calculate the ordered pitch intervals, then the pc intervals (pcis) between each note. Write these underneath and between each pc integer. Refer to this information when identifying transformations of P. Before proceeding check your work with the answer key.
- Listen to and notate all of the segments (b-e). Calculate the ordered pitch intervals and the pcis between each note.
- Compare the answer with your analysis of P. How does this segment relate to P? Is it another form of P, or is it some form of I, R, or RI?

NAME ______________________________

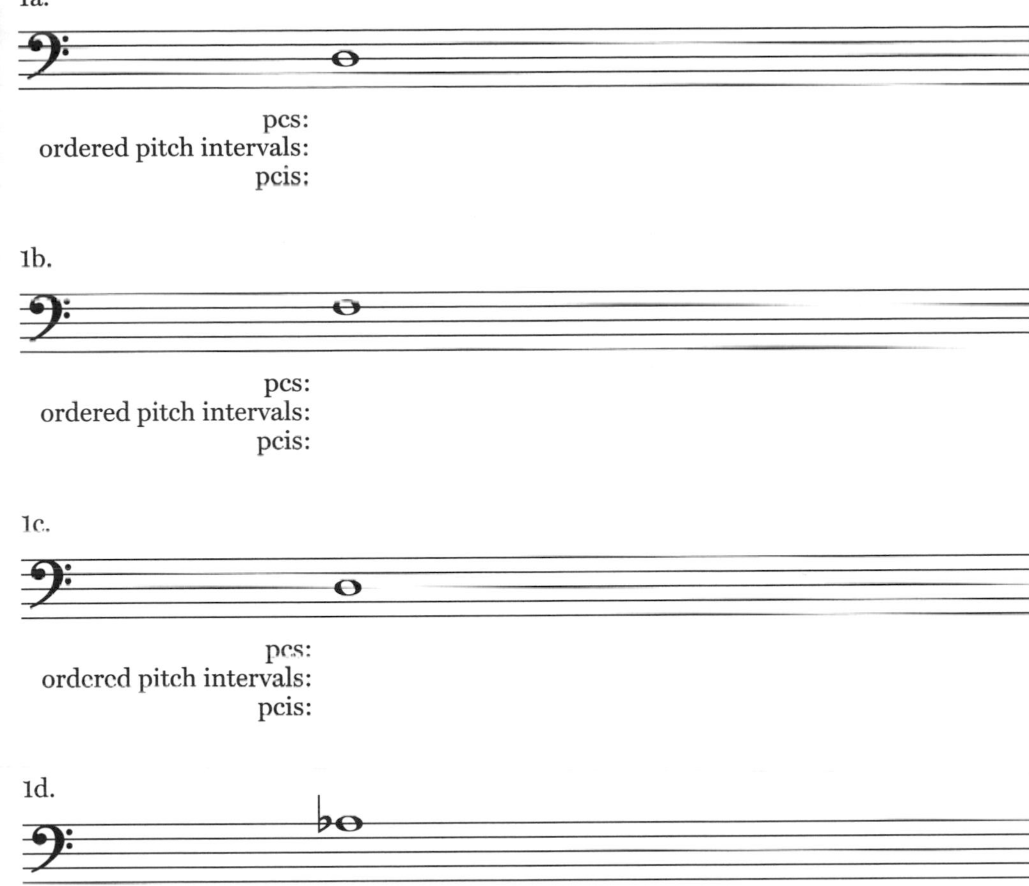

1a.

pcs:
ordered pitch intervals:
pcis:

1b.

pcs:
ordered pitch intervals:
pcis:

1c.

pcs:
ordered pitch intervals:
pcis:

1d.

pcs:
ordered pitch intervals:
pcis:

1e.

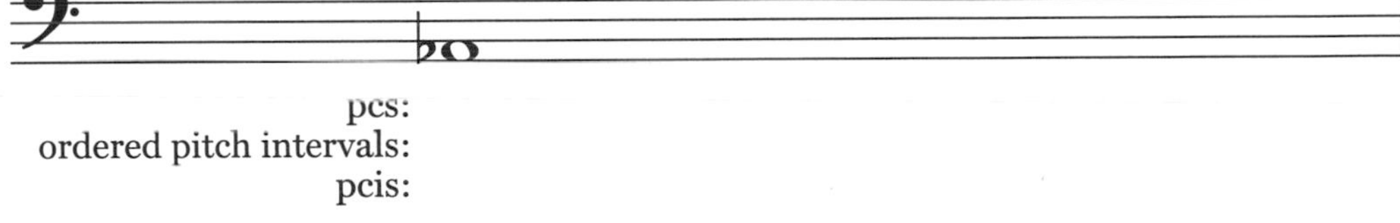

pcs:
ordered pitch intervals:
pcis:

NAME ______________________

Contextual Listening 38.1

In this CL exercise you will:

- Identify the meter of a twentieth-century piano work
- Segment its main theme and identify the pitch intervals between its successive pitches
- Consider the theme as an unordered pitch-class set and identify its normal order
- Analyze the interval content using an interval-class vector
- Identify scale and mode types
- Describe relationships between different statements of the theme

Listen to a work for piano, and complete the following exercises.

1. Which of these represents the meter at the beginning of this excerpt?
   (a) simple triple (b) simple quadruple
   (c) compound duple (d) compound triple

Exercises 2-6 are based only on the higher part.

2. (a) The theme consists of the first ten pitches in the higher part. *All later comparisons will be made to this initial statement of the theme.* Notate the pitches and rhythm of the theme next, and begin on A4. Write the appropriate clef, meter signature, and accidentals.

   (b) Label the first four pitches of the theme as segment 1 and the remaining six pitches as segment 2.

   (c) Write the pitch interval between each pair of successive pitches of the theme. Write the interval in semitones, and include + for *above* and – for *below*. This will help you listen for changes in the theme, such as melodic inversion.
   < ___ ___ ___ ___ ___ ___ ___ ___ ___ >

   (d) If we consider segment 1 to be an *unordered* pcset, what is its normal order? What are its Forte number and prime form? (To find Forte numbers, consult the appendix.)

   (e) Think of every possible way to create trichord subsets of segment 1. Notate these subsets next. To which set class do these subsets belong?

   (f) If we consider segment 2 to be an *unordered* pcset, what is its normal order? What are its Forte number and prime form?

3. How is the second statement of the theme varied?
   (a) The pitches change in segment 1. (b) The pitches change in segment 2.
   (c) The rhythm changes in segment 1. (d) The rhythm changes in segment 2.

4. How is the third statement of the theme related to the first statement?

(a) The pitches are transposed up a tritone. (b) There are more dotted rhythms.

(c) The melodic contour is inverted. (d) The rhythm is augmented.

5. Listen again, and compare the fourth statement (and those that immediately follow it) with the original statement of the theme. Which compositional device does the composer employ?

(a) fragmentation (b) melodic inversion

(c) rhythmic diminution (d) parallel chords

6. Beginning with the fourth statement and continuing through the ninth statement, the theme descends from the piece's highest pitch, B♭5. Starting on this B♭, notate just the *first* pitch of each of these entrances on the following staff.

7. To which scale do these initial pitches belong?

(a) pentatonic (b) whole-tone (c) harmonic minor (d) octatonic

8. The final statement of the theme features which process?

(a) The contour is inverted.

(b) Some pitches are rhythmically augmented.

(c) The order of segments 1 and 2 is reversed.

(d) The entire theme is heard in retrograde.

Listen to the piece again. Focus on the lower part and its relationship to the theme statements in the higher part.

9. The first entrance of the lower part is

(a) a rhythmic augmentation of the higher part.

(b) a rhythmic diminution of the higher part.

(c) an imitation of the higher part at the octave.

(d) a melodic inversion of the higher part.

10. The second entrance of the lower part is

(a) a melodic inversion of the higher part.

(b) an imitation of the higher part a M6 below.

(c) a rhythmic augmentation of the higher part.

(d) a fragmentation of the higher part.

11. The third entrance of the lower part is

(a) an imitation of the higher part a M9 below.

(b) a melodic inversion of the higher part.

(c) a rhythmic diminution of the higher part.

(d) a fragmentation of the higher part.

NAME ______________________________

Contextual Listening 38.2

In this CL exercise you will:

- Notate a two-part texture from a twelve-tone choral work
- Identify the pitch intervals between its successive pitches
- Determine the twelve-tone row on which the composition is based
- Construct a 12 × 12 row matrix

The dove descending breaks the air
With flame of incandescent terror,
Of which the tongues declare
The one discharge from sin and error.

Listen to the beginning of a twelve-tone composition for mixed chorus, in which only the women's voices are heard. Then complete the following exercises.

1. Notate the pitches and rhythm of both parts on the following staves in simple triple meter. The first pitches of each part are given. For help, listen to a piano reduction (CL 38.2a).

   Divide this task into steps.

   (a) Sketch the rhythm lightly in the staff, to guide you in placing the pitches.

   (b) Notate the interval succession to help you determine the pitches.

   (c) Confirm the melodic pitches by checking them against the harmonic pitch intervals.

   (d) Finally, transcribe the melodies onto the staff.

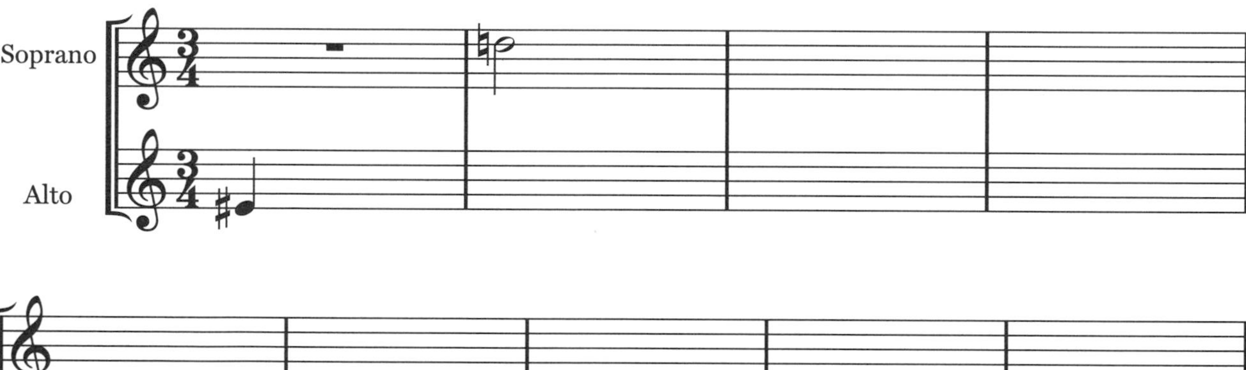

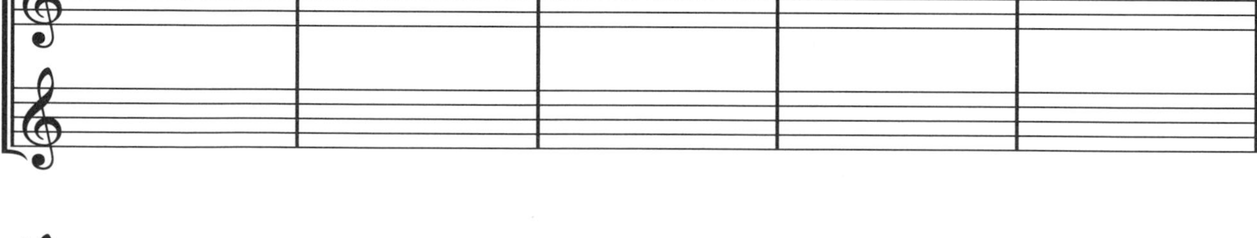

NAME ______________________________

2. Knowing that composers might choose P, I, R, and RI row forms, study your notation and see if the pitch relationships become apparent. Before examining the excerpt in detail, write a verbal description of how the composer treats his row.

3. (a) Notate the first twelve distinct pitches of the alto part on the following staff (to the text "The dove descending breaks the air"). Call these pitches P_5, meaning the row form that begins on pc 5.
   (b) Write the pc integer beneath each pitch.
   (c) Write the pc interval number between each successive pair of pc integers. This will help you compare this initial statement of the row with other statements.
   (d) Write the row order numbers, 1-12, above each pitch. This will help you find your location in the row.

4. (a) Notate the first twelve distinct pitches of the soprano part on the following staff ("The dove . . . terror").
   (b) Write the pc integer beneath each pitch.
   (c) Write the pc interval number between each successive pair of pc integers.
   (d) Write the row order numbers, 1-12, above each pitch.

   (e) How is this second row related to P_5, the original row? Use any of the information given to help you answer this question.

5. (a) Notate the last twelve distinct pitches of the soprano part on the following staff ("Of which . . . error"). This section begins immediately after the section you analyzed in question 4.
   (b) Write the pc integer beneath each pitch.
   (c) Write the pc interval number between each successive pair of pc integers.
   (d) Write the row order numbers, 1-12, above each pitch.

(e) How is this row related to P_5, the original row? Use any of the information given to help you answer this question.

6. (a) Notate the distinct pitches of the end of the alto part on the following staff ("Of which . . . error"). Note that there are only eleven pitches.
   (b) Write the pc integer beneath each pitch.
   (c) Write the pc interval number between each successive pair of pc integers.
   (d) Write the row order numbers, 1-11, above each pitch.

   (e) How is this row related to P_5, the original row? Use any of the information given to help you answer this question.

   (f) As the music continues beyond this excerpt, the altos sing the next pitch. With which pc would the altos begin their next phrase? Why?

7. (a) Examine the alto pitches in the middle of the excerpt ("air with flame of incandescent terror"). To which row form do they belong? (The row begins in the middle of the notes sung to "air.")

   (b) Compare your answer with that of question 3. How are the first two row statements in the alto part linked?

8. Create a 12 × 12 matrix based on the row. Notate the pcs with integers.
   (a) Transpose the first row (your answer to question 3) to begin on pc 0 by subtracting 5 from each element in the row.
   (b) Write P_0 in the top line of your matrix.
   (c) Write the I form of the row down the left column in the matrix. To find I, take the inverse of each pc in the top row.
   (d) Consider each pc in the left column the first pc of a new transposition of the row.
   (e) Make sure that the diagonal from top left to bottom right contains only zeros. Make sure each row or column includes one each of the twelve pc integers. (No pcs may be duplicated.)

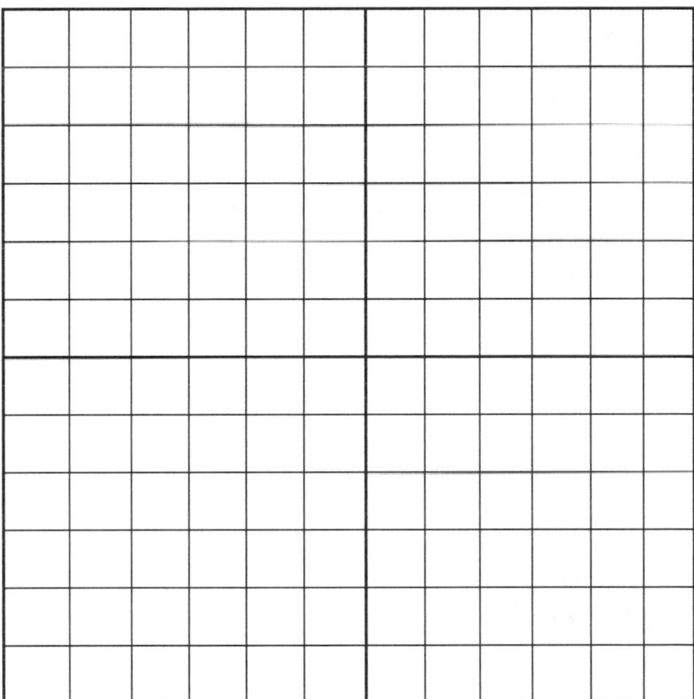

CHAPTER 39

Rhythm, Meter, and Form After 1945

In this chapter you'll learn to:

- Aurally identify and notate music written in polymeters and changing meters
- Identify relationships between musical phrases
- Create a 12 × 12 matrix for a twelve-tone composition
- Transpose twelve-tone rows

Preparatory Listening

Complete the *Try It* dictations to review the following concepts and skills:

- Aurally identifying polymeters
- Notating sets, scales, and modes in polymeters.

Try It

In each of the following exercises, the upper voice features one type of beat division and the lower voice another, which creates a simple example of polymeter.

- Listen to the example several times to determine a repeated grouping of strong and weak notes in each part. The lower voice is comprised entirely of eighth notes.
- Write a composite eighth-note meter signature, for example $\frac{3}{4}$ in the upper staff and $\frac{9}{8}$ in the lower.
- Sketch the rhythm of each part in a meter that matches its beat division (no tuplets will appear in either part).
- Sketch the rhythms above and below the staves, using beams to show the groupings that you hear, and indicate all bar lines.
- Sketch the pitches on the staff as you listen for repeated notes and patterns.
- Combine rhythm and pitches to complete the notation of the example.
- Finally, identify the scale or mode from which all melodic pitches are derived.

NAME ________________________________

1.

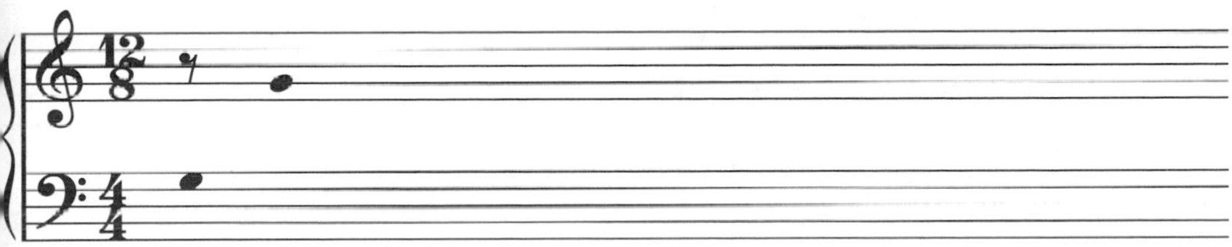

2.

3.

4.

5.

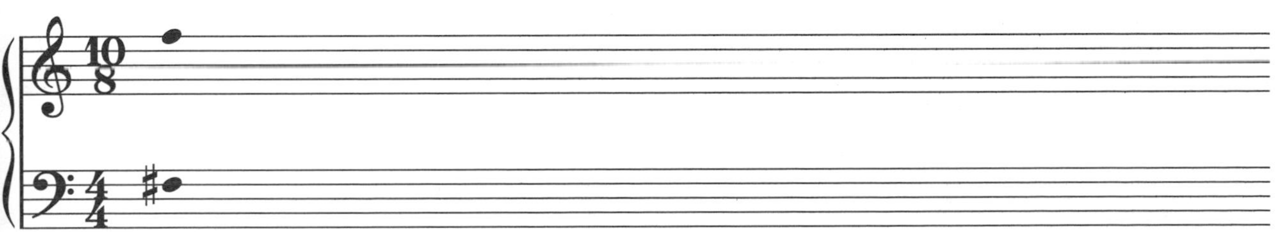

NAME ____________________

Contextual Listening 39.1

In this CL exercise you will:

- Determine the changing meter of an excerpt from a musical
- Notate the melody
- Explain how the chromaticism is derived

Listen to an excerpt from a musical, and complete the following exercises.

This excerpt consists of eight measures, and the meter changes every measure.

1. In which two meter signatures (in which order) would the music be notated?

   (a) $\frac{2}{4}$ and $\frac{3}{4}$ (b) $\frac{3}{4}$ and $\frac{6}{8}$ (c) $\frac{6}{8}$ and $\frac{3}{4}$ (d) $\frac{3}{4}$ and $\frac{2}{4}$

2. Use the workspace provided to capture the excerpt.

   (a) Notate the rhythm of the melody on the single-line staves in the meters you chose for question 1. Write the meter signature, and include bar lines. Beam notes to show beat grouping.

   (b) Below the single-line staves, and under each note, write the solfège syllables or scale-degree numbers for the melody beginning on *sol* ($\hat{5}$).

   (c) Combine your answers to complete the notation of the pitches and rhythm of the vocal melody beginning on G4. Include the appropriate clef, meter signatures, and accidentals.

Workspace

Rhythm:

Melody:

Solfège syllables:
Scale-degree numbers:

Solfège syllables:
Scale-degree numbers:

Notation:

NAME ______________________________

3. In the second half of the excerpt, the chromaticism is due to which of the following?

   (a) A6 chords (b) modal mixture (c) CT°7 (d) chromatic voice exchanges

4. The bass line alternates between two pitch classes. Which are their scale-degree numbers?

   (a) $\hat{1}$ and $\hat{3}$ (b) $\hat{1}$ and $\hat{5}$ (c) $\hat{5}$ and $\hat{1}$ (d) $\hat{3}$ and $\hat{1}$

5. The melody is always doubled in such a way as to create a chord of which quality?

   (a) major triad (b) minor triad (c) MM7 (d) Mm7

NAME ______________________________

Contextual Listening 39.2

In this CL exercise you will:

- Determine the meter of a jazz composition
- Notate its rhythm and melody
- Explain how phrases relate to each other
- Identify the keys that are tonicized

Listen to an excerpt from a jazz composition, and complete the following exercises.

1. In which meter signature can the entire excerpt best be notated?

   (a) $\frac{5}{8}$ (b) $\frac{7}{8}$ (c) $\frac{8}{8}$ (d) $\frac{9}{8}$

2. Use the workspace provided to capture the excerpt.

   (a) Notate the rhythm of the first phrase of the melody on the single-line staff in the meter you chose for question 1. Write the meter signature, and include bar lines. Beam notes to show beat grouping.

   (b) Below the single-line staves, and under each note, write the solfège syllables or scale-degree numbers for the melody beginning on *mi* ($\hat{3}$).

   (c) Combine your answers to complete the notation of the pitches and rhythm of the vocal melody beginning on A4. Include the appropriate clef and meter signature.

Workspace

Rhythm:

Melody:

Solfège syllables:
Scale-degree numbers:

Solfège syllables:
Scale-degree numbers:

Notation:

3. Which is the implied quality of the first chord of the excerpt?

   (a) major triad (b) minor triad (c) MM7 (d) Mm7

Phrase 2 is a repetition of phrase 1.

4. In phrase 3, which scale degree is tonicized?

   (a) $\hat{3}$ (b) $\hat{4}$ (c) $\hat{5}$ (d) $\hat{6}$

5. Use the workspace provided to capture the excerpt.

   (a) Notate the rhythm of the melody for phrase 3 on the single-line staves in the meter you chose for question 1. Write the meter signature, and include bar lines. Beam notes to show beat grouping.

   (b) Below the single-line staves, and under each note, write the solfège syllables or scale-degree numbers for the melody beginning on *sol* ($\hat{5}$).

   (c) Combine your answers to complete the notation of the pitches and rhythm of the vocal melody beginning on C5. Include the appropriate clef, meter signature, and accidentals.

Workspace

Rhythm:

Melody:

Solfège syllables:

Scale-degree numbers:

Solfège syllables:

Scale-degree numbers:

Notation:

Phrase 4 is a repetition of phrase 3.

6. How does phrase 5 relate to the phrases that precede it?

   (a) repetition of phrase 1 (b) repetition of phrase 3

   (c) varied repetition of phrase 3 (d) entirely new phrase

Phrase 6 is a repetition of phrase 5.

7. Which key is tonicized in phrase 7?

   (a) tonic (b) dominant (c) mediant (d) relative minor

8. Use the workspace provided to capture the excerpt.
   (a) Notate the rhythm of the melody for phrase 7 on the single-line staves in the meter you chose for question 1. Write the meter signature, and include bar lines. Beam notes to show beat grouping.
   (b) Below the single-line staves, and under each note, write the solfège syllables or scale-degree numbers for the melody beginning on *mi* ($\hat{3}$).
   (c) Combine your answers to complete the notation of the pitches and rhythm of the vocal melody beginning on A4. Include the appropriate clef, meter signature, and accidentals.

Workspace

Rhythm:

Melody:

Solfège syllables:
Scale-degree numbers:

Solfège syllables:
Scale-degree numbers:

Notation:

Phrase 8 is a repetition of phrase 7.

9. How is the melody of phrase 9 related to any previous material?
   (a) identical to phrase 1
   (b) transposition of phrase 1 up a third
   (c) identical to phrase 3
   (d) transposition of phrase 5 down a second

NAME ________________________

Contextual Listening 39.3

In this CL exercise you will:

- Determine and notate the row on which an art song is based
- Determine the relationship between various statements of the row
- Transpose the row
- Create a 12 × 12 matrix for the song
- Determine the rhythmic relationships between various statements of the row

Laß deinen süßen Rubinenmund	*Let not your sweet ruby mouth*
Zudringlichkeiten nicht verfluchen;	*Condemn me for being so importunate;*
Was hat Liebesschmerz andern Grund,	*What other reason does heartache have*
Als seine Heilung zu suchen?	*Than to look for its own healing?*

Listen to a twelve-tone song for soprano and E♭ and B♭ clarinets in which the treatment of durational values plays a significant structural role. Though these clarinets are transposing instruments, notate them at concert pitch.

1. (a) On the following staff, notate the first twelve pitches of the voice (to the text "Laß deinen süßen Rubinenmund"). Begin on E4. This original row is called P_4. For help, listen to CL 39.3a, the excerpted clarinet part.
   (b) Write the pc integer beneath each pitch.
   (c) Write the pc interval number between each successive pair of pc integers.
   (d) Write the row order numbers, 1-12, above each pitch.

2. (a) Notate the first twelve pitches of the B♭ clarinet (the first clarinet you hear) on the following staff. Begin on concert pitch C♯4.
   (b) Write the pc integer beneath each pitch.
   (c) Write the pc interval number between each successive pair of pc integers.
   (d) Write the row order numbers, 1-12, above each pitch.

   (e) How does this second row relate to the original row, P_4?

(f) Transpose the concert pitches in 2 (a) to the pitches that would appear in the B♭ clarinet part. (Add 2 to each integer in the row.)

3. (a) Notate the *last* twelve pitches of the B♭ clarinet on the following staff. (These pitches begin immediately after those in your answer to question 2.) Begin on concert pitch D4.

   (b) Write the pc integer beneath each pitch.

   (c) Write the pc interval number between each successive pair of pc integers.

   (d) Write the row order numbers, 1-12, above each pitch.

   (e) How does this row relate to the original row, P_4?

4. Listen again to the beginning of the voice part and compare what you hear with the *beginning* of the B♭ clarinet part. What is the *rhythmic* relationship between these two parts?

5. Listen again to the beginning of the voice part and compare what you hear with the *end* of the B♭ clarinet part. What is the *rhythmic* relationship between these two parts?

6. In question 1, you determined the original form of the row, P_4. Create a 12 × 12 matrix based on this row. Notate the pcs with integers.

   (a) Transpose the first row (your answer to question 1) to begin on pc 0 by subtracting 4 from each element in the row.

   (b) Write P_0 in the top line of your matrix.

   (c) Write the I form of the row down the left column in the matrix. To find I, take the inverse of each pc in the top row.

   (d) Consider each pc in the left column the first pc of a new transposition of the row.

NAME ______________________________

(e) Make sure that the diagonal from top left to bottom right contains only zeros. Make sure each row or column includes one each of the twelve pc integers. (No pcs may be duplicated.)

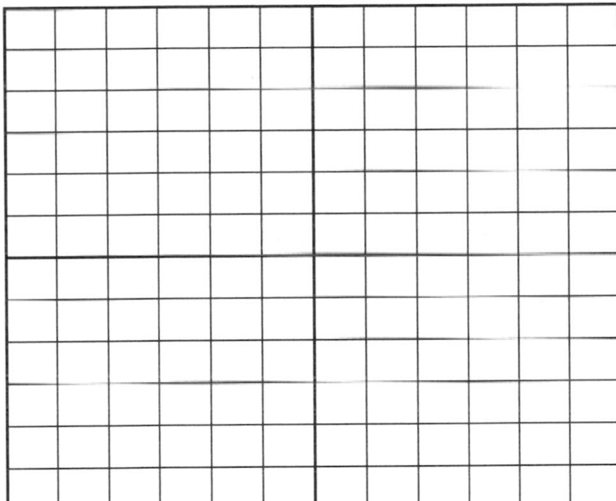

Refer to your matrix to help you complete exercises 7-11.

7. (a) Beginning on B♭3, notate the pitches of the voice that are sung to the text "Zudringlichkeiten nicht verfluchen." This music begins *immediately* after the first twelve pitches of the voice (your answer to question 1.) Note that there are only eleven pitches. Find the "missing" pitch!

   (b) Write the pc integer beneath each pitch.

   (c) What is the name of this row form? (Refer to your matrix.)

   (d) Which pc is missing?

   (e) Listen again to both the voice and the B♭ clarinet. Follow your notation or the row form in the matrix. What happens in the music at the point when you expect to hear the missing pc? Briefly describe the composer's solution to this "missing" pc.

8. (a) Beginning on F4, notate the pitches of the voice that are sung to the text "Was hat Liebesschmerz andern Grund" (the music following your answer to question 7) (ca. 23″).

   (b) Write the pc integer beneath each pc.

(c) Compare this music with the beginning of the voice part. Focus on the contour and intervals of each melody. Relying only on your ears and without consulting your matrix, decide how these two row forms are related.

(1) P (2) R (3) I (4) RI

(d) Consult your matrix to confirm what you heard. Which row form is sung to these words?

9. (a) Beginning on G♭5, notate the final pitches of the voice that are sung to the text "Als seine Heilung zu suchen, zu suchen?" (ca. 34″). Note that there are only eleven pitches; find the missing pitch.

(b) Write the pc integer beneath each pitch.

(c) What is the name of this row form? (Refer to your matrix.)

(d) Which pc is missing?

(e) At the end, listen again to both the voice and the B♭ clarinet (the lower-sounding clarinet). Follow your notation or the row form in the matrix. What happens in the music at the point when you expect to hear the missing pc? Briefly describe the composer's solution to this "missing" pc.

10. (a) The first entrance of the E♭ clarinet (the higher-sounding clarinet) occurs while the singer holds the last syllable of "verfluchen" (ca. 18″). Beginning on concert pitch A4, notate the first twelve pitches of the E♭ clarinet.

(b) Write the pc integer beneath each pitch.

(c) Listen to the beginning of the voice again and compare it with the entrance of the E♭ clarinet. Focus on the contour and intervals of each melody. Relying only on your ears and without consulting your matrix, decide how these two row forms are related.

(1) P (2) R (3) I (4) RI

(d) Consult your matrix to confirm what you heard. Which row form does the E♭ clarinet play?

(e) Transpose the concert pitches given to the pitches that would appear in the E♭ clarinet part. (Subtract 3 from each integer in the row.)

11. (a) The E♭ clarinet's second row begins immediately after its first statement (simultaneously with the singer's syllable "-schmerz"). Beginning on concert pitch F5, notate the remaining pitches of the E♭ clarinet part. For help, listen to CL 39.3a. Note that there are only eleven pitches. Once again, find the missing pc.

(b) Write the pc integer beneath each pitch.

(c) What is the name of this row form? (Refer to your matrix.)

(d) Which pc is missing?

(e) At the end, listen again to both the voice and the E♭ clarinet (the higher-sounding clarinet). Follow your notation above or the row form in the matrix. What happens in the music at the point when you expect to hear the missing pc? Briefly describe the composer's solution to this "missing" pc.

Recent Trends

In this chapter you'll learn to:

- Apply a variety of analytical tools studied throughout the text to understand works composed in the latter half of the twentieth century
- Notate melodic pitches from instrumental and vocal works
- Determine the normal order and prime form of unordered pitch-class sets, and identify them by their set classes
- Determine relationships between structurally significant ordered and unordered pitch class sets
- Transfer pitches from concert pitch to notation written for a transposing instrument

Preparatory Listening

Complete the *Try It* dictations to review the following concepts and skills:

- Hearing relationships in twelve-tone rows that have been manipulated through serial processes
- Notating pitch rows on the staff
- Determining the ordered pitch intervals and pitch-class intervals between adjacent notes of rows
- Determining the relationships between a row and its transformations

Try It

In the following exercises, you will identify and analyze row P, as well as four row forms related to P.

- Listen to the first example (a). This is row P, which begins with the given pitch.
- Notate all the pitches of P. Beneath each pitch, write its pc integer number.
- Calculate the ordered pitch intervals, then the pc intervals (pcis) between each note. Write these underneath and between each pc integer. Refer to this information when identifying transformations of P. Before proceeding check your work with the answer key.
- Listen to and notate all of the other row forms (b-e). Calculate the ordered pitch intervals and the pcis between each note.

NAME ________________________________

- Compare the answer with your analysis of P. How does this row form relate to P? Is it another form of P, or is it some form of I, R, or RI? Supply the level of transposition for each segment (for example, P_3, I_2, R_9, RI_6, etc.).

1a.

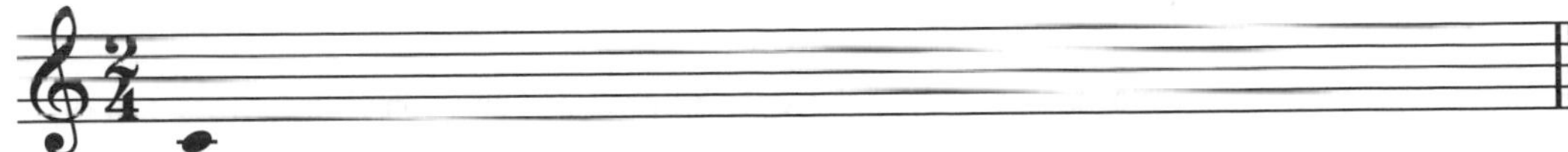

pcs:
ordered pitch intervals:
pcis:

1b.

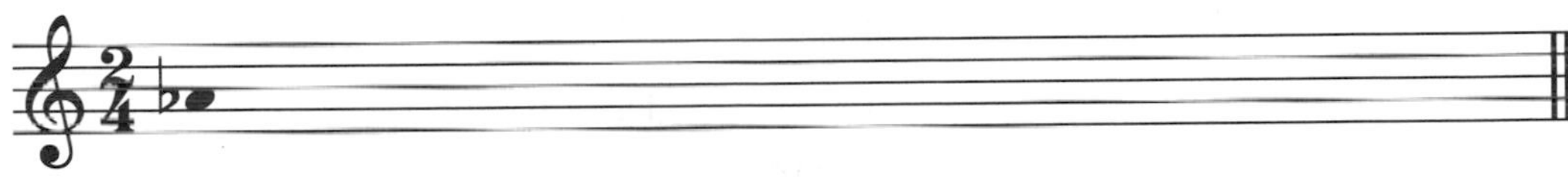

pcs:
ordered pitch intervals:
pcis:

1c.

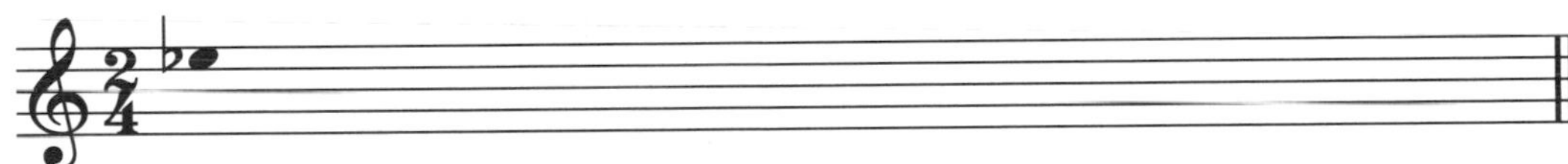

pcs:
ordered pitch intervals:
pcis:

1d.

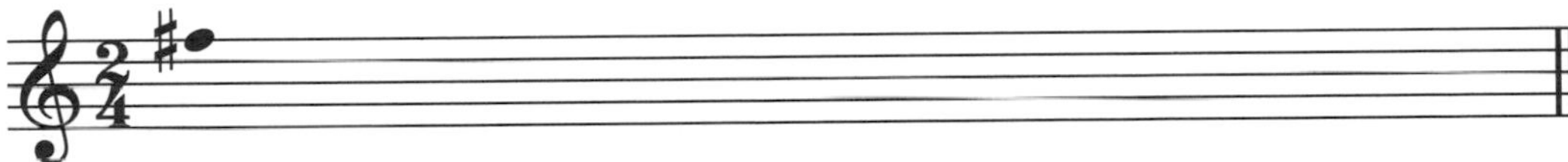

pcs:
ordered pitch intervals:
pcis:

1e.

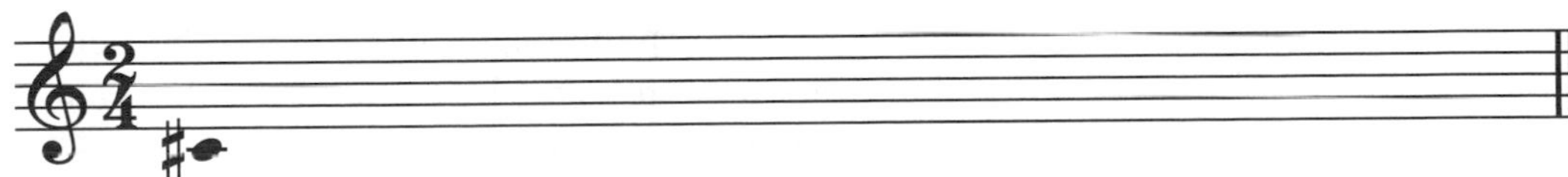

pcs:
ordered pitch intervals:
pcis:

Contextual Listening 40.1

In this CL exercise you will:

- Identify the meter type of an *a cappella* choral work
- Identify the mode on which the excerpt is based
- Identify parallel intervals and chord types
- Determine the pitch-classes or scale-degree numbers, and convert this to notation on the staff

Listen to an excerpt from a choral work, and complete the following exercises.

1. Which of these represents the meter of this excerpt?

   (a) simple duple (b) simple triple
   (c) compound duple (d) compound triple

2. At the beginning, the women's voices are doubled at which harmonic interval?

   (a) M3 (b) P4 (c) P5 (d) M6

3. The women sing "and the bridesmaids all wore" to which of these parallel harmonic intervals?

   (a) all thirds (b) 3-3-3-6-6-6 (c) 6-6-6-3-3-3 (d) all sixths

4. At the entrance of the men's voices ("bridesmaids all wore"), which is the quality of the chord

   (a) major triad (b) minor triad (c) MM7 (d) mm7

5. When the men first sing "green, green," the alternating harmonies are of which qualities?

   (a) minor triad, then Mm7 (b) minor triad, then mm7
   (c) major triad, then MM7 (d) major triad, then mm7

6. The last chord is of which quality?

   (a) major triad (b) minor triad (c) MM7 (d) mm7

7. From the entry of the men's voices until the end of the excerpt, which is the mode?

   (a) Dorian (b) Phrygian (c) Lydian (d) Mixolydian

8. Use the workspace provided to capture the excerpt.

   (a) Notate the rhythm of the soprano and bass on the single-line staves in the meter you chose for question 1 with the quarter note as the beat unit. Write the meter signature, and include bar lines. Beam notes to show beat grouping.

   (b) Below the single-line staves, and under each note, write the pitch classes or letter names of the soprano and bass. Begin on 9 (A) for the sopranos and determine the first pitch in the basses from listening to the women's parts.

   (c) Combine your answers to complete the notation of the soprano and bass. Begin on A4 for the soprano. Write the appropriate clefs, key signature (and any accidentals), and meter signature.

NAME ______________________________

Workspace

Rhythm:

Soprano:

Pitch classes:

Letter names:

Pitch classes:

Letter names:

Pitch classes:

Letter names:

Notation:

Rhythm:

Bass:

Pitch classes:

Letter names:

Pitch classes:

Letter names:

Pitch classes:

Letter names:

NAME ______________________

Contextual Listening 40.2

In this CL exercise you will:

- Determine the meter of a work for chorus and orchestra
- Identify the design of melodic segments of the melody
- Notate vocal segments on the staff
- Determine the normal order and prime form of unordered pitch-class sets, and identify their set class
- Identify the scale or mode from which the melodic segments are derived

Listen to an excerpt from a work for chorus and orchestra.

The excerpt consists of eight melodic segments, though you will focus on only the first four. Segments 1-3 contain eight melodic pitches each. Segment 4 contains ten melodic pitches.

1. Which is the rhythmic notation of the first melodic segment?

2. Notate the pitches and rhythm of the first four segments of the melody on the following staves. Begin on G5. (After segment 4, there is a repetition of segment 1.) Write the appropriate clef and accidentals.

3. Which is the design of the first four melodic segments?

   (a) **a a a a** (b) **a a a′ b** (c) **a b a b** (d) **a b a c**

4. Consider the first half of segment 1 to be an unordered pcset. Call this trichord set A. Play the rotations of set A at the keyboard, or notate them on the following staff. What are the normal order, prime form, and set class for this trichord?

NAME ______________________________

5. Consider the second half of segment 1 to be an unordered pcset. Call this trichord set B. Play the rotations of set B at the keyboard, or notate them on the following staff. What are the normal order, prime form, and set class for this trichord?

6. Consider all the pcs of melodic segment 1 to be unordered pcset C. Play the rotations of set C at the keyboard, or notate them on the following staff. What are the normal order, prime form, and set class for this pentachord?

7. Add pc e to set C to create a hexachord. (Pc e is present in the harmony of the first segment.) Call this hexachord set D. Play the rotations of set D at the keyboard, or notate them on the following staves. What are the normal order, prime form, and set class for this pentachord?

8. In traditional terms, set D might be thought of as two same-quality triads a half step apart. Which of the following is the quality of these two triads?

   (a) major (b) minor (c) augmented (d) diminished

9. To which traditional scale do the pitches of melodic segments 3 and 4 belong? In segment 4, be sure to include the men's parts as part of the melody.

   (a) E major (b) C♯ ascending melodic minor

   (c) G♯ Aeolian mode (d) G♯ Lydian mode

10. Consider the pcs of melodic segment 3 to be unordered pcset E. Play the rotations of set E at the keyboard, or notate them on the following staff. What are the normal order, prime form, and set class for this trichord?

11. Melodic segment 4 consists of two traditional pentachords of which quality?

    (a) major (b) minor (c) harmonic (d) Phrygian

12. The pentachords of melodic segment 4 belong to which set class?

    (a) [0 1 3 5 7] (b) [0 1 4 5 7] (c) [0 2 3 5 7] (d) [0 2 4 6 8]

NAME ______________________

Contextual Listening 40.3

In this CL exercise you will:

- Notate instrumental and vocal segments of an art song
- Transfer pitches from concert pitch to notation written for a transposing instrument
- Identify sets by their common name
- Determine the normal order of unordered pitch-class sets
- Determine relationships between selected pitch-class sets

Listen to an excerpt from an art song, and complete the following exercises.

1. Notate the pitches of the alto flute from the beginning until the soprano enters. Begin on B♭4. Write the appropriate clef and accidentals. Call the four distinct pitch classes set A. For an audio hint, listen to CL 40.3a.

2. Notate the pitches of the alto flute as flutists would read them. The alto flute sounds a P4 below its written pitches.

3. Find the intervals between each pc in set A. Use this information to create its interval-class vector. Perform the intervals between the pcs, or realize set A as pitches on the following staff to help you visualize the process.

   The interval-class vector for set A is [__ __ __ __ __ __].

4. What is another name for set A?

   (a) whole-tone tetrachord (b) Phrygian tetrachord

   (c) all-interval tetrachord (d) octatonic tetrachord

5. Play the rotations of set A at the keyboard, or notate them on the following staff. Find the normal order and prime form. To which set class does this tetrachord belong?

NAME ________________________________

6. When the soprano enters, she sings the same motive four times. Which is the interval of this opening motive in semitones? (The third and fourth occurrences are easiest to hear.)

   (a) 1 (b) 2 (c) 3 (d) 4

7. After the soprano's first entrance, the flute plays again, adding one pitch to set A. Call set A plus this new pitch: set B. Realize set B as pitches and play its rotations at the keyboard, or notate them on the following staves. What is the normal order for set B? To which set class does B belong? For an audio hint, listen to CL 40.3b.

8. After the flute performs set B, the antique cymbals repeat the first interval of the composition, to which one new pitch is added in the glockenspiel. Call this trichord set C. Realize the set as pitches and play its rotations at the keyboard, or notate them on the following staves. What is the normal order for set C? To which set class does C belong?

9. Notate the five distinct pitches of the soprano part on the staff provided. Begin on D5. Write the appropriate clef and accidentals. Call these pcs set D. Realize the set as pitches and play its rotations at the keyboard, or notate them on the following staves. What is the normal order for set D? To which set class does D belong? For an audio hint, listen to CL 40.3c.

10. Realize the pcs of sets B, C, and D as pitches in the order in which they appear. What is the musical significance of the soprano's last pitch?

11. Listen to the soprano's last pitch several times. The percussion adds three pitches to the soprano part to create a tetrachord. Call this tetrachord set E. While the soprano sustains the last pitch, the flute adds three pitches to create a different tetrachord. Call this tetrachord set F. For an audio hint, listen to CL 40.3d.

Realize each set as pitches and play the rotations at the keyboard, or notate them on the following staves. What are the normal orders for sets E and F? To which set classes do E and F belong?

12. How is set E related to set C?

13. How is set F related to set A?

Composition

Elements of Music

Composition 1: Rhythm (Chapters 2 and 4)

A. Simple meter

(1) On your own paper, notate the rhythm of the following nursery rhyme in simple duple meter. First use the symbols / and ˘ (for strong and weak) to mark the metric accents and beat divisions of the poem, then transfer the rhythm to staves, drawing all the note heads on the middle line. Use only beat patterns you have studied.

/ ˘ / ˘ / ˘ / ˘
Pat a cake, pat a cake, ba - ker's man,

Bake me a cake as fast as you can.

Pat it and prick it,

And mark it with a B,

And put it in the oven for Baby and me.

(2) Compose a rhythmic duet, eight measures in simple duple meter, on your own paper. Be prepared to perform both parts together, and tap on different surfaces to produce two different sounds. Choose from these seven patterns, including three or four of them in each part. Use no ties.

Choose patterns whose composite (combined) rhythm is pattern 2, but include pattern 2 itself only minimally. Add musical interest with dynamics and other markings. If you like, write a text to be recited with your rhythm.

(3) Compose another rhythmic duet, this time eight measures in simple triple meter. Choose patterns whose composite rhythm creates the pattern of 2 or 5.

B. Compound meter

Follow the procedure you used in A(1) to set the same text as a rhythmic duet in compound duple meter. Choose only beat patterns from those given next.

Which version do you prefer and why? Which version fits best with the text?

C. Team composition (group)

Choose a meter type—simple or compound. Then have teams of three to four students compose a sixteen-measure rhythmic duet, using only the beat patterns you have studied. Each student notates one measure, then passes the marker (or chalk) to the next person. Repeat until the duet is complete. All compositions should be performed and critiqued in class.

Composition 2: Major-Key Melody (Chapters 3ff.)

Explore the following palette of compositional choices, then compose short melodies accordingly. Start simply and challenge yourself to create expressive, musical statements according to the criteria you've selected. As you become more comfortable, move on to criteria that are new to you.

Choose a tonic pitch that will keep your melody within the range of your voice. Practice playing your compositions at the keyboard with both hands while singing them with solfège syllables or scale-degree numbers.

RANGE OF MELODIES

- Major pentachord (*do-re-mi-fa-sol*; $\hat{1}$-$\hat{2}$-$\hat{3}$-$\hat{4}$-$\hat{5}$).
- Major scale from *ti* to *la;* $\hat{7}$-$\hat{6}$. Such melodies often save *la* ($\hat{6}$) until near the end, where it becomes the high point of the line.
- Major scale from *do* to *do;* $\hat{1}$-$\hat{1}$. These melodies often employ only the pentachord in the beginning, saving the upper tetrachord for the high point of the line.
- Major scale from *sol* to *sol;* $\hat{5}$-$\hat{5}$. Consider saving the top notes of the pentachord for the high point. For more drama, extend beyond *sol* ($\hat{5}$) to peak on *la* ($\hat{6}$).
- Major pentatonic scale. Recall that this scale excludes *ti* ($\hat{7}$) and *fa* ($\hat{4}$).

Meter choices: simple duple, simple triple, simple quadruple.
Beat units: quarter note, half note, eighth note.

Choose from these palettes of rhythmic values:

Always remember to do the following in your compositions:

- Write the appropriate clef(s), key signature (and any accidentals), meter signature, and include bar lines.
- Group beats according to the meter, and beam divisions and subdivisions to show beat grouping.
- Add dynamics, articulations, and phrasing to make your work as musical as possible.

VARIATIONS

- Prepare your melody for class presentation. For example, notate it on manuscript paper and copy to share with others, or use notation software and display it with a projector.
- Show a composition and have the class silently imagine its sound before you perform it aloud.
- Critique each composition. Correct any technical errors, and suggest improvements to the melody.
- Sing a melody aloud with solfège syllables or scale-degree numbers, as a solo or as a group performance.
- Show a melody and play from it, introducing one or more errors. Ask classmates to identify the nature of each error.
- Perform a melody instead of showing the notation, and have classmates take melodic or rhythmic dictation or aurally analyze its features.

Composition 3: Melody in Minor Keys and the Diatonic Modes (Chapters 5ff.)

Following the guidelines from Composition 2, compose short melodies in minor keys, diatonic modes, and using minor pentatonic scales. Make your compositions as musical as possible by marking the score with dynamics, articulations, and phrasing.

Composition 4: Two-Voice Counterpoint (Chapters 9–10)

A. 1:1 counterpoint

Compose a two-voice setting of the following text by John Keats, according to the criteria that follow.

"Bright star, would I were steadfast as thou art–"

- Speak the line several times, and experiment to find an appropriate meter; conduct as you do this. Which words or syllables are stressed?
- Invent a rhythm for the line, then notate it with the text underneath.
- With the rhythm you have created, compose a melody in a major or minor key. Set the text syllabically: that is, one note per syllable.
- On a grand staff, notate your melody on the top staff, in the appropriate clef with the text below the staff.
- In the lower staff, compose a counterpoint in first species to fit the voice range of a classmate; write the text below the staff.

B. 2:1 counterpoint

Convert your 1:1 composition from Part A into 2:1 counterpoint by altering one part at a time.

- Add one or two consonant skips, keeping in mind the overall shape of your melody.
- Where melodic thirds occur, fill them in with weak-beat passing tones.
- Wherever both voices move downward by step, create a suspension by sustaining one of the voices over a strong beat and resolving it on the beat afterward.

VARIATIONS

- Prepare your melody for class presentation. For example, notate it on manuscript paper and copy to share with others, or use notation software and display it with a projector.
- Show a composition and have the class silently imagine its sound before you perform it aloud.
- Correct any technical errors, and suggest improvements to the melody.
- Sing the counterpoint in groups, with several persons on each part, making sure that performers sing in the exact range indicated in the composition—that is, no octave doubling.
- Perform a melody instead of showing the notation, and have classmates take melodic or rhythmic dictation or aurally analyze its features.

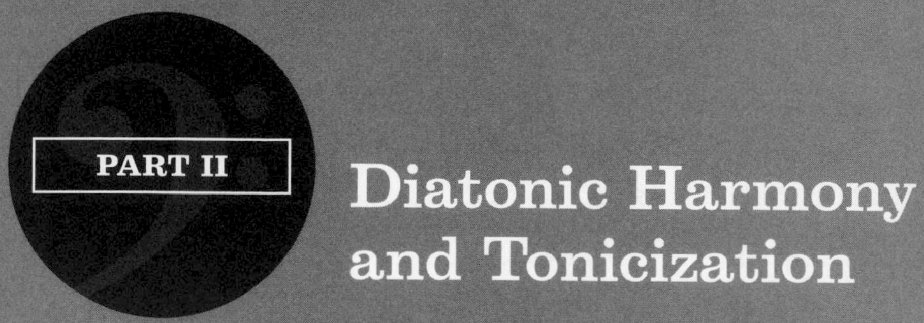

PART II

Diatonic Harmony and Tonicization

Composition 5: Vocal Melodies (Chapters 11-12)

Follow the guidelines given to compose four melodies, each one two phrases long, in a comfortable vocal range.

(1) major key, bass clef, simple quadruple meter

(2) minor key, treble clef, simple quadruple meter

(3) major key, treble clef, compound duple meter

(4) minor key, bass clef, compound duple meter

Prepare to sing and play your pieces in class. In each melody:

- End phrase 1 with an inconclusive cadence and phrase 2 with a conclusive cadence.
- Limit yourself to rhythmic values ranging from eighth notes to dotted-half notes.
- Group and beam rhythms in patterns characteristic of the meter.
- Mark the score with the dynamics, articulation, and phrasing that best express the musical statements you create.
- Incorporate sight-singing, keyboard, and improvisation ideas from *The Musician's Guide to Aural Skills: Sight-Singing*, Third Edition that correspond to Chapters 11-12. The strategies for team improvisation are also good guidelines for completing this melody.

Composition 6: Phrases in Two-Voice Counterpoint (Chapters 11-12)

From the following outline, create two compositions in simple triple meter, each one two phrases long. Embellish each part of the outline with passing (P) and neighbor (N) tones and chordal skips (CS). Conclude phrase 1 with a half cadence as shown here (melody falls to $\hat{2}$), and phrase 2 with a perfect authentic cadence (melody falls to $\hat{1}$). Follow the guidelines from Composition 5.

Outline (based on Mozart, Piano Sonata in C Major, K. 309, first movement)

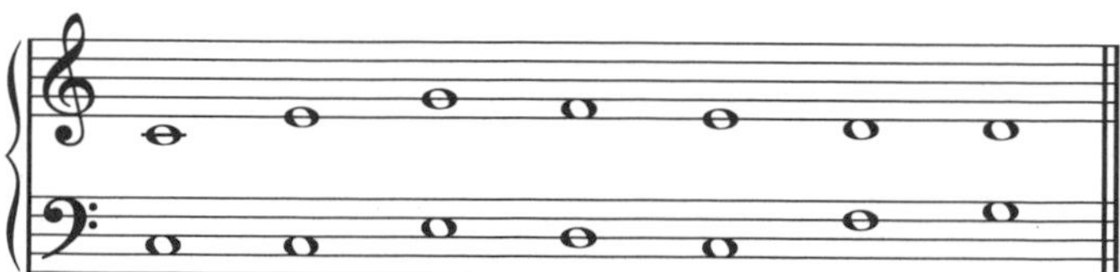

Composition 7: Two-Phrase Choral Piece (Chapter 13)

Compose a two-phrase choral work that includes predominant chords. Set the following text—from "At Last," by Helen (Fiske) Hunt Jackson—or one similar in its scope.

All lost things are in the angels' keeping, Love;
No past is dead for us, but only sleeping, Love.

Write for four voices, SATB style. Employ voice-leading as found in Keyboard Lesson 11.1 from *The Musician's Guide to Aural Skills: Sight-Singing*, Third Edition. Sing the work in class.

- First analyze the text's accentuation. Mark a / for strong accents. Make the musical rhythm similar to that of the text.
- Choose a minor key.
- Choose a simple meter, and write rhythmic patterns characteristic of that meter. Use eighth notes as the smallest rhythmic value.
- Conclude phrase 1 with a HC, phrase 2 with a PAC.
- Include at least one example of IV and ii^6, as well as an example of the progression iv-ii$^{\circ 6}$.
- Follow only the voice-leading you studied in Chapter 13 of *The Musician's Guide to Aural Skills: Sight-Singing*, Third Edition.

Composition 8: Phrase Pairs for Keyboard (Chapters 13-15)

Compose a two-phrase piece that includes dominant-function chords featured in Keyboard Lessons 12-13 from *The Musician's Guide to Aural Skills: Sight-Singing*, Third Edition.

- Write for piano, in four voices, keyboard style (three notes in the right hand, one in the left).
- Choose a minor key.
- Choose a compound meter, and write rhythmic patterns characteristic of that meter.
- Conclude phrase 1 with a HC, phrase 2 with a PAC.
- Include at least one example of V$^6_5$, V$^4_3$, or V$^4_2$ and its correct resolution.
- Perform your work, singing each part as you play with solfège syllables, scale-degree numbers, or letter names.

Composition 9 (Chapters 15, 18)

A. Vocal melodies

Following the guidelines from Composition 5, create four melodies—one in each of the following phrase structures: (1) parallel period, (2) contrasting period, (3) parallel double period, and (4) contrasting double period. Choose a comfortable vocal range. Prepare to perform your work in class.

B. Keyboard-style compositions

Compose two minor-key works in four parts, keyboard style—one from each of the following plans. Use voice-leading from Keyboard Lessons 12-15 from *The Musician's Guide to Aural Skills: Sight-Singing*, Third Edition. Prepare to perform your works in class.

(1) Parallel period

- Choose a compound meter.
- Organize each phrase with a sentence structure.
- Conclude phrase 1 with a Phrygian cadence.
- Conclude phrase 2 with a PAC followed by a plagal extension.

(2) Contrasting period

- Choose a simple meter.
- Within each phrase, create two four-measure subphrases.
- Conclude phrase 1 with a Phrygian cadence.
- Include a deceptive resolution in phrase 2, but end it with a PAC.

Composition 10: Trio (Chapters 19ff.)

Compose a one-phrase trio in C minor, simple quadruple meter, that features the descending-fifth progression, delayed resolutions, and voice-leading from Keyboard Lessons 16-19 in *The Musician's Guide to Aural Skills: Sight-Singing*, Third Edition. Conclude with a PAC. Write for the instrumentalists who are in your class. Use Corelli's Allegro as a model. Perform your work in class.

Corelli, Allegro, from Trio Sonata in F Minor, Op. 3, No. 9 (adapted)

STRATEGIES

- Look at Keyboard Lessons 12-13 for ideas for progressions that will establish the tonic key (C minor). The simplest is i-V-i.
- Choose a simple motive that reinforces the voice-leading outline.
- To make a strong cadence, conclude with T-PD-D-T (see Keyboard Lesson 14.2).
- Option: Write a different phrase that ends with a Phrygian half cadence (Keyboard Lesson 15.2).

Composition 11 (Chapters 18, 20-21)

A. Vocal melodies

Compose three parallel periods for voice. Include one or more accidentals that imply the tonicization of a nontonic scale degree. In each period, include some form of motivic development in both phrases, and some form of phrase expansion in phrase 2.

- Choose a major-key signature in the range of three flats to three sharps.
- Choose a simple-meter signature.
- Limit yourself to rhythmic values from sixteenth notes to dotted-half notes.
- Group and beam rhythms in patterns characteristic of the meter.
- Make your compositions as musical as possible by marking the score with dynamics, articulations, and phrasing.
- Variation: Compose one of the melodies in $\frac{5}{8}$ meter, grouping and beaming rhythms in patterns characteristic of the meter.

B. Keyboard-style composition from Roman numerals or figured bass

Create a two-phrase composition from one of the following progressions. As you play, sing each part with solfège syllables and scale-degree numbers.

- To create a motive, choose a simple melodic idea and a distinctive rhythm.
- Improve your counterpoint by making the rhythm of each hand distinct.
- Embellish your ideas with chordal skips, neighbor tones, and passing tones.
- Prepare to perform in both simple and compound meters.
- Prepare to transpose your compositions to major and minor keys ranging from three flats to three sharps.

Progression 1 (Roman numerals)

Phrase 1: i–IV$^{6}_{5}$–V$^{6}_{5}$–i. Phrase 2: i–iv^{7}–VII–III^{7}–VI–ii^{ø7}–V–(V)$^{4}_{2}$–i^{6}–ii^{o6}–V$^{6-5}_{4-3}$–i.

Base phrase 2 on the motivic idea of phrase 1. Also, since internal repetition is often the way in which phrase expansions occur, consider the sequence in phrase 2 to be the means of realizing an expansion.

Sample realization

6
V 4/2 i6 ii°6 V6/4 5/3 i
V 4/2 i6 ii°6 V6/4 5/3 i
Progression 2 (figured bass)
d:

Chromatic Harmony and Form

Part III features two large composition projects, each of which may be completed in steps. After each step, work with a partner and critique each other's work.

Composition 12: Minuet (Chapters 23ff.)

Compose two minuets, each one sixteen measures long, one in a major key and the other in minor. Each minuet consists of an eight-measure, two-phrase modulatory period followed by an eight-measure phrase that begins with a sequence and returns to a PAC in the tonic key. Plans specific to each tonality appear next.

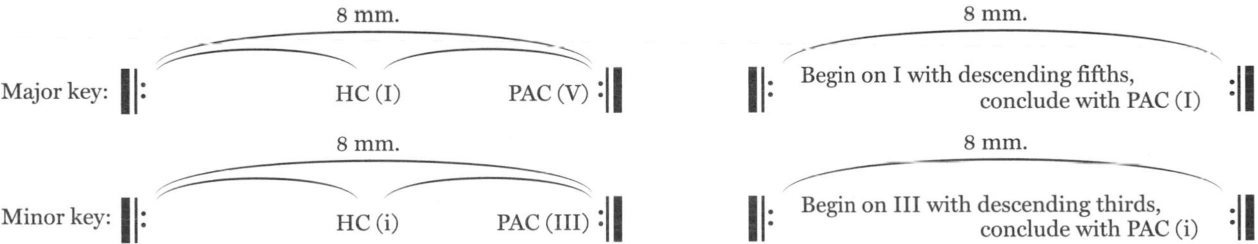

Before you start, review the following lessons, which are directly applicable to this project: Compositions 6, 8, 9, and 11, as well as Improvisations 11, 14, 16, and Keyboard Lessons 19 and 22 from *The Musician's Guide to Aural Skills: Sight-Singing*, Third Edition.

Peer review: After completing one minuet, exchange your work with a partner. Each composer offers suggestions for improvement. Look for and report any common problems—such as notation errors, improper voice-leading, and conflicts between melody and harmony. Suggest aesthetic improvements as well: for example, more rhythmic drive prior to the cadence; an appropriate place for a suspension; and so on. In their final drafts, composers should correct any technical errors, such as missing accidentals or parallel fifths. Any aesthetic suggestion may be taken or discarded at your discretion; after all, it's your name that will appear on the final composition.

Composer ______________________

Major Key

Step 1: Analyze this melodic and harmonic outline.

Step 2: Add some consonant skips to the melodic and harmonic outline in step 1.

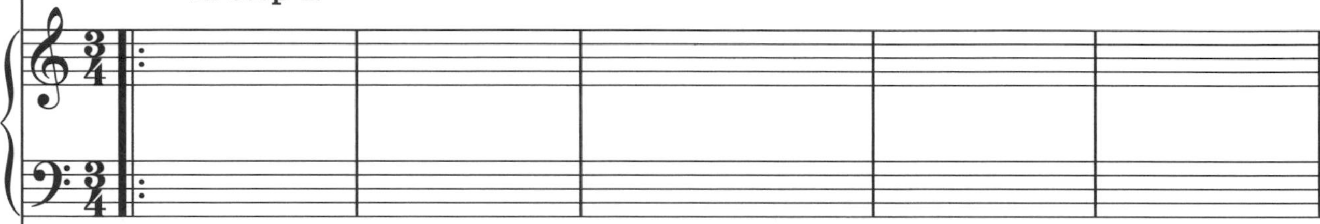

Step 3: To the embellishment in step 2, add some passing tones between select thirds.

Step 4: To the embellishment in step 3, add some neighboring tones to complete the piece.

6
1.
2.

9

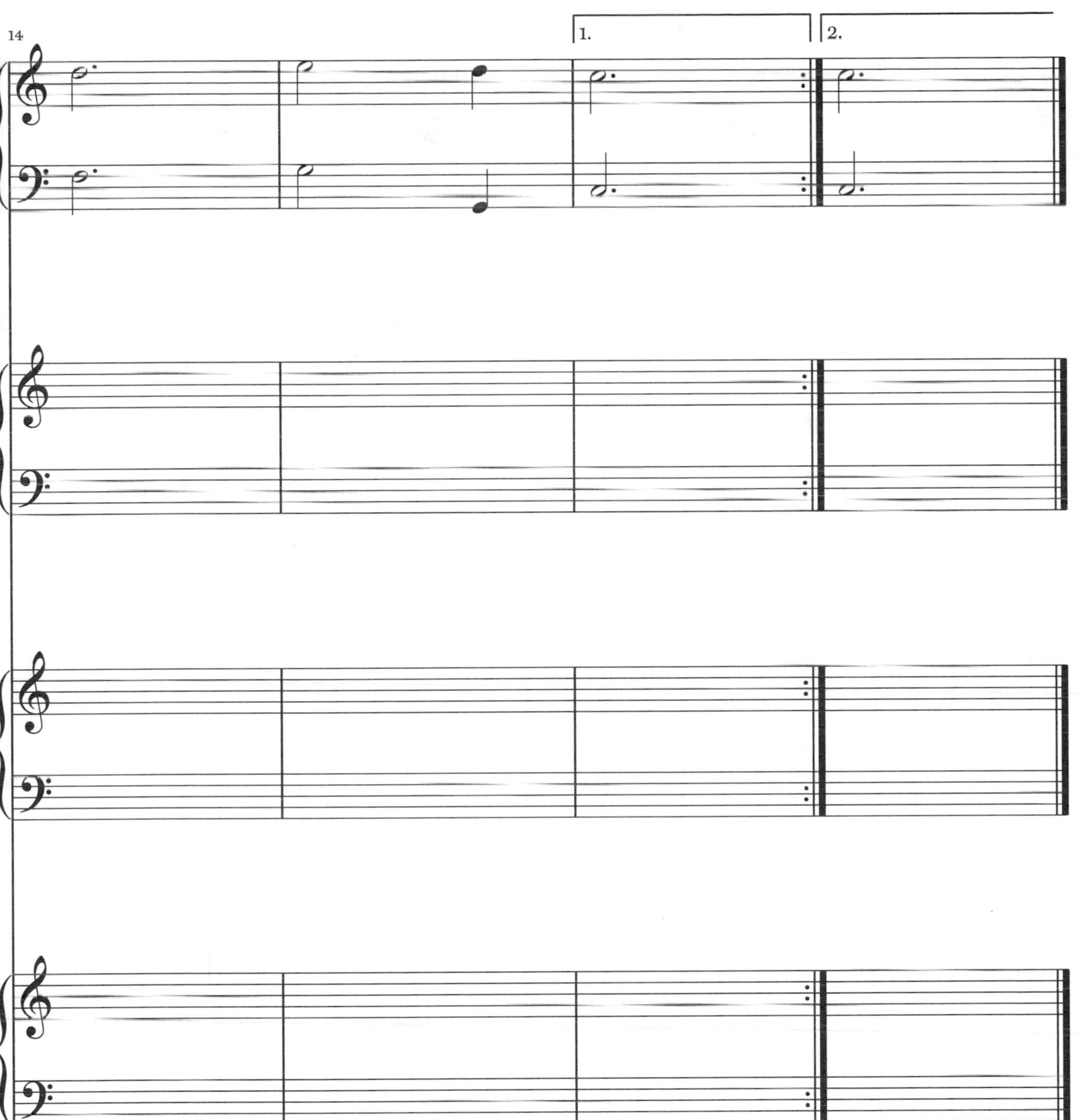
14
1.
2.

Composer ______________________

Minor Key

Step 1: Analyze this melodic and harmonic outline.

Step 2: Add some consonant skips to the melodic and harmonic outline in step 1.

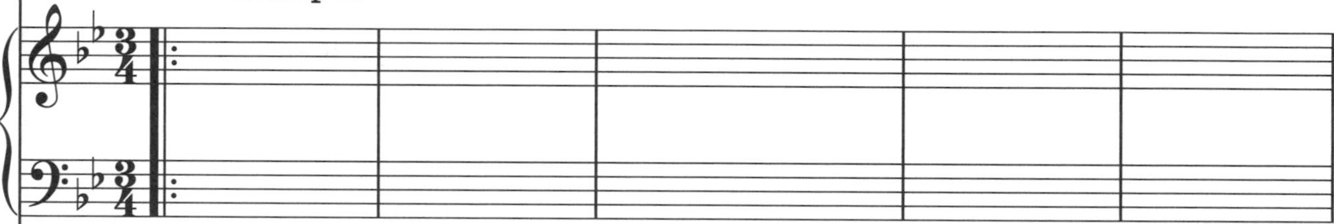

Step 3: To the embellishment in step 2, add some passing tones between select thirds.

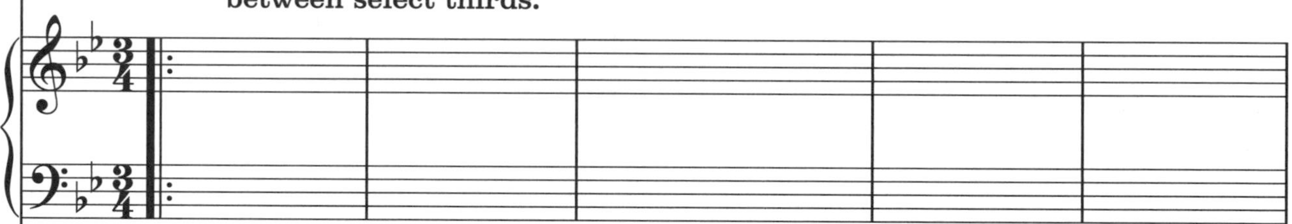

Step 4: To the embellishment in step 3, add some neighboring tones to complete the piece.

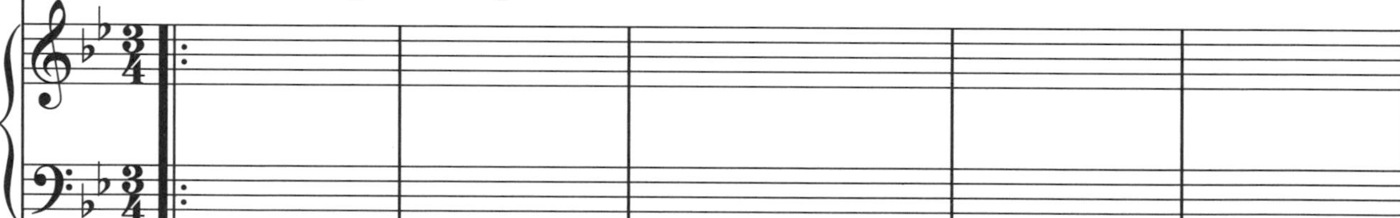

6
1.
2.

9

14
1.
2.

Composition 13: Sonata-Form Movement (Chapter 32)

In this project, you will compose a sonata-form movement for piano in four steps. After each step, exchange your work with a partner. Offer each other suggestions for improvement in the manner described in Composition 12. Perform your finished composition in class.

Step 1. Exposition: First theme group (FTG) and transition (TR)

1. Choose a major key and a meter type.
2. In phrase 1 (FTG):
   (a) Establish the tonic key.
   (b) Introduce the motive of (FTG), the first theme group.
   (c) Conclude with a PAC in I.
3. In phrase 2 (TR):
   (a) Begin with the motive of phrase 1 (FTG), creating a dependent transition.
   (b) Modulate to V by means of a sequence or linear intervallic pattern (LIP).
   (c) Conclude with a HC *in the key of V.*

Step 2. Exposition: Second theme group (STG)

1. List the attributes of FTG (character, register, dynamics, articulation, texture, tempo, type of accompaniment, harmonic rhythm, etc.).
2. Choose the opposite of three or more of these attributes. Let these opposites help you create a motive for STG.
3. With this new motive, compose a parallel period *in the key of V.*
4. In phrase 2 of your period:
   (a) Create an internal expansion by repeating a subphrase.
   (b) Conclude with a PAC in V.
   (c) Compose a cadential extension (codetta) that contains a "flourish."

Step 3. Development

1. In phrase 1:
   (a) Begin in the key of V.
   (b) Use an embellished form of FTG's motive.
   (c) Conclude with an IAC in V.
2. In phrase 2:
   (a) Begin like phrase 1 of the development.
   (b) Create a descending-fifth sequence.
   (c) Conclude with the progression A6–V in the key of I.
   (d) Repeat the progression to create a cadential extension.
   (e) Write a lead-in to connect the end of the development to the beginning of FTG in the recapitulation.

Step 4. Recapitulation

1. Copy phrase 1 of FTG and embellish it.
2. Rewrite TR so that it cadences on V instead of V/V.
3. Transpose STG to the key of the tonic.

For help, review the lessons where you acquired the skills needed to complete the tasks in this project.

Task	*Keyboard Lesson*	*Improvisation*	*Composition*
Creating a phrase	11.1, 12.1	12.1, 13.1, 16.1	5, 6
Modulating with a sequence	19.1, 22.1	22.1, 23.1	12
Making a period	18.1	18.1	8, 9, 12
Phrase expansion	14.2	14.1	11
A6 chords	27.2	31.1	

If you want to compose a minor-key sonata-form movement: The secondary key is III, so TR moves to a HC in III, STG is in the key of III, and the development may begin in III.

PART IV

The Twentieth Century and Beyond

Composition 14: Modes and Scales (Chapters 34ff.)

Compose a short **A B A′** piece for soloist and an accompanying instrument (piano or other keyboard, computer with instruments, etc.). Choose one of the following scales for the **A** section and another for **B**: pentatonic, octatonic, whole-tone, any mode, or construct your own scale.

Vary several of these elements in the **A′** section:

- melodic contour (inversion, same shape but wider leaps, etc.)
- dynamics
- register
- amount of repetition (e.g., sequences)
- nature of the accompaniment (e.g., block chords versus arpeggios)
- melodic embellishment
- articulation
- doubling (e.g., parallel chords)
- transposition of scale or melody or both
- change of motivic rhythm

Here are three examples.

	A	**B**	**A′**
(1)	Dorian mode	Pentatonic scale	Dorian mode: Invert the contour of the melody.
(2)	Whole-tone scale	Octatonic scale	Whole-tone scale: Augment the rhythm of the melody.
(3)	Lydian-Mixolydian mode	Your own scale	Lydian-Mixolydian mode: Change thc accompaniment.

This project may be completed in stages. Compose a draft to be critiqued in class, then incorporate appropriate suggestions into the work's final version. Perform your composition so the class can practice dictation, analysis, score-reading, and error-detection.

Composition 15: Pitch-Class Sets (Chapters 37ff.)

Compose a short **A B A′** piece for soloist and an accompanying instrument (piano or other keyboard, computer with instruments, etc.). Choose one of the following sets for the **A** section and a different set for **B**: 4-3 [0 1 3 4], 4-9 [0 1 6 7], 4-Z15 [0 1 4 6], 5-28 [0 2 3 6 8], 5-31 [0 1 3 6 9]. In each section, base all of your melodic and harmonic ideas on that single set, together with its transpositions and inversions.

STRATEGIES

- As a precompositional strategy, transpose and invert your set to begin on each of the twelve pcs. Choose from among these possibilities those you think sound best.
- Consider using the order of the pcs in the set as the basis for organizing your transpositions or inversions. For example, say you choose 4-Z15, transpose it to begin in F♯, and realize the pitches, in this order: {t 7 0 6}. The whole notes in measures 2-5 (shown next) are the ordered elements of the original set.

- Consider using unordered pcsets instead (put the whole notes in the preceding example in any order).
- Remember, you may realize pcs in any octave in the range of your instruments.
- Timbre is a very important element in recent music. Mark your scores with articulations, bowings, or special effects such as flutter-tonguing, harmonics, and so forth.
- Feature your sets both melodically and harmonically. (What chords can you make from your sets?)
- For extended instrumental techniques, consult with your soloist and an orchestration book, such as Samuel Adler's *The Study of Orchestration*, 4th ed. (New York: W. W. Norton, 2016).
- An older but still useful resource for nontraditional ideas of how to notate music is Gardner Read's *Music Notation: A Manual of Modern Practice*, 2nd ed. (New York: Taplinger, 1979).

Composition 16: Twelve-Tone and Serial Piece (Chapters 38ff.)

Choose a twelve-tone row from Contextual Listening or the *Sight-Singing* volume, or create one of your own. Compose a duet for yourself and a classmate. Express the row in relatively simple ways, such as those shown next.

- Overlap the end of one row form with the beginning of another.
- Choose row forms that permit you to overlap a pc (or pcs) in the middle of two simultaneous expressions of the row.
- Create a melody that is nonretrogradable: that is, a melody in which the pcs occur in the same order whether performed forward or backward.
- Compose a canon, making one part a rhythmic augmentation of the other.
- Create a matrix to help you explore the possibilities for your row choices.

VARIATIONS

- Include rows of lengths other than twelve pcs.
- Create a piece that is both twelve-tone *and* pitch-centric (that is, a piece that is not functionally tonal but one in which we perceive a "tonic").
- Choose a row based on combinatorial hexachords (hexachords that combine with other versions of themselves to complete the chromatic scale, or aggregate) to ensure that you express the aggregate both melodically and harmonically.
- Choose three instruments, and compose a trio that features combinatorial tetrachords.
- Serialize other aspects of your composition—for example, rhythm, dynamics, register, and timbre.

To serialize other aspects of your composition, use each interval class in your series to determine duration. Let the sixteenth note represent the shortest duration. In the following series, the order numbers are shown above the row and the interval classes below.

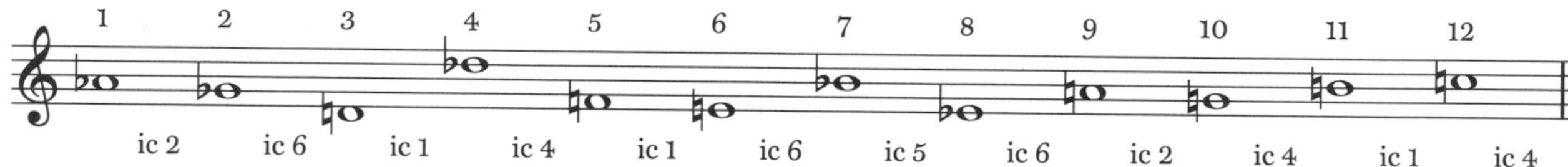

Use the interval class to determine the duration, dynamics, and articulation. For example, when the ic between two pcs is 5, notate the first pitch so that it lasts for five sixteenth notes, and add a ***f*** and > to the pitch.

	ic 1	ic 2	ic 3	ic 4	ic 5	ic 6
Duration in sixteenth notes	1	2	3	4	5	6
Dynamics	***pp***	***p***	***mp***	***mf***	***f***	***ff***
Articulations	·	^	*gliss.*	–	>	*tr*

(Why include ic 3? That ic might occur *between* two forms of the row later in the work.)

Flute

Whimsical

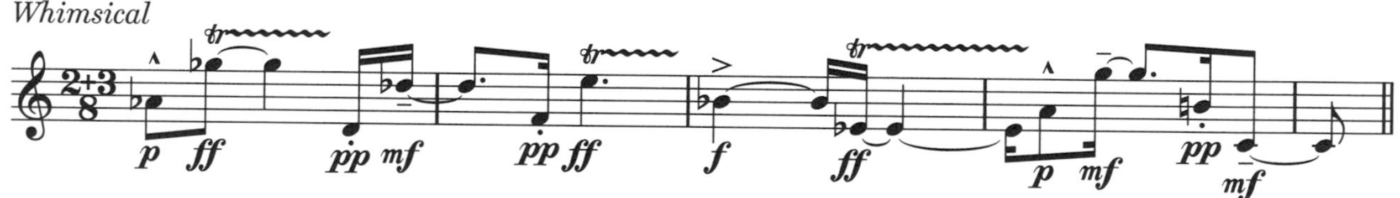

Composition 17: Rhythms (Chapters 39ff.)

A. Percussion duet

Compose a percussion duet in **A B A′** form. In the **A** section, include both changing and asymmetrical meters. Characterize section **B** by the use of polymeter. Incorporate the following ideas:

- Use classroom objects such as pencils, books, and desks as percussion instruments.
- Create a motive that is nonretrogradable (sounds the same when played backward and forward, like a rhythmic palindrome).

- Plan the length of your duet according to the golden mean. That is, the piece divides into two unequal parts where the ratio of the smaller part (YZ) to the larger (XY) is about the same as the larger part (XY) is to the whole piece (XZ).

Three adjacent Fibonacci numbers (1, 1, 2, 3, 5, 8, 13, 21, 34, 55, 89, etc.) may be used to approximate this proportion. For example, if the smaller part (YZ) is 21 measures and the larger part (XY) is 34 measures, the entire composition (XZ) is 55 measures; 21/34 is about the same proportion as 34/55.

One way to apply the proportion shown in the diagram to your **A B A** duet is to plan for the recapitulation of **A** at point Y, or about 62 percent of the total duration of the piece.

B. Ametric composition

Compose an ametric work that you will perform in class. Your composition may feature any or all of the following techniques.

- Feathered beaming: gradual acceleration gradual deceleration

- Timed proportions

- Graphic notation (this example includes timed proportions, too)

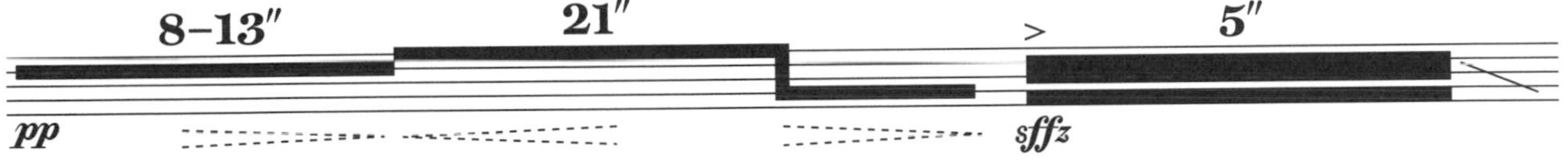

Try It Answers

Chapter 1

Chapter 2

Chapter 3

Chapter 4

Chapter 5

Chapter 6

Chapter 7

Chapter 8

Chapter 9

1.

2.

3.

Chapter 10

Chapter 11

5.
6.
7.
8.
9.
10.
Chapter 12
1.
A: I V8—7 I
2.
g: i V8—7 i
3.
D: I V8—7 I
4.
c: i V8—7 i
5.
c: i V6 i
6.
C: I V6 I
7.
E♭: I V6 I
Chapter 13
1.
c: i V4/3 i6
2.
G: I V6/5 I
3.
c: i V6/5 i
4.
C: I V4/3 I6
5.
D: I V4/3 I6
6.
e: i V4/3 i6
7.
e: i V4/3 i6
8.
C: I V4/2 I6
9.
C: I ii6 V8−7 I
10.
c: i iiø6 V8−7 i
11.
a: i iv V8−7 i
12.
c: i iv V i
Chapter 14
1.
G: I V8/6/4 7/5/3 I
2.
b: i V8/6/4 7/5/3 i
3.
D: I V6/4 I6
4.
a: i5/3 6/4 5/3
5.
G: I IV I6
6.
C: I IV I6 ii6 V
7.
e: i V4/3 i6
8.
c: i V6/5 i
9.
D: I vi ii6 V8/6/4 7/5/3 I
10.
c: i VI iiø6 V8−7 i

Chapter 15

1.

2.

3.

4.

5.

6.

7.

8.

9.

10.

Chapter 16

1.

2.

3.

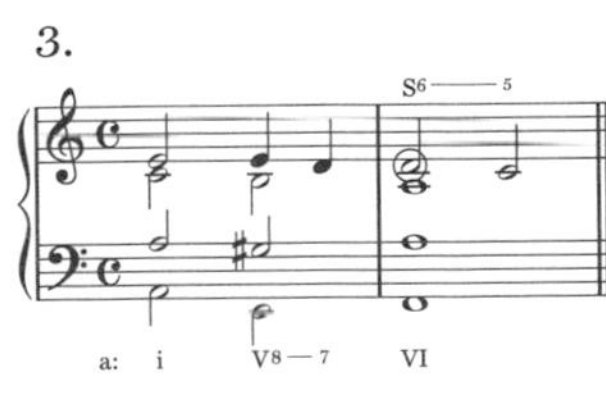

4.

5.

6.

7. 8.

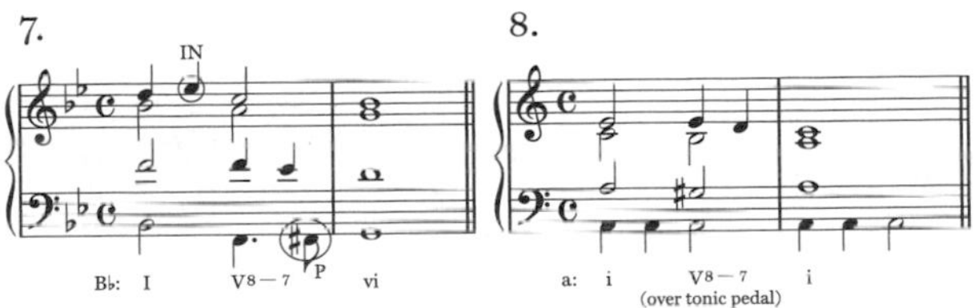

9.

Chapter 17

1.

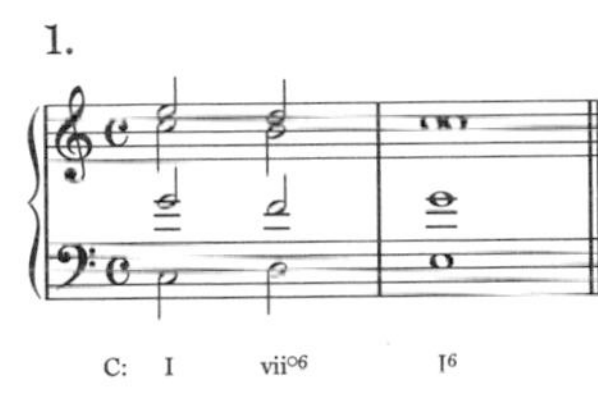

2.

3.

4.

5.

6.

7.

8.

Chapter 18

1.

2.

3.

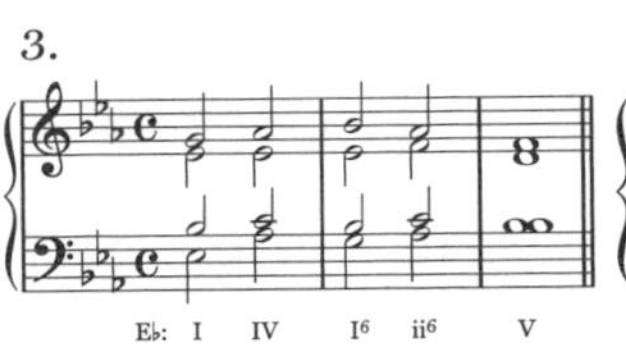

4.

Chapter 19

Chapter 20

Chapter 21

Chapter 22

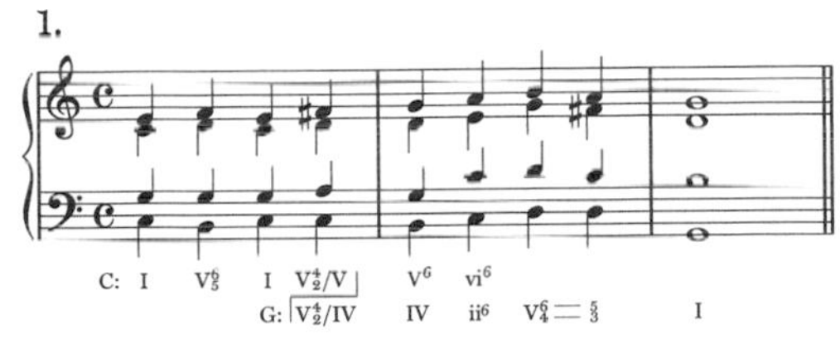

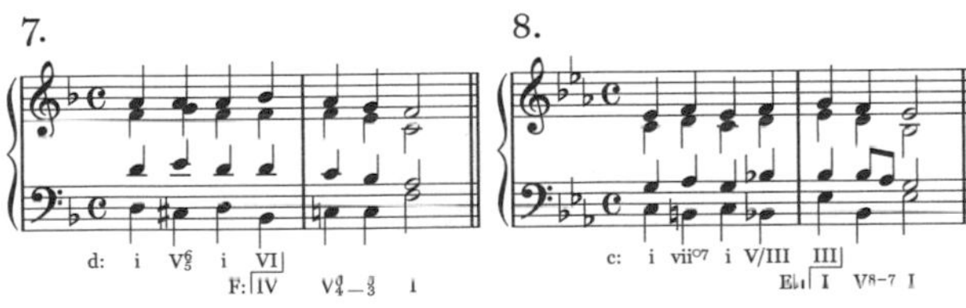

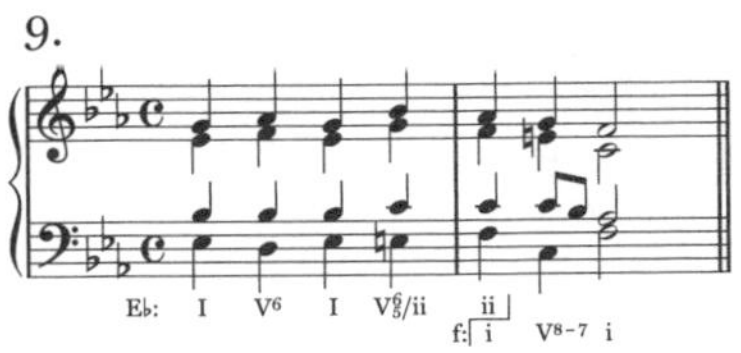

Chapter 23

Chapter 24

Chapter 25

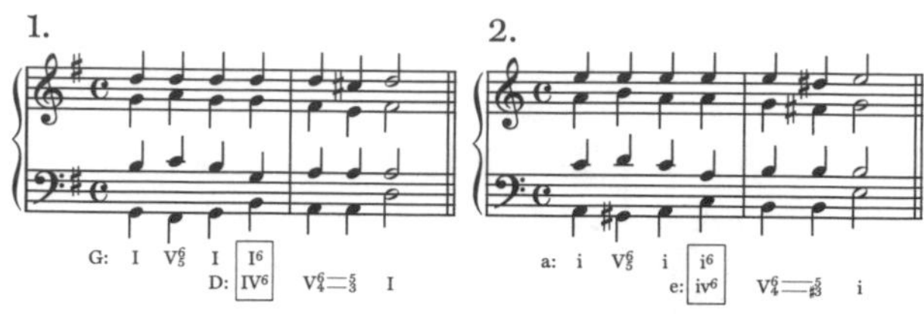

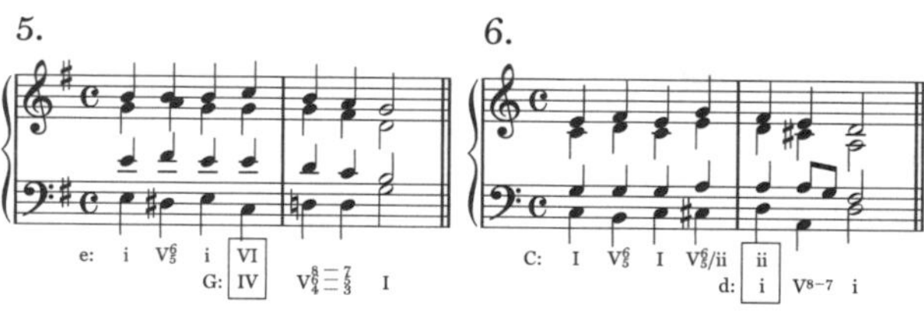

Chapter 26

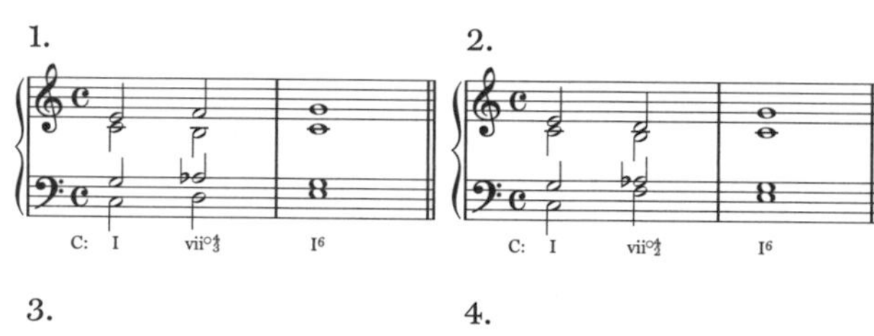

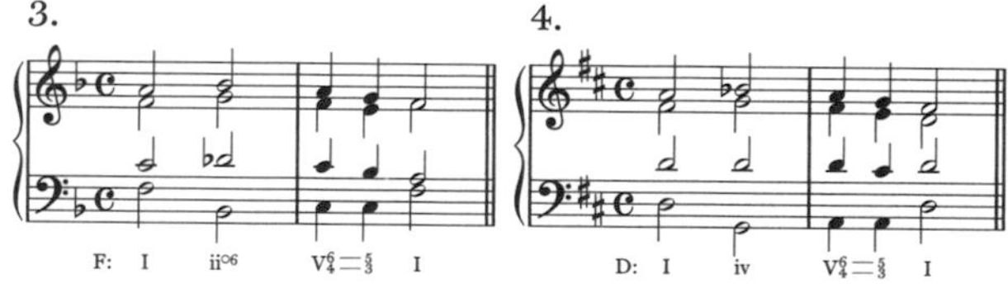

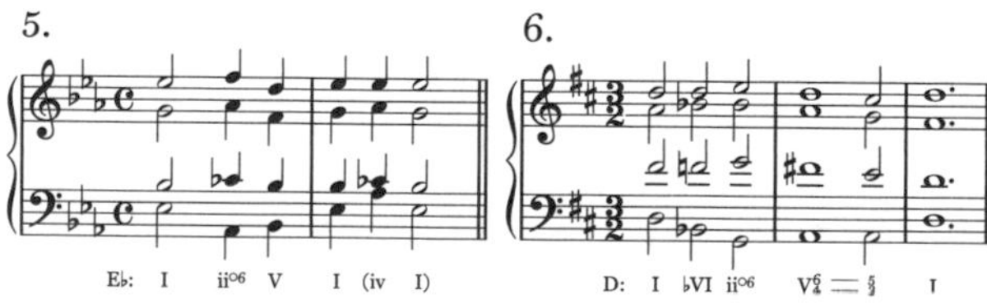

Chapter 27

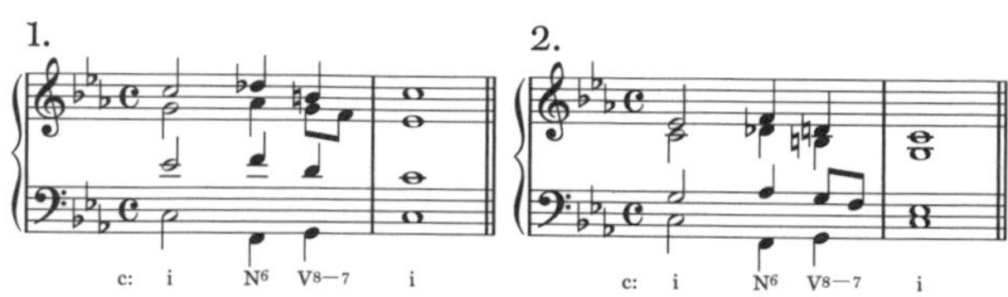

Chapter 28

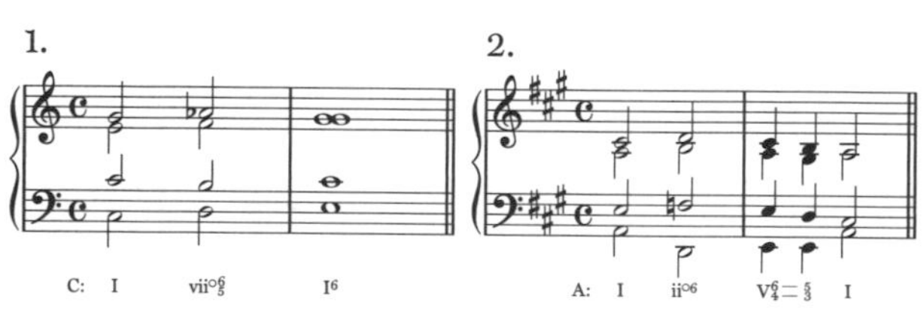

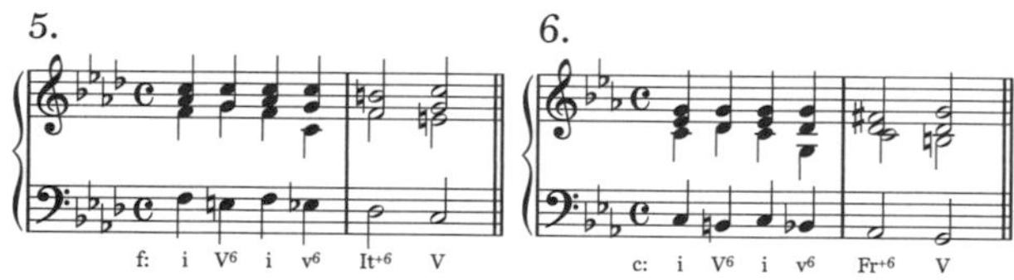

Chapter 29

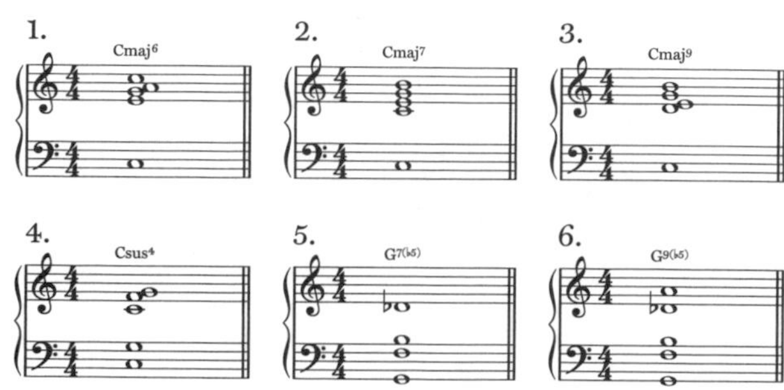

7.

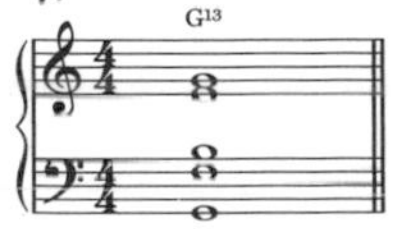
G13

8.

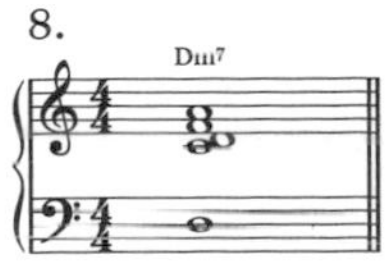
Dm7

9.

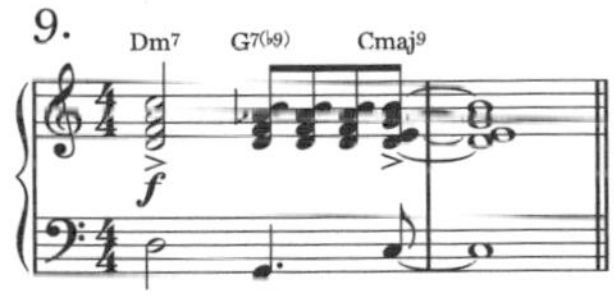
Dm7
G7(♭9)
Cmaj9
f

10.

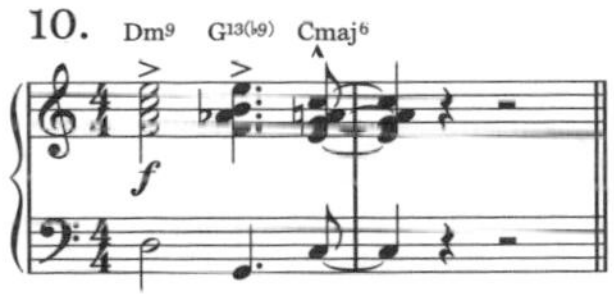
Dm9
G13(♭9)
Cmaj6
f

11.

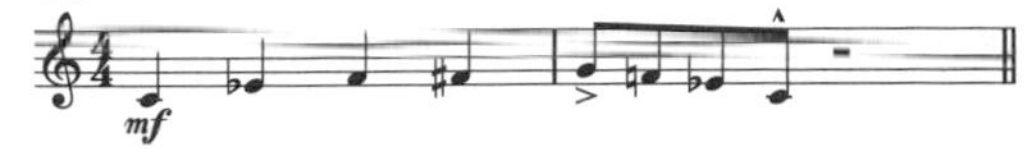
mf

12.

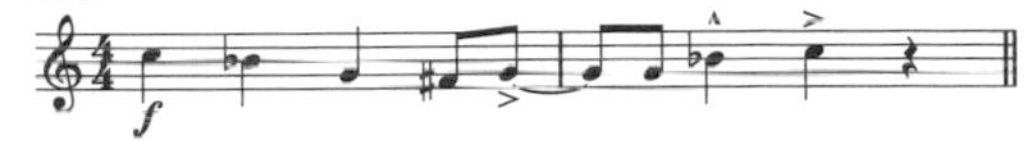
f

Chapter 30

1\.

Chromatic Falling Fifths

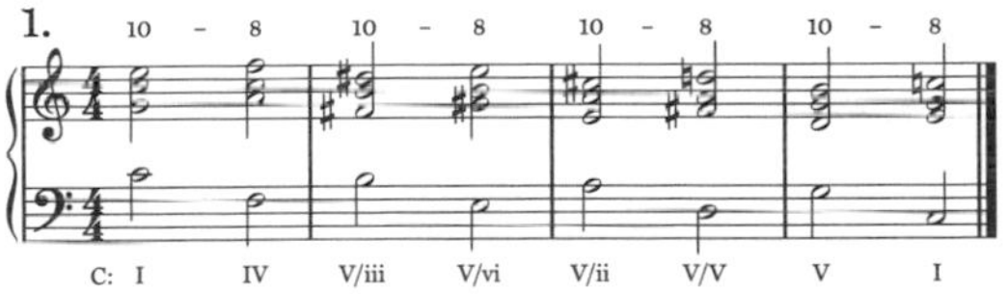
10 – 8 10 – 8 10 – 8 10 – 8
C: I IV V/iii V/vi V/ii V/V V I

2\.

Chromatic Falling Fifths

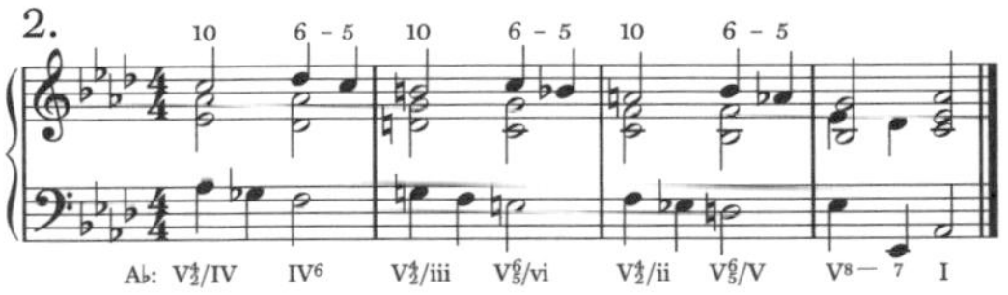
10 6 – 5 10 6 – 5 10 6 – 5
A♭: V4/2/IV IV6 V4/2/iii V6/5/vi V4/2/ii V6/5/V V8 — 7 I

3\.

Chromatic Falling Thirds

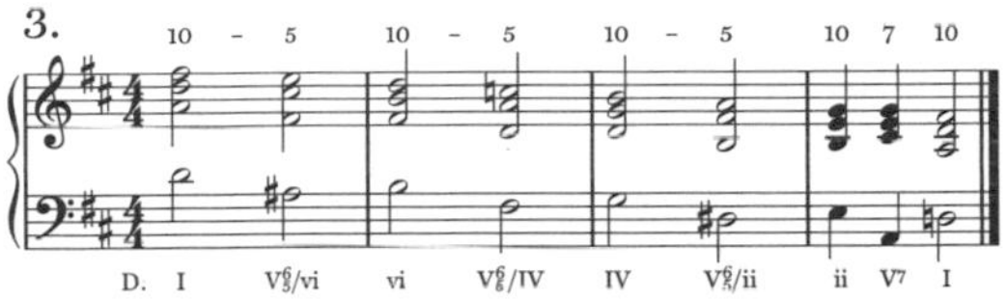
10 – 5 10 – 5 10 – 5 10 7 10
D: I V6/5/vi vi V6/5/IV IV V6/5/ii ii V7 I

4\.

Chromatic Falling First-Inversion Thirds

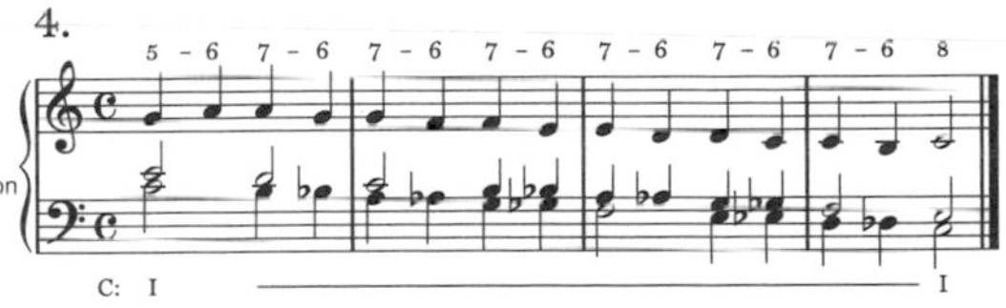
5 - 6 7 - 6 7 - 6 7 - 6 7 - 6 7 - 6 7 - 6 8
C: I I

5\.

Chromatic Falling First-Inversion Thirds

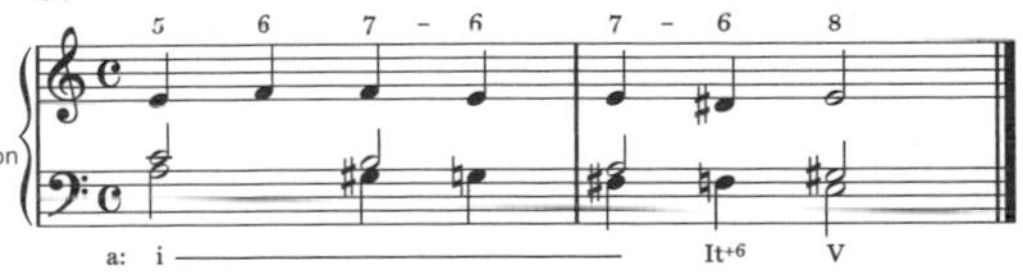
5 6 7 – 6 7 – 6 8
a: i It+6 V

6\.

Chromatic 5-6

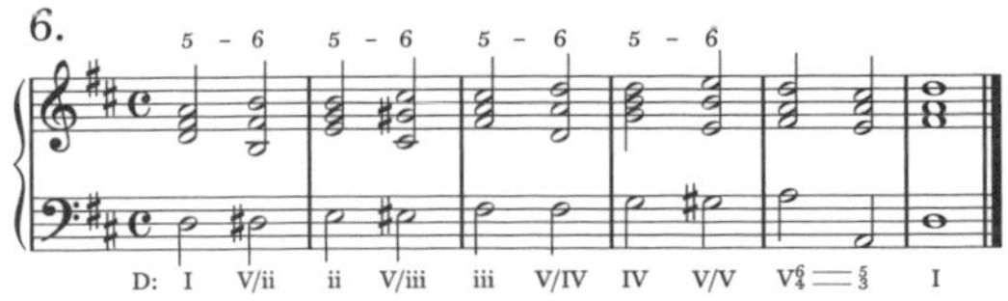
5 - 6 5 - 6 5 - 6 5 - 6
D: I V/ii ii V/iii iii V/IV IV V/V V6/4 — 5/3 I

Chapter 31

1\.

c: i V6 i (4/2) Gr6 V6/4 — 5/3

2\.

c: i V6 i (4/2) Gr6 D♭:V7 I

3\.

f: i V6 i V7 i V7 i

4\.

f: i V6 i V7 e: V8/6/4 — 7/5/3 i

5\.

C: I V I viiø6/5 I6 V7 I

6\.

C: I V I E♭:viiø7 I V7 I

Chapter 32

1\.

Chromatic Falling First-Inversion Thirds

5 6 7 – 6 7 – 6 8
b: i It+6 V

2\.

Chromatic Falling Fifths

10 – 7 10 – 7 10 – 7 10
D: I (V7/IV) V7/♭VII V7/iii V7/vi V7/ii V7/V V7 I

3\.

Chromatic Falling Thirds

C: I V6/4–3/vi vi9 – 8 V6/4–3/IV IV9 – 8 V6/4–3/ii ii9–8 V I8/4 — 8/3

4\.

Chromatic 5-6 Sequence

10 – 5 10 – 5 10 – 5 10 – 5
D: I V6/5/ii ii V6/5/iii iii V6/5/IV IV V6/5/V V6/4 — 5/3 I

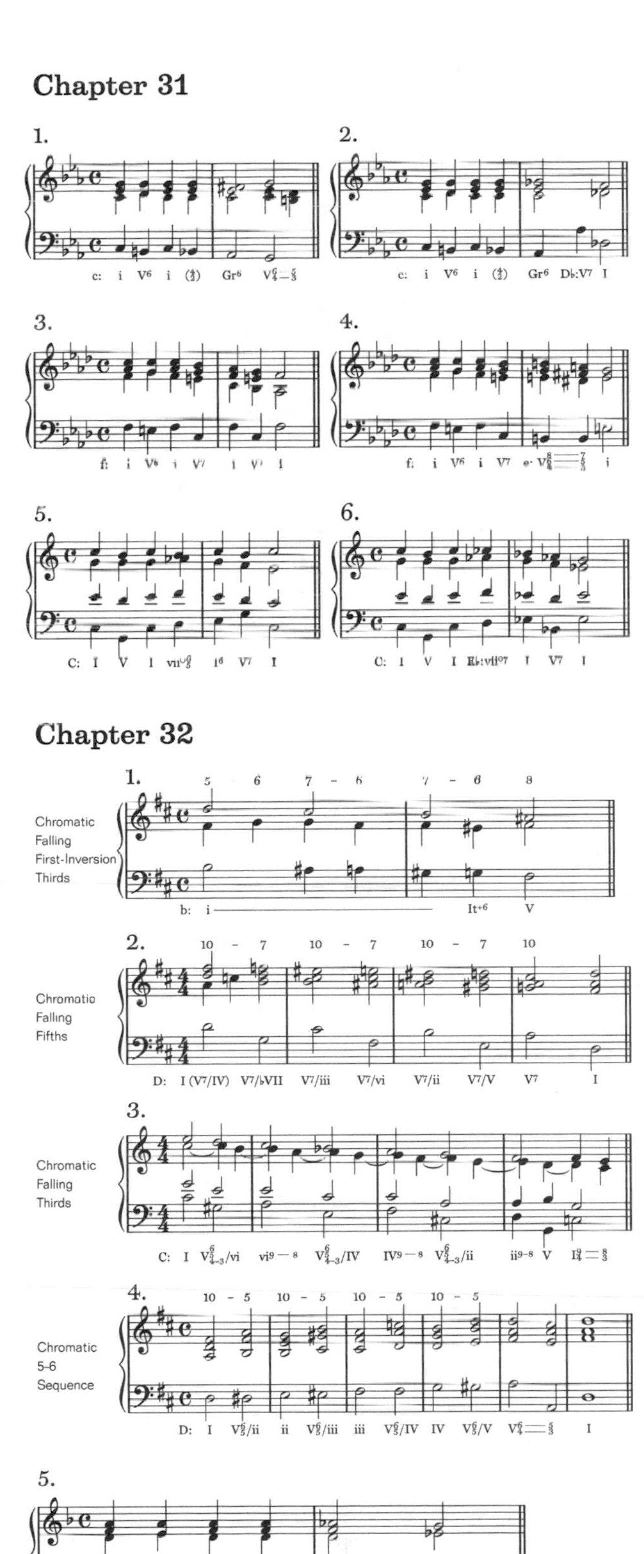

5\.

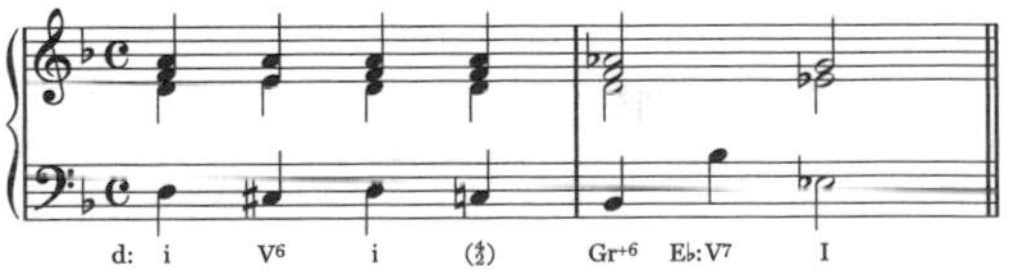
d: i V6 i (4/2) Gr+6 E♭:V7 I

6\.

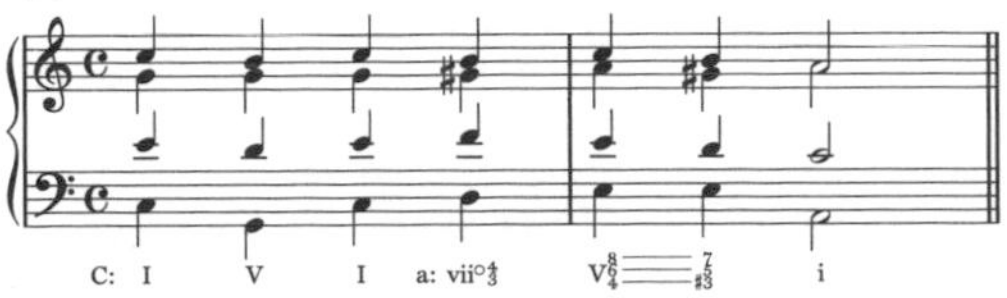
C: I V I a: viiø4/3 V8/6/4 — 7/5/3 i

Chapter 33

1. 2. 3.

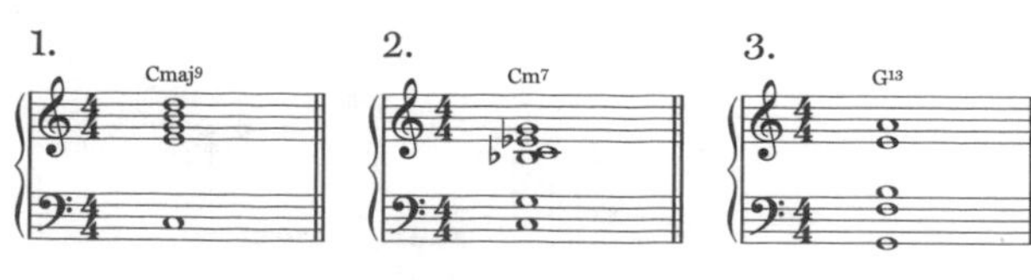

4. 5.

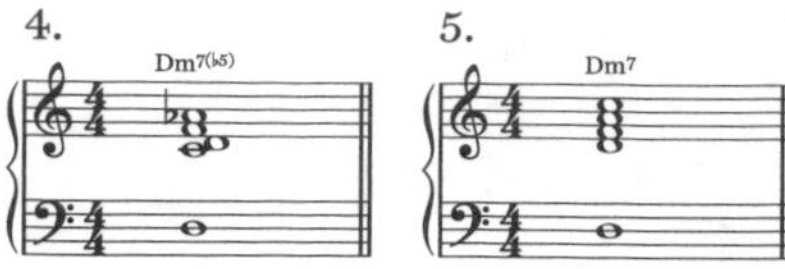

6. 7.

8.

9.

10.

Chapter 34

1. major tetrachord

2. minor tetrachord

3. Phrygian tetrachord

4. harmonic tetrachord

5. whole-tone tetrachord

6. Dorian mode = minor + minor

7. Phrygian mode = Phrygian + Phrygian

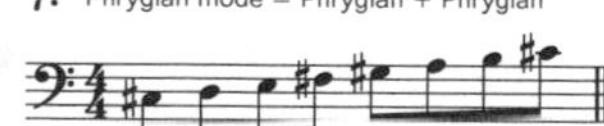

8. Lydian mode = whole-tone + major

9. Mixolydian mode = major + minor

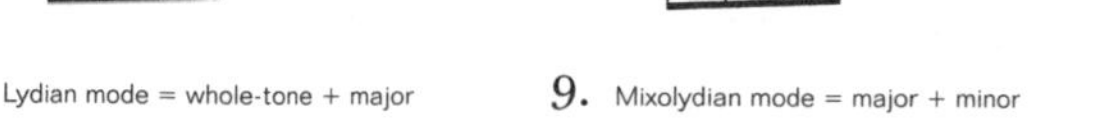

10. Aeolian mode = minor + Phrygian

11. melodic minor = minor + major

12. harmonic minor = minor + harmonic

Chapter 35

1. normal order { 3 4 7 9 }; prime form [0 1 4 6]; Forte SC 4-Z15; ic vector [111111]

2. normal order { 9 e 0 2 }; prime form [0 2 3 5]; Forte SC 4-10; ic vector [122010]

3. normal order { e o 2 3 }; prime form [0 1 3 4]; Forte SC 4-3; ic vector [212100]

4. normal order { 3 4 7 e }; prime form [0 1 4 8]; Forte SC 4-19; ic vector [101310]

5. normal order { 8 t 0 2 }; prime form [0 2 4 6]; Forte SC 4-21; ic vector [030201]

6. normal order { e 1 2 5 7 }; prime form [0 2 3 6 8]; Forte SC 5-28; ic vector [122212]

7. normal order { 6 8 t 1 3 }; prime form [0 2 4 7 9]; Forte SC 5-35; ic vector [032140]

8. normal order { 2 3 8 9 }; prime form [0 1 6 7]; Forte SC 4-9; ic vector [200022]
normal order { 8 9 2 3 }

9. normal order { 9 t 0 1 4 5 }; prime form [0 1 3 4 7 8]; Forte SC 6-Z19; ic vector [313431]

10. normal order { 0 1 4 6 7 }; prime form [0 1 3 6 7]; Forte SC 5-19; ic vector [212122]

Chapter 36

1.

normal order {7 8 e} ic vector [101100]

2.

normal order {9 e 3} ic vector [010101]

3.

normal order {1 3 6} ic vector [101100]

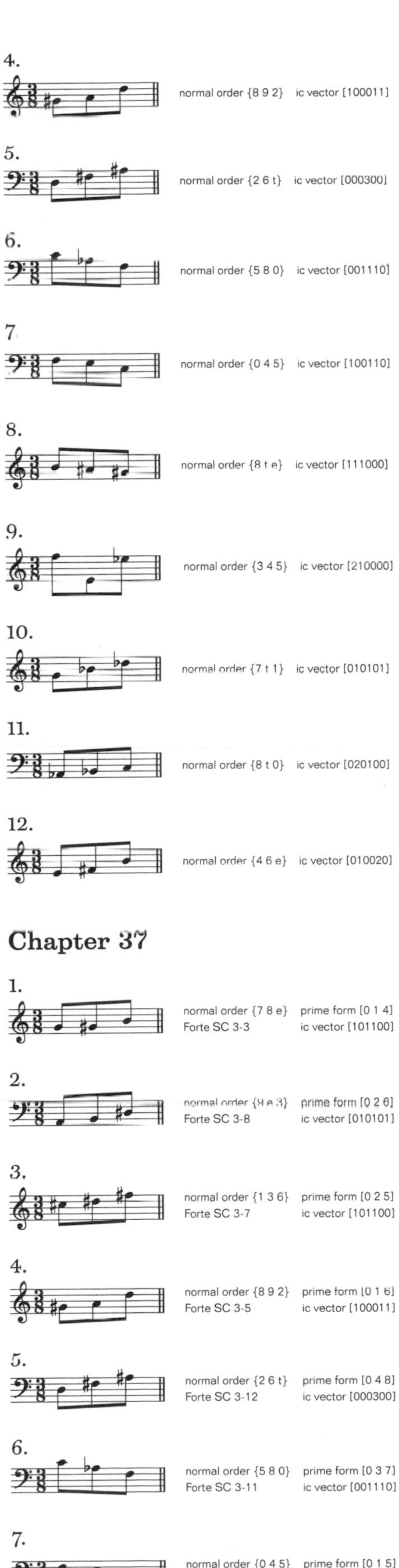

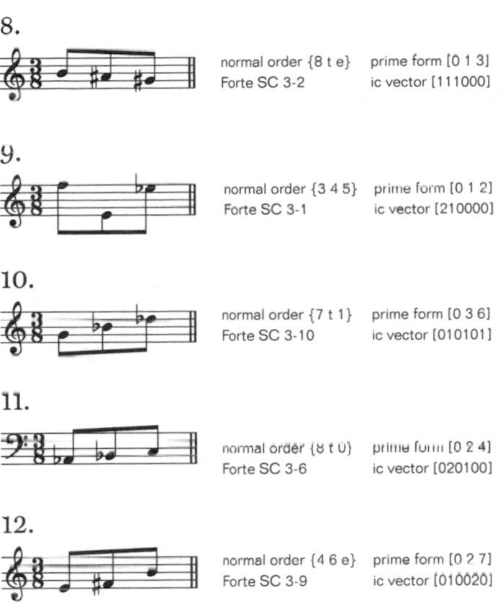

Chapter 38

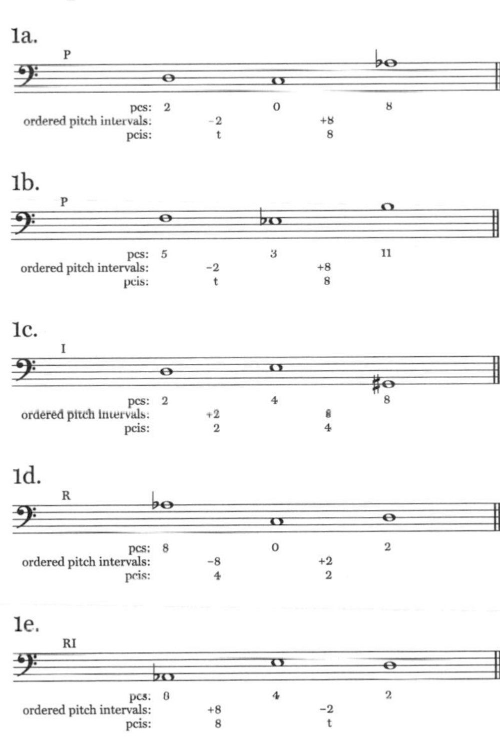

Chapter 39

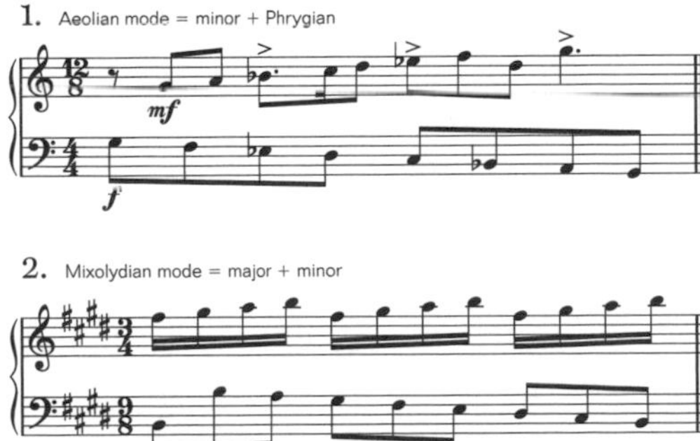

4. overtone (Lydian-Mixolydian mode) = whole tone + minor

5. octatonic = two minor tetrachords a tritone apart

Chapter 40

APPENDIX

Set-Class Table

NAME	PCS	IC VECTOR
3-1(12)	0,1,2	210000
3-2	0,1,3	111000
3-3	0,1,4	101100
3-4	0,1,5	100110
3-5	0,1,6	100011
3-6(12)	0,2,4	020100
3-7	0,2,5	011010
3-8	0,2,6	010101
3-9(12)	0,2,7	010020
3-10(12)	0,3,6	002001
3-11	0,3,7	001110
3-12(4)	0,4,8	000300
4-1(12)	0,1,2,3	321000
4-2	0,1,2,4	221100
4-3(12)	0,1,3,4	212100
4-4	0,1,2,5	211110
4-5	01,2,6	210111
4-6(12)	0,1,2,7	210021
4-7(12)	0,1,4,5	201210
4-8(12)	0,1,5,6	200121
4-9(6)	0,1,6,7	200022
4-10(12)	0,2,3,5	122010
4-11	0,1,3,5	121110
4-12	0,2,3,6	112101
4-13	0,1,3,6	112011
4-14	0,2,3,7	111120
4-Z15	0,1,4,6	111111
4-16	0,1,5,7	110121
4-17(12)	0,3,4,7	102210
4-18	0,1,4,7	102111
4-19	0,1,4,8	101310
4-20(12)	0,1,5,8	101220
4-21(12)	0,2,4,6	030201
4-22	0,2,4,7	021120
4-23(12)	0,2,5,7	021030
4-24(12)	0,2,4,8	020301
4-25(6)	0,2,6,8	020202
4-26(12)	0,3,5,8	012120
6-34	0,1,3,5,7,9	142422
6-35(2)	0,2,4,6,8,t	060603
9-1	0,1,2,3,4,5,6,7,8	876663
9-2	0,1,2,3,4,5,6,7,9	777663
9-3	0,1,2,3,4,5,6,8,9	767763
9-4	0,1,2,3,4,5,7,8,9	766773
9-5	0,1,2,3,4,6,7,8,9	766674
9-6	0,1,2,3,4,5,6,8,t	686763
9-7	0,1,2,3,4,5,7,8,t	677673
9-8	0,1,2,3,4,6,7,8,t	676764
9-9	0,1,2,3,5,6,7,8,t	676683
9-10	0,1,2,3,4,6,7,9,t	668664
9-11	0,1,2,3,5,6,7,9,t	667773
9-12	0,1,2,4,5,6,8,9,t	666963
8-1	0,1,2,3,4,5,6,7	765442
8-2	0,1,2,3,4,5,6,8	665542
8-3	0,1,2,3,4,5,6,9	656542
8-4	0,1,2,3,4,5,7,8	655552
8-5	0,1,2,3,4,6,7,8	654553
8-6	0,1,2,3,5,6,7,8	654463
8-7	0,1,2,3,4,5,8,9	645652
8-8	0,1,2,3,4,7,8,9	644563
8-9	0,1,2,3,6,7,8,9	644464
8-10	0,2,3,4,5,6,7,9	566452
8-11	0,1,2,3,4,5,7,9	565552
8-12	0,1,3,4,5,6,7,9	556543
8-13	0,1,2,3,4,6,7,9	556453
8-14	0,1,2,4,5,6,7,9	555562
8-Z15	0,1,2,3,4,6,8,9	555553
8-16	0,1,2,3,5,7,8,9	554563
8-17	0,1,3,4,5,6,8,9	546652
8-18	0,1,2,3,5,6,8,9	546553
8-19	0,1,2,4,5,6,8,9	545752
8-20	0,1,2,4,5,7,8,9	545662
8-21	0,1,2,3,4,6,8,t	474643
8-22	0,1,2,3,5,6,8,t	465562
8-23	0,1,2,3,5,7,8,t	465472
8-24	0,1,2,4,5,6,8,t	464743

NOTE: Numbers in parentheses show the number of distinct sets in the set class if other than 48.
All brackets are eliminated here for ease of reading.

NAME	PCS	IC VECTOR
4-27	0,2,5,8	012111
4-28(3)	0,3,6,9	004002
4-Z29	0,1,3,7	111111
5-1(12)	0,1,2,3,4	432100
5-2	0,1,2,3,5	332110
5-3	0,1,2,4,5	322210
5-4	0,1,2,3,6	322111
5-5	0,1,2,3,7	321121
5-6	0,1,2,5,6	311221
5-7	0,1,2,6,7	310132
5-8(12)	0,2,3,4,6	232201
5-9	0,1,2,4,6	231211
5-10	0,1,3,4,6	223111
5-11	0,2,3,4,7	222220
5-Z12(12)	0,1,3,5,6	222121
5-13	0,1,2,4,8	221311
5-14	0,1,2,5,7	221131
5-15(12)	0,1,2,6,8	220222
5-16	0,1,3,4,7	213211
5-Z17(12)	0,1,3,4,8	212320
5-Z18	0,1,4,5,7	212221
5-19	0,1,3,6,7	212122
5-20	0,1,3,7,8	211231
5-21	0,1,4,5,8	202420
5-22(12)	0,1,4,7,8	202321
5-23	0,2,3,5,7	132130
5-24	0,1,3,5,7	131221
5-25	0,2,3,5,8	123121
5-26	0,2,4,5,8	122311
5-27	0,1,3,5,8	122230
5-28	0,2,3,6,8	122212
5-29	0,1,3,6,8	122131
5-30	0,1,4,6,8	121321
5-31	0,1,3,6,9	114112
5-32	0,1,4,6,9	113221
5-33(12)	0,2,4,6,8	040402
5-34(12)	0,2,4,6,9	032221
5-35(12)	0,2,4,7,9	032140
5-Z36	0,1,2,4,7	222121
5-Z37(12)	0,3,4,5,8	212320
5-Z38	0,1,2,5,8	212221
6-1(12)	0,1,2,3,4,5	543210
6-2	0,1,2,3,4,6	443211
6-Z3	0,1,2,3,5,6	433221
6-Z4(12)	0,1,2,4,5,6	432321
6-5	0,1,2,3,6,7	422232
6-Z6(12)	0,1,2,5,6,7	421242
6-7(6)	0,1,2,6,7,8	420243
6-8(12)	0,2,3,4,5,7	343230
6-9	0,1,2,3,5,7	342231
6-Z10	0,1,3,4,5,7	333321
6-Z11	0,1,2,4,5,7	333231
6-Z12	0,1,2,4,6,7	332232
6-Z13(12)	0,1,3,4,6,7	324222

NAME	PCS	IC VECTOR
8-25	0,1,2,4,6,7,8,t	464644
8-26	0,1,2,4,5,7,9,t	456562
8-27	0,1,2,4,5,7,8,t	456553
8-28	0,1,3,4,6,7,9,t	448444
8-Z29	0,1,2,3,5,6,7,9	555553
7-1	0,1,2,3,4,5,6	654321
7-2	0,1,2,3,4,5,7	554331
7-3	0,1,2,3,4,5,8	544431
7-4	0,1,2,3,4,6,7	544332
7-5	0,1,2,3,5,6,7	543342
7-6	0,1,2,3,4,7,8	533442
7-7	0,1,2,3,6,7,8	532353
7-8	0,2,3,4,5,6,8	454422
7-9	0,1,2,3,4,6,8	453432
7-10	0,1,2,3,4,6,9	445332
7-11	0,1,3,4,5,6,8	444441
7-Z12	0,1,2,3,4,7,9	444342
7-13	0,1,2,4,5,6,8	443532
7-14	0,1,2,3,5,7,8	443352
7-15	0,1,2,4,6,7,8	442443
7-16	0,1,2,3,5,6,9	435432
7-Z17	0,1,2,4,5,6,9	434541
7-Z18	0,1,2,3,5,8,9	434442
7-19	0,1,2,3,6,7,9	434343
7-20	0,1,2,4,7,8,9	433452
7-21	0,1,2,4,5,8,9	424641
7-22	0,1,2,5,6,8,9	424542
7-23	0,2,3,4,5,7,9	354351
7-24	0,1,2,3,5,7,9	353442
7-25	0,2,3,4,6,7,9	345342
7-26	0,1,3,4,5,7,9	344532
7-27	0,1,2,4,5,7,9	344451
7-28	0,1,3,5,6,7,9	344433
7-29	0,1,2,4,6,7,9	344352
7-30	0,1,2,4,6,8,9	343542
7-31	0,1,3,4,6,7,9	336333
7-32	0,1,3,4,6,8,9	335442
7-33	0,1,2,4,6,8,t	262623
7-34	0,1,3,4,6,8,t	254442
7-35	0,1,3,5,6,8,t	254361
7-Z36	0,1,2,3,5,6,8	444342
7-Z37	0,1,3,4,5,7,8	434541
7-Z38	0,1,2,4,5,7,8	434442
6-Z36	0,1,2,3,4,7	*
6-Z37(12)	0,1,2,3,4,8	
6-Z38(12)	0,1,2,3,7,8	
6-Z39	0,2,3,4,5,8	
6-Z40	0,1,2,3,5,8	
6-Z41	0,1,2,3,6,8	
6-Z42(12)	0,1,2,3,6,9	

NAME	PCS	IC VECTOR	NAME	PCS	IC VECTOR
6-14	0,1,3,4,5,8	323430			
6-15	0,1,2,4,5,8	323421			
6-16	0,1,4,5,6,8	322431			
6-Z17	0,1,2,4,7,8	322332	6-Z43	0,1,2,5,6,8	
6-18	0,1,2,5,7,8	322242			
6-Z19	0,1,3,4,7,8	313431	6-Z44	0,1,2,5,6,9	
6-20(4)	0,1,4,5,8,9	303630			
6-21	0,2,3,4,6,8	242412			
6-22	0,1,2,4,6,8	241422			
6-Z23(12)	0,2,3,5,6,8	234222	6-Z45(12)	0,2,3,4,6,9	
6-Z24	0,1,3,4,6,8	233331	6-Z46	0,1,2,4,6,9	
6-Z25	0,1,3,5,6,8	233241	6-Z47	0,1,2,4,7,9	
6-Z26(12)	0,1,3,5,7,8	232341	6-Z48(12)	0,1,2,5,7,9	
6-27	0,1,3,4,6,9	225222			
6-Z28(12)	0,1,3,5,6,9	224322	6-Z49(12)	0,1,3,4,7,9	
6-Z29(12)	0,1,3,6,8,9	224232	6-Z50(12)	0,1,4,6,7,9	
6-30(12)	0,1,3,6,7,9	224223			
6-31	0,1,3,5,8,9	223431			
6-32(12)	0,2,4,5,7,9	143250			
6-33	0,2,3,5,7,9	143241			

*Z-related hexachords share the same ic vector; use vector in the third column

SOURCE: Allen Forte, *The Structure of Atonal Music* (New Haven: Yale University Press, 1973) (adapted)